ON AIR

KT-415-221

ON AIR

Methods and Meanings of Radio

MARTIN SHINGLER

Senior Lecturer in Media Studies, Staffordshire University

and

CINDY WIERINGA

*Senior Lecturer in Radio, London College of Music and
Media, Thames Valley University*

A member of the Hodder Headline Group
LONDON · NEW YORK · SYDNEY · AUCKLAND

First published in Great Britain in 1998 by
Arnold, a member of the Hodder Headline Group,
338 Euston Road, London NW1 3BH

http://www.arnoldpublishers.com

Co-published in the United States of America by
Oxford University Press Inc.,
198 Madison Avenue, New York, NY10016

© 1998 Martin Shingler and Cindy Wieringa

All rights reserved. No part of this publication may be reproduced or
transmitted in any form or by any means, electronically or mechanically,
including photocopying, recording or any information storage or retrieval
system, without either prior permission in writing from the publisher or a
licence permitting restricted copying. In the United Kingdom such licences
are issued by the Copyright Licensing Agency: 90 Tottenham Court Road,
London W1P 9HE.

The advice and information in this book are believed to be true and accurate
at the date of going to press, but neither the authors nor the publisher
can accept any legal responsibility or liability for any errors or omissions.

British Library Cataloguing in Publication Data
A catalogue entry for this book is available from the British Library

Library of Congress Cataloging-in-Publication Data
Shingler, Martin, 1965–
    On air : methods and meanings of radio / Martin Shingler and Cindy
Wieringa.
        p.   cm.
    Includes bibliographical references and index.
    ISBN 0-340-65232-2 (hardcover).—ISBN 0-340-65231-4
    1. Radio broadcasting—History. I. Wieringa, Cindy. II. Title.
PN1991.2.S55 1998
791.44'09—dc21   98-18248
                                                                CIP

ISBN 0 340 65232 2 (hb)
ISBN 0 340 65231 4 (pb)

1 2 3 4 5 6 7 8 9 10

Production Editor: Rada Radojicic
Production Controller: Priya Gohil
Cover Design: Mouse Mat Design

Composition by Phoenix Photosetting, Chatham, Kent
Printed and bound in Great Britain by
MPG Books, Bodmin, Cornwall

Contents

This book is dedicated to
Simon J. Ruston
and Stephanie

Acknowledgements

The Introduction and Chapters 2, 3, 4 and 6 were written by Martin Shingler. Chapters 1, 5, 7 and the Glossary were written by Cindy Wieringa. The authors and publishers would like to thank the following for permission to use copyright material in this book.

Cambridge University Press for extracts from Frances Gray, 'Giles Cooper the Medium and the Moralist' and Peter Lewis, 'The Road to Llareggub' in John Drakakis (ed.) *British Radio Drama* (1981); David Higham Associates and New Directions Publishing Corporation for extracts from Dylan Thomas, *Under Milk Wood* (1956); Addison Wesley Longman for extracts from Frances Gray, 'The Nature of the Radio Drama' and Jonathan Raban, 'Icon or Symbol: the Writer and the "Medium"' in Peter Lewis (ed.) *Radio Drama* (1981); Sylvère Lotringer and Semiotext(e) for extracts from Jody Berland, 'Contradicting Media: Toward a Political Phenomenology of Listening' in Neil Straus (ed.) *Radiotext(e)* (1993); Routledge for extracts from Dorothy Hobson, 'Housewives and the Mass Media' in Stuart Hall (ed.) *Culture, Media, Language* (1980); Sage for extracts from Paddy Scannell (ed.) *Broadcast Talk* (1991); Richard Scott Simon Ltd. (Sheil Land Associates) for extracts from *Rabbi Lionel Blue: 50 Thoughts for the Day*, BBC Radio Collection, BBC Enterprises Ltd. (1990).

The authors would also like to thank Staffordshire University for its help and support throughout this project, in particular Professor Derek Longhurst, Christine Gledhill and Peter Hames. We would also like to express our special thanks to Mel Hill for being instrumental in the origination of this project and for inspiring many of the ideas developed here.

Introduction

Radio is one of the world's most pervasive mass media, reaching the most far-flung corners of the planet (even beyond it) and heard by millions of people every minute of every day. It is such an everyday and familiar aspect of modern life that most of us take it entirely for granted and, in so doing, underestimate its power. Yet radio is a powerful cultural influence in the modern world and has an important role to play in the lives of millions of people. It is also a fascinating medium, flexible and versatile. It has a rich heritage, certainly, having played a very significant part in twentieth-century history; but it also has an exciting future before it. Since its emergence from the laboratories in the late 1800s and its development as a popular mass medium in the 1920s, radio has proved itself capable of great changes, almost continually reinventing itself in order to take its place alongside new forms of electronic media. In the ever-changing world of mass information and entertainment, radio has remained one of the most vital and popular forms. This being the case, why is it so taken for granted? Why, for instance, did its centenary pass almost unnoticed, while cinema's one-hundredth birthday was celebrated with three years of film festivals and publications in the mid-1990s?

Radio has a number of unique characteristics which make it successful and ensure its longevity but at the same time encourage people to underestimate its importance and take it for granted. Chief among these is its ubiquity: it gets everywhere. Often (to adapt a famous advertising slogan) it reaches parts that other mass media cannot reach: it can be heard out in the middle of vast oceans or on the top of remote mountain peaks. Of course, most of us hear it in more mundane locations. Virtually any room in our home may be furnished with a radio set, including the garage and the potting shed. We hear it all over the place: in our cars, in shops, offices and factories, in the street, in the park and on the beach. We can also hear it at any time of day: morning, noon and night. For many of us, it is the first thing we hear on waking and the last thing we hear before falling asleep. So there is nothing special about listening to the radio. The second characteristic which results in us quite literally failing to recognise the value of radio is that it costs most of us virtually nothing to consume. Few of us actually pay for the privilege of enjoying a rich diet of up-to-the-minute news, chat, music, information, comedy and drama. The third characteristic is the fact that it is invisible. When we do stop and think about radio and what it actually consists of, probably the first thing that strikes us is the fact that there is nothing to see. As we shall discuss in more detail in Chapter 4, listeners consume radio blind. Consequently, our attention (like our eyes) is often focused on something other than the radio itself (such as the road ahead, the ironing, the meal we are preparing) and this is true even when we our listening attentively to one of our favourite radio programmes. For all these reasons then, it is easy to see why radio's importance (and even its presence) as a mass medium in the modern world is so easily taken for granted and, consequently, underestimated.

Many of the commentators who have given radio serious thought have described it as a 'secondary activity' or a 'secondary medium'. At the inception of British radio broadcasting, in the early 1920s, the BBC (British Broadcasting Company and later, from 1927, Corporation) expressed concern that radio should not be used simply as background noise. They insisted, for instance, that listeners should minimise distractions to the point of sitting in their most comfortable armchair in a darkened room in order to give radio programmes as much of their attention as they would a play at the theatre. However, the BBC's attempts to achieve a higher level of audience concentration on radio programmes have invariably met with failure as the vast majority of listeners have preferred to use radio as a background to other activities – usually manual, mundane and repetitive tasks. The BBC's eventual recognition of this reality was perhaps signified most forcefully during the Second World War with the introduction of 'Music While You Work', a daily broadcast of instrumental music aimed at improving the productivity of munitions factories by providing a background conducive to sustained and unbroken activity. Since that time, employers (large and small) have recognised the beneficial effects of music on both staff and customers; hence in-house factory music systems and the playing of non-stop music stations (including BBC Radio 1) in hairdressers, garages, cafes, shops, etc.

Since the 1950s, radio has also assumed the role of a 'secondary medium' in the sense that it has been superseded by television as the primary source of entertainment and information within modern western society. But the rise of television in the post-war period has not brought about, as many people anticipated, the death of radio; the ability of radio to assume the function of a secondary medium in the sense discussed above (i.e., as an accompaniment to other activities such as driving, housework, various forms of manual labour, shopping, etc.) has proved to be of vital importance to its survival in the modern world. As men and women work increasingly longer hours and make increasingly long journeys to and from their places of work, the time they have free to dedicate undivided attention to leisure and entertainment has been reduced and the consumption of the mass media has become ever more fragmented. Radio is, however, an excellent means for busy people to gain information and entertainment in short bursts either during breaks from work or whilst on the move.

Most radio producers recognise an essentially distracted listenership and, with only a few exceptions (e.g., drama, news and features), much of mainstream radio broadcasting is designed not only to accommodate listening as a secondary activity but positively to exploit the advantages of a semi-attentive audience. For instance, it is evident that advertisers have become increasingly aware of the advantages of reaching an audience whose lives are pervaded with sounds and information without them really noticing. This has entailed a virtual revolution in thinking within the advertising industry, which since the advent of commercial television in Britain in 1955 had regarded radio as a less effective medium for advertising than television, press and even posters. Advertising on the radio had tended to be viewed as something that smaller and more parochial advertising agencies specialised in or had been used as a training ground for more junior members of staff, prior to their moving on to higher-profile and more expensive television commercials. In consequence, many radio advertising campaigns had been little more than an extension of, or supplement to, larger television and press campaigns. However, in recent years there have been signs of a growing recognition of the effectiveness of radio as an advertising medium, particularly with the long-awaited introduction of national commercial stations in Britain (e.g., Classic FM, Virgin 1215 and Talk Radio). Moreover, the effectiveness of radio advertising would seem to lie, ironically, in its taken-for-grantedness – the thinking being that listeners are likely to have less resistance to messages that they perceive to be making little impact on their consciousness but which are actually charting a more direct route to the unconscious (or preconscious) mind. True or false, this is an argument that has persuaded many advertisers to adopt a new attitude to radio as a marketing medium, and this change of attitude has resulted in radio being the only medium in the 1990s whose share of advertising has expanded, particularly in Europe.

Radio has undergone significant changes in the 1990s. In Britain today, more than at any other time since the 1950s, there is a range of exciting opportunities opening up in the field of radio, due largely to industrial and institutional change. In particular, the impact of the 1990 Broadcasting Act, which brought in its wake new national commercial radio stations and increasing opportunities for independent radio productions on the existing BBC networks, has breathed new life into the British radio industry. With the establishment of the Radio Authority as the main regulatory body (overseeing developments in British radio broadcasting, regulating both programmes and advertising, issuing licences and setting frequencies, etc.), radio seems to be throwing off many of its former inhibitions as it moves out of television's shadow. Given the Radio Authority's remit to encourage

competition and increase listener choice, we would hope to see (as is generally anticipated) greater diversification within the British radio industry in
future, attracting practitioners and audiences from a much wider range of
the social spectrum.

look at what social spectrum u have asked.

Clearly, new technology has a principal role to play in radio's recent and
on-going renaissance. Recent improvements in digital technology have
enabled a greater range of high-quality frequencies to be used and, hence,
more national commercial stations to emerge. However, the driving force
behind new developments in radio broadcasting has tended to be more
social than technological. The birth of broadcasting in both Britain and the
United States came long after the technology for radio broadcasting had
been invented. What is generally believed to have led to the setting up of
regular radio broadcasting stations in America and Britain after the First
World War were essentially social factors, such as increased leisure time,
surplus income, extension of voting rights and improvements in education.
Thus, in considering the motivating forces behind the rejuvenation of radio
broadcasting we should pay as much attention to social factors as to technological ones.

If we are to understand the ways in which radio works and, from there,
grasp its potential (creative, persuasive, communicative, political, etc.) we
must first understand what has shaped it and what factors have determined
its conventions. Radio may seem to come from nowhere, its signals appearing miraculously out of thin air, but actually its form is shaped by a host of
factors: physical, technological, social. In the first chapter of this book we
shall be exploring in some detail the conditions under which radio emerged
as a mass medium of information and entertainment. This provides a brief
history of radio to the present day and highlights the key events in radio's
past which have made the medium what it is today.

Throughout its history, radio has proved itself to be eminently adaptable
to new social, economic and industrial circumstances. Voices have frequently been heard heralding the imminent demise of the medium in the face
of competition from new forms of communication, mass information and
entertainment. But radio has consistently reemerged stronger from periods
of decline. For instance, the recent rapid expansion of the market for audio-
cassettes of both new and classic radio shows suggests a recognition by both
listeners and the industry of radio's abiding fascination and interest. Also, in
both publishing and education we can see increasing interest in radio and its
history. The study of radio's institutional framework and modes of production constitutes one area of academic engagement. There is also a need for
an informed and in-depth examination of the medium itself, its inherent
properties, its codes and conventions, its textual practices and modes of
reception. This type of study (which might constitute a field of 'radio studies' akin to film studies) is long overdue. Radio has not been given anything
like the academic or critical attention devoted to film or television, and to
date a 'critical theory' of radio is lacking. *On Air* is intended to contribute

towards the establishment of a more wide-ranging theoretical, analytical and 'academic' approach to radio.

In order to provide a more critical assessment of radio, much of our book is given over to examining the basic codes of the medium (namely, speech, music, noise and silence) and the conventions which have developed for employing these codes in specific ways in order to create radiogenic effects. In Chapter 2, for instance, we look in detail at the uses of the spoken word on radio. This involves a discussion of the speech policies adopted by radio stations, along with our own attempts to define the specific nature of 'radio speech', including an exploration of the effects of expressivity of speech (i.e., accent, intonation, timbre, pitch, volume and speed) and a consideration of the ideology of the 'radio voice'. In Chapter 3, on the other hand, we investigate the non-verbal codes of radio. Here we look at music, noise (acoustics and sound effects) and silence as distinct categories before moving on to a consideration of the ways in which they can be used in conjunction with speech to produce vivid moments of radio drama. Having examined both the problems and the benefits of invisibility in Chapter 4, in Chapter 5 we consider how invisibility disguises the constructedness of radio programmes, making them seem live, spontaneous and natural when they may actually be recorded, edited and heavily fabricated packages. Here we shall consider some of the ethical issues involved in editing and examine constructions of 'realism' and 'naturalism' that are produced by both 'live' and pre-recorded programming. This chapter will raise concerns about the manipulation or deception of audiences as a prelude to a more detailed consideration of the relationship between radio stations and their listeners in Chapter 6.

Throughout this book we examine the codes and conventions of mainstream radio broadcasting. In so doing, one of our principal aims is to articulate and draw attention to the formal strategies employed by radio broadcasters and the inherent features of radio as a broadcasting medium. Another of our aims is to provide a vocabulary with which to analyse radio programmes. So, for instance, in Chapter 2 we examine a range of terms for understanding the peculiar nature of radio speech: e.g., 'mundane', 'institutional' and 'intermediate'. Also, at the end of the book we provide a glossary as a guide to commonly used terminology, including terms used throughout *On Air* and those employed widely within the radio industry itself.

Radio's codes (speech, music, noise and silence) remain constant however much the technology, the industry and its regulatory policies change. But radio itself is always changing in order to meet the needs of an ever-changing audience. Ultimately, radio is shaped not by the technology that makes wireless communication possible, not even by industrial and institutional structures, but by those who tune in and listen. Their needs, desires, ideologies and habits ultimately determine the conventions of radio broadcasting more than any other factor and radio is in an almost constant state of redevelopment as it attempts to adapt itself to the most significant changes in modern society, to the ideals and lifestyles of those who like to listen to music, noise and speech. In Chapter 6 we examine the specific relation radio has with its audience and explore some of the ways in which people use and relate to this medium. We consider the influence audiences exert on radio stations and discuss intimacy and feedback, including the opportunities radio provides for direct interaction. With specific reference to phone-ins and talk-back radio, we also consider whether or not radio is (as some have claimed) a democratic medium capable of emancipating its listeners by providing them with greater access to the airwaves and creating listening communities. Finally in Chapter 6 we also look at how audiences relate to radio broadcasters (e.g., presenters and disc jockeys). Chapter 7 extends this examination with a number of case studies of talk-back radio to provide a more tangible sense of how listeners are treated by presenters and radio-station personnel. Cindy Wieringa's experiences of working on morning/daytime talk-back radio and news and current affairs in Australia and Hong Kong demystify many of the 'behind-the-scenes' processes by explaining the techniques, ideology and mission behind much radio production and both support and exemplify the theories discussed in the book.

Throughout *On Air* we have attempted to strike a balance between a more theoretical approach to radio (e.g., Higgins and Moss 1982; Dyson 1994; Valentine and Saint Damian 1988) and insights derived from professional broadcasters and trainers (e.g., Hayes 1994; Evans 1977; McWhinnie 1959). This approach is not simply a matter of the material and sources we've drawn on in the course of our discussion but also reflects our own expertise. As authors of this book, we represent two ends of the theory/practice spectrum. Prior to contributing to this book, Cindy Wieringa had worked for many years as a broadcast journalist. At the time of writing, she was a university lecturer involved in teaching a variety of radio, journalism, writing and production courses. Martin Shingler, on the other hand, came to the subject of radio after several years as an academic, researching and lecturing in (ironically) the visual arts, film in particular. The way we have divided up our work on the book has enabled us to pursue our own areas of expertise and interest and develop a dialogue between theory and practice rather than segregate the two issues as has been the tradition in the past.

Pooling our experiences of and interests in radio, we have endeavoured to provide what we consider to be a wide-ranging account of the medium. Although we may come at our subject from rather different angles, one of the things that unites our approach to radio is our respect for it, our belief in its significance for people throughout the world, in the past, the present and, of course, the future. This does not mean that we have produced a eulogy to (or defence of) radio, however. In fact, we have found it necessary in various instances to be critical of some of the positive claims that have been made: for instance, on the subject of radio as a democratic and emancipatory medium. Balance has once again been our objective here, attempting to put forward for consideration the cases for and against. On many occasions we leave readers to draw their own conclusions when assessing contentious subjects that have divided practitioners, analysts, commentators and theorists. It has, in fact, been our objective to encourage readers not only to consider certain issues relating to radio broadcasting but also to pursue their own investigations and analyses of the medium. Our 'Things to do' sections at the end of each chapter are intended as only a first step in this direction. We hope that our ideas and analyses will provoke a much more far-reaching consideration of this undeservedly neglected mass medium, resulting in a better understanding of the past and future of radio, its strengths and weaknesses and both its positive and its negative effects.

Things to do

Consider for a moment how many radios you have in your home (not forgetting your car). How many rooms in your house have a radio? Beyond your home, in what other places do you come into contact with radio? It might prove instructive if, for the rest of today, you make a mental note of all the different places (and all the different times) that you hear a radio (even just as snatches of sound in the distance from an unknown source).

| 1 |

Radio time-line: history at a glance

Radio is generally seen as the 'poor relation' of society's most popular form of home entertainment, television; and nowadays even television is competing with home videos, computer games and the internet. Humankind seems to have lost the art of listening and instead relies on visual stimuli for entertainment and information. Television has become the focal point of many of our lives. Our homes and in many cases our budgets are arranged to accommodate 'the box', and conversation all but disappears when the set is switched on. In fact, after some fifty years of popularity the role of radio in our lives is so marginalised that even in our education we are led to believe that radio is 'second best': the most popular radio texts discuss the medium in terms of 'blindness' (Crisell 1992), suggesting that radio is 'handicapped', that the listener is faced with some kind of disadvantage if she chooses to listen rather than 'see'. This chapter will challenge such views by examining the various highs and lows throughout the medium's illustrious history. This history has been recounted in full by reputable scholars and practitioners in several very good textbooks. Instead of presenting yet another full version of the 'Marconi to satellite' story, this chapter will take a glimpse at the key events that have shaped the development of the radio medium.

The radio time-line[1]

1830s–40s   Samuel Morse refines the semaphore system by devising a code (Morse Code) in which each letter of the alphabet can be represented by a series of dots and dashes signalled by flashing lights, sounds or, most importantly, electrical impulses; the latter to become known as the telegraph.

1850s   The telegraph becomes the principal means of distributing news and information in most industrial nations, its growth tied up with the expansion of the railways.

1870s	Alexander Graham Bell demonstrates his telephone which transmits the human voice from one apparatus to another via a cable or wire. By the 1890s, Bell's telephonic apparatus becomes a standard piece of household equipment amongst the middle and upper classes. The invention gives birth to the concept of 'broadcasting', i.e., the sending of a single message or sound which can be simultaneously received by large numbers of people in different locations.
1887	In Germany, Heinrich Rudolf Hertz successfully transmits electromagnetic waves without any other form of conduction. His discoveries are publicised through lectures and articles in scientific journals. Subsequently, Hertz's name is adopted as the measure of all radio frequencies (i.e., MHz – Mega Hertz).
1893	In the USA, Reginald Aubrey Fassenden conducts a series of experiments into 'Hertzian waves' at the University of Pittsburgh. He goes on to work for one of America's earliest and largest electrical manufacturing companies, Westinghouse.
1894	In Italy, Guglielmo Marconi studies articles on Hertzian waves and conducts his own experiments near Bologna (he was 20 years old at the time), transmitting Morse dots and dashes from one side of the valley to the other. However, when the Italian Minister of Post and Telegraph declares no interest in his experiments, he leaves Italy for England.
1897	In Britain, Marconi receives support for his experiments from the General Post Office. He stays in Britain and patents his invention, the wireless telegraphy, and sets up the Wireless Signal & Telegraph Company when he is only 23 years old. He moves his equipment to the Isle of Wight, where he transmits to the mainland, fourteen miles away.
1899	Marconi transmits Morse Code across the English Channel to France and on 2 November sets up the Marconi Wireless Company of America.
1901	Marconi receives the first transatlantic wireless signal, sent from England to Newfoundland. His companies exploit the commercial potential of wireless telegraphy with ship-to-ship and ship-to-shore communication (Marconigrams).
	In the USA, Fassenden successfully superimposes a voice on to a continuous radio wave using a telephonic microphone, enabling the transmission of speech and music.

(Marconi had been using intermittent or broken waves to send Morse signals.)

1902   Marconi's signal is developed enough to span the Atlantic to North America.
        In America, Fassenden forms the National Electric Signaling Company.

1904   At the British Marconi works, John A. Fleming develops a glass bulb called the diode tube which becomes the basis for transmitting wireless voice signals; however, it fails to amplify electronic signals. The Post Master General is empowered to control wireless telegraphy.

1906   Inventor Lee De Forest devises a three-element or triode vacuum tube (known as the audion) which becomes the basis for radio signal amplification of voice transmissions. On Christmas Eve Fassenden makes one of the earliest known radio broadcasts. The broadcast is picked up within a radius of several hundred miles by ships, shore stations and amateur wireless enthusiasts and wins him not only considerable publicity in newspapers across the country but also lucrative contracts with the American Navy and with the United Fruit Company, which picked up the broadcast as far away as the West Indies.

1907   De Forest sets up his own company, the De Forest Radio Telephone Company.

1908   De Forest broadcasts phonograph records from the Eiffel Tower in Paris; his transmissions are received within a 500-mile radius and help to publicise the new invention of 'wireless'.

1910   De Forest broadcasts Enrico Caruso (at that time, the world's most famous tenor) live from the Metropolitan Opera House in New York City. Amateur wireless-making becomes a growing trend (particularly amongst adolescent males).

1912   The American Armed Forces, anxious at the level of interference caused by amateur enthusiasts transmitting on the same wavelengths as the Navy, puts pressure on Congress to regulate and restrict the use of wireless in the USA. Consequently, the Radio Law of 1912 empowers the Department of Commerce to issue transmitting licences and set wavelengths and time limits; but the department is unable to actually refuse a licence. In April, the sinking of the

Titanic foregrounds the potential of wireless as a lifesaver when the rescue operation is coordinated by Marconi wireless telegraphy.

1913   The USA develops its first music-licensing organisation, the American Society of Composers, Authors, and Publishers (ASCAP). ASCAP aims to protect the creative works of musicians and music publishers broadcast on the new experimental radio stations.

1917   Over 8000 transmitting licences are issued by the US Department of Commerce. When America enters the war in Europe (in April), all of Marconi's American operations are taken over by the armed services and a ban is imposed on amateur radio. Consequently developments in radio are steered away from the home and towards improving the efficiency of point-to-point, or two-way, communication.

1919   The American Government returns all radio stations to their former companies and the ban on amateurs is lifted, but concern is raised about the number of enthusiasts cluttering the airwaves. That same year, the American Marconi Company, General Electric, Western Electric and the American Telegraph and Telephone Company (AT&T) merge. The new organisation, the Radio Corporation of America (RCA), acquires all the stations, equipment and employees of the Marconi Wireless Company of America. The largest radio company in the USA is now American rather than British. All amateur radio operators are banned in a bid to develop uncluttered communication lines for military purposes. By the 1920s RCA becomes the largest radio company in the world. David Sarnoff is the major force behind the move.

1920   (Feb.) In Britain, the Marconi Company sets up a series of irregular broadcasts from a transmitter in Chelmsford. The most significant broadcast is made on 15 July, when the opera singer Dame Nellie Melba gives a radio recital sponsored by the *Daily Mail*. Enthusiasm for wireless grows rapidly.

In the USA, wireless receiving sets are advertised for the first time. In November, the Westinghouse Electric & Manufacturing Company launches America's first regular broadcasting station, KDKA.

1922   The Radio Society of Great Britain is formed. The Marconi Company begins a regular broadcast from Writtle, London (2LO) and the south east. Meanwhile, Metropolitan Vickers sets up a station in Manchester and Western Electric establishes another in Birmingham. Later that year the largest British radio and electrical companies form a single broadcasting organisation and on 15 December the British Broadcasting Company is registered, receiving its licence on 18 January 1923.

In the USA, Westinghouse joins RCA and Sarnoff is made General Manager. By the summer of 1922 over 400 broadcasting licences are issued by the Department of Commerce. The Secretary of Commerce, Herbert Hoover, holds a Radio Conference in Washington. Also in that year AT&T sets up the first 'toll station', designed to broadcast advertisements.

1923   The BBC is the sole broadcasting company in Britain with 2LO in London, 2ZY in Manchester and 5IT in Birmingham. In its first year it opens new stations in Newcastle-upon-Tyne, Cardiff, Glasgow, Aberdeen, Bournemouth and Belfast in a bid to offer 'universal coverage' throughout the British Isles. 2LO moves from the Strand to Savoy Hill. The first outside broadcast (OB) transmits from Covent Garden with *The Magic Flute*. *Twelfth Night* is the first play on British radio. The chimes of Big Ben are broadcast. The Post Office issues 80,000 radio licences and between 400,000 and 500,000 radios sets are in use. By the end of that year the BBC can be heard by 80 per cent of the British population. The first public inquiry into British broadcasting (by the Sykes Committee) rejects any form of advertising being carried on BBC stations.

1924   The BBC establishes a series of relay stations in Sheffield, Plymouth, Edinburgh, Liverpool, Leeds–Bradford (a twin station), Hull, Nottingham, Dundee, Stoke-on-Trent and Swansea. These stations carry programmes directly from London, offering listeners in some areas an alternative to their local regional station. The BBC publishes the *Radio Times* in order to respond to listeners' comments and criticisms. It employs 300 staff and adopts an official policy of received pronunciation and anonymous announcing, ensuring standardisation and a 'BBC voice'. One million licences are issued and an expected one million sets are in use. The BBC time pips are heard for the first time and the Crawford Committee is set up to consider the future of broadcasting.

In America, commentator Lowell Thomas makes his first radio appearance and is recognised as the pioneer of news broadcasting. Sales of radio sets reach US$350 million, the most popular being RCA's 'Radiola'.

1925   BBC presenters are told to wear dinner jackets on air and a
            second public broadcasting inquiry is launched (the
            Crawford Committee).
                In the USA, AT&T launches toll stations in Pittsburgh,
            Detroit and Washington and RCA permits its announcers to
            use their own names on air.

1926,   The Control Board approves a plan put forward by Peter
            Eckersley, the BBC Chief Engineer, to establish five main sta-
            tions – London, Manchester, Birmingham, Cardiff and
            Glasgow – all of which would be able to transmit simultane-
            ously their local programmes and a national programme
            produced and broadcast from London. The two-tier system
            of national and regional programming is born and with this
            the BBC's first Director General John Reith's personal con-
            trol over British broadcasting is consolidated. That same
            year sees a breakthrough for radio news with the beginning
            of the General Strike; the Crawford Committee finds that the
            BBC should remain as the sole broadcaster.
                In the USA, RCA takes over all AT&T toll stations and
            establishes a system of network broadcasting. RCA forms
            the National Broadcasting Corporation (NBC), which oper-
            ates two networks (Blue & Red, each made up of a coast-to-
            coast chain of over sixty stations). Stations increase their
            level of advertising and sponsorship.

1927   The American Congress establishes the Federal Radio
            Commission (FRC) to regulate radio and introduces a new
            radio law (the Radio Act of 1927). One of the commission's
            mandates is to ensure that stations operate in the 'public
            interest, convenience or necessity' and safeguard against
            monopolistic control whilst simultaneously reducing the
            number of broadcasting stations and the interference caused
            by so many stations operating in densely populated areas.
            The Columbia Broadcasting System (CBS) is established as a
            'chain broadcaster' or network and quickly becomes the
            major rival to NBC.
                In Britain, the British Broadcasting Company becomes the
            British Broadcasting Corporation when the government
            buys out all private shares and ensures that it becomes a
            non-profit-making organisation. The BBC then receives a
            new ten-year licence and broadcasts the first sports com-
            mentary (England v Wales rugby). John Reith is knighted.

1930   An anti-trust suit is brought against RCA by the US
            Department of Justice, claiming monopolistic practices. In
            Britain, the BBC experiments with trial transmissions of

television using two systems, one devised by John Logie Baird and another by the American company EMI.

1931   Radio Normandy begins broadcasting from the north coast of France.

1932   The BBC moves to Broadcasting House and in the course of this decade quadruples its staff and raises salaries. The corporation now serves Britons at home and overseas with its Empire Service (Australia, Canada, India, Africa). It aims to supply all its listeners with a mix of entertainment, information and education catering for all tastes, remaining impartial and culturally 'uplifting' but much of the programming is thought to be too 'highbrow' due to middle-class and Oxbridge producers. The principles of Public Service Broadcasting are cemented under the influence of Reith.

1933   Radio Luxembourg begins broadcasting to Britain (December), and becomes very popular with audiences (particularly amongst female and working-class listeners) tired of the BBC's 'stuffiness'.
          In the USA, inventor Major Edwin H. Armstrong experiments with Frequency Modulation (FM) to offer greater fidelity and truer sound as radio companies seek more sophisticated technology within a booming industry.

1934   The USA forms its fourth radio network (CBS, NBC's Blue & Red, MBS). Congress passes a new broadcasting law, the Communications Act of 1934, and transforms the Federal Radio Commission (FRC) into the Federal Communications Commission (FCC), extending its powers to include the telephone industry.

1935   RCA demonstrates FM broadcasting. Sarnoff (head of RCA), however, turns his attention to television, delaying the entry of FM into the marketplace.

1936   The third public inquiry into broadcasting is undertaken (by the Ullswater Committee), and recommends the renewal of the BBC's ten-year licence and the continuation of its broadcasting monopoly. Crystal Palace fire demonstrates the potential of radio news through its immediacy and ability to broadcast 'live' reports.

1937   The effectiveness of recorded and live location broadcasts is recognised when Chicago reporter Herb Morrison records the Hindenburg disaster.

1938   The BBC's first foreign-language service begins with the Arabic Service. John Reith retires.

Orson Welles's *The War of the Worlds* is broadcast in America, creating national panic as listeners believe the world is being invaded by Martians.

1939   General Electric begins marketing the first commercial FM receivers and one year later the FCC authorises the first FM radio stations.

In Britain, the Home Service begins with the Second World War, replacing national and regional programmes. An estimated 9 million radio sets exist.

1940   The BBC operates two stations, the Home Service for civilians and the Forces Programme for service personnel stationed abroad, and flourishes unchallenged, strengthened by its services during the Second World War. This popularisation sees a more light-hearted approach to programming along with the adoption of such American techniques as fixed schedules and series formats. The Empire Service becomes the World Service and increases its number of foreign-language services to over forty.

In the USA, some stations begin broadcasting on FM.

1943   The American Armed Forces Network (AFN) is set up in London to cater for US military personnel stationed in Europe and carries many popular American shows including 'Top 40' music programmes. AFN rapidly attracts many BBC listeners.

In the USA, the Supreme Court forces NBC to sell one of its networks in answer to the FCC's report on 'chain broadcasting'. Edward Noble buys NBC Blue and founds the American Broadcasting Company (ABC).

1944   The first BBC foreign news correspondents are employed.

1945   The BBC launches the Light Programme, formerly the Forces Programme, as listeners demand 'lighter', more entertaining programming. The broadcasting of news during the Second World War leads to the development of public affairs programming.

Luxembourg is liberated by the Allied Forces and its radio station and transmitter are used by the Americans to broadcast Allied propaganda to Germany prior to invasion.

In the USA, the FCC moves the FM band from its 42–52 MHz spot to its present 88–108 MHz frequency, allowing VHF-TV (Very High Frequency-TV) allocations. The move makes all FM receivers and transmitting equipment obsolete, hindering the growth of FM.

1946   A third BBC station is launched and is the Corporation's first minority channel, catering for fans of serious music, literature and drama; but it attracts only 4 per cent of the audience share. The BBC re-launches a regular television service.

1948   The transistor is discovered and for the first time radio becomes portable, cheaper and more reliable.

1949   Radio Luxembourg broadcasts the first ever 'Top 20' on commercial radio.

1950   Radio Luxembourg becomes increasingly popular with British audiences and begins to poach some of the BBC's best talent. Yet another investigation into broadcasting is undertaken by the Beveridge Committee, but its findings are ignored by an incoming Tory Party which launches its own inquiry.

In the USA, radio bosses are forced to seek new formats in a bid to attract audiences turning to television as former radio stars, advertisers and producers flock to the new medium. To survive, radio stations seek niche markets, e.g., jazz, rock 'n roll, classical, etc., as well as drumming up listener loyalty by forging stronger ties with local communities and achieving more distinct local identities.

1951   The BBC launches 'The Archers'.

1952   'The Future of British Broadcasting' white paper is published, opening the way for commercial television. The impact of television is felt one year later.

1953   More than 20 million people, or 56 per cent of the population, watch the live telecast of the coronation of Elizabeth II.

1954   The introduction of BBC Television sees a decline in radio listeners. Dylan Thomas's *Under Milk Wood* is broadcast.

1955   A second television station, ITV, is introduced and Radio Luxembourg attracts a peak British audience of around 9 million. The BBC opens two VHF transmitters, one of which uses FM, but there is little public demand because very few listeners have the technology necessary for receiving the transmissions. (FM broadcasting does not take off until the 1990s.) Both the BBC and Radio Luxembourg continue to feel the competitive pinch of television.

Formatted radio develops in America with the introduction of a new music genre that combines elements of country and rhythm and blues. Cleveland disc jockey Alan Freed dubs it 'rock 'n roll'.

1956 The Suez conflict sees some recovery in audience numbers for the BBC as it reports vital information.

1957 Radio is reorganised in order for it to complement television rather than compete with it, focusing on daytime week-day slots and specialist programmes for smaller audiences at evenings and weekends. Radio Luxembourg sees its audience figures drop by 6 million, having lost some of its best talent to ITV and as the BBC begins to take its youth programming more seriously with specialist programming ('Pick of the Pops', 'Easy Beat').

1961 American radio innovator Gordon McLendon launches an all-news format in southern California and develops specialised programming. FM stereo is authorised and the transistor revolution is in full swing, both factors rendering radio 'trendier' and giving it youth appeal.

1962 Re-vamping of 'Pick of the Pops'.

1964 Radio Caroline, the first British pirate radio station, begins broadcasting from a ship off the coast of Essex in March. By 1967 there are no fewer than nine ships and forts on the air.

1966 US FM stations experiment with newer forms of rock music called 'progressive rock', offering more music and fewer commercials than Amplitude Modulation (AM) stations.
In Britain, the first regular broadcasts in stereo are made on the BBC.

1967 A Labour government outlaws offshore pirates under the Marine Offences Act. Later that year, in a bid to fill the gap left by the retreating pirates, the BBC launches its fourth station, Radio 1. The Light Programme becomes Radio 2, the Third Programme, Radio 3 and the Home Service, Radio 4. BBC local radio adopts the 'phone-in', enabling listeners to participate in live on-air discussions.

1969 Prince Charles gives his first broadcast interview, to Jack de Manio on the 'Today' programme.

1970 In the USA, automated tape/cartridge systems penetrate

many FM studios, particularly those with a mostly instrumental format. The systems prove to be economical and lead to a number of tape-supplied music services.

1971   The Conservative Party is back in power under Ted Heath. It abolishes radio-only licences and publishes a white paper entitled 'An Alternative Source of Broadcasting' which is aimed at curtailing the BBC's expansion of local radio in favour of Independent Local Radio (ILR) or commercial radio; this culminates in the Sound Broadcasting Act of 1972. By now virtually all new cars are fitted with radios as standard, creating a whole new culture of radio listeners and programming (e.g., 'Drive Time').

1973   The Independent Broadcasting Authority (IBA) is formed to oversee developments in ILR and two major ILR stations are launched, Capital Radio and LBC. Seventeen other ILR stations quickly follow.

1974   A new Labour Government in Britain halts the development of ILR by awarding local radio licences to the BBC, enabling it to further expand its local radio network across the country.

1977   The British Community Communications Group (ComCom) is formed to campaign for the introduction of non-commercial (non-IBA, non-BBC) local radio which truly serves the needs of local communities. Its formation coincides with a public inquiry (by the Annan Committee) into the future of radio and television broadcasting. The craze for dance music (disco) and reggae gives birth to a number of land-based black music pirate stations operating in major cities, particularly London (e.g., Radio Invicta and the DBC or Dread Broadcasting Company).

1978   Broadcasting from parliament begins.

1979   The Tory Party returns to office and is committed to expanding the role of commercial radio in the economy
          In the USA, FM audience levels surpass AM audiences for the first time as popular contemporary music settles into the FM band and AM adopts more news/talk formats. The Sony Walkman goes on sale, heralding the new era of personal stereo.

1980   Throughout the early part of this decade a host of UK terrestrial pirates appear, often city-based, specialising in the latest dance crazes (house, hip-hop, etc.). ILR becomes more and more regional and there is some growth in the community radio movement. Speech-based programming, particularly phone-ins, prove more cost-effective than music programmes (due to copyright fees). This trend is also popular across the Atlantic.

In the USA, radio networks begin using satellite technology to link affiliated stations, replacing cable and telephone lines which enable only one programme at a time to be simulcast.

1983   The Community Radio Association is formed.

1984   The Thatcher Government introduces the Telecommunications Act of 1984 and sets up the radio investigation service to wipe out the illegal broadcasters or pirates. The government introduces Restricted Service Licences (RSLs), which are twenty-eight-day, short-distance broadcasting licences. Many former 'pirates' apply for RSLs and are eventually granted permanent licences. The Radio Academy is formed.

1986   The Home Office cancels the community radio experiment.

1989   The government relaxes restrictions and allows more commercial radio. Atlantic 252 begins broadcasting.

1990   The Broadcasting Act sets up the Radio Authority, whose job it is to promote the expansion of commercial radio. Radio 5 begins and Radio 2 becomes the first national programme to go out on FM only.

In the USA, FM broadcasting now accounts for around 85 per cent of the audience. Station operators introduce 'Local Marketing Agreements' (LMAs) with neighbouring stations, paying a monthly fee in order to simulcast programming (and advertising) on a designated proportion of its neighbour's airtime. This represents a new form of syndication.

1991   Radio Luxembourg closes after fifty-eight years of broadcasting, unable to compete with independent radio stations.

1992   Classic FM is the first national commercial station to receive an eight-year broadcasting licence. Its light, popular approach to classical music appeals to the ageing 'baby-boom' audience which has the leisure time and disposable income to attract national and multi-national advertisers.

1994   The BBC launches Five Live. Urban pirates are prosecuted, seeing a decline in the number of terrestrial pirates and an expansion in FM services.

1995   Independent radio's audience share overtakes the BBC's for the first time in British radio history. More and more advertisers are looking to radio with renewed interest; at this time advertising revenue has doubled since the earlier part of the decade. The BBC launches a digital radio service which eliminates transmission noise – however, listeners require special receivers.

1996   The new style of the 'Shock Jock' made popular in the USA by Howard Stern and adopted by London's Talk Radio shows signs of failure. It seems that the more conservative British listener is not ready for this rather anarchic interviewing style. Independent radio's advertising revenue shows an annual increase of 23 per cent. The 1996 Broadcasting Act reveals a loosening of the laws restricting cross-media ownership.

The Secretary of State for Heritage reassigns 225 kHz, a frequency previously used by the BBC, for possible use for a fourth Independent National Radio Service.

1997   Since the summer of 1996 to the end of 1997, the Radio Authority awards 21 new local radio licences. More licences are advertised through 1997/98 to utilise FM frequencies between 105–108 Mhz.

In the summer/autumn of 1997, the Radio Authority prepares for the first licence advertisements in Digital Radio. Digital Radio is already operating in Canada, Mexico, Australia, Singapore and China.

Themes and implications

The history of radio can be traced through 'stepping stones' or landmark events that have played a key role in the development and popularisation of the medium over the past 100 years. The radio student can retrospectively examine those events in order to understand the impact they had on the metamorphosis of a technology that began with a series of electronic 'dots and dashes' and evolved into the sophisticated medium of today. These themes can be identified as follows.

1 *Vision.* It was vision and foresight that the early pioneers of radio, such as Marconi and Sarnoff, possessed when they recognised the potential of radio waves to be transformed from a technology of military necessity to one of social benefit and pleasure.

2 *Ethics*. The pioneering days of radio in Britain are synonymous with the development of Public Service Broadcasting (PSB). PSB was based on principles of truth, freedom, accessibility and quality; in short, *ethical* broadcasting.

3 *Democracy*. In a democratic society such as Britain, citizens have the right to freedom of speech and access to information. Radio news offered a platform and access at a time when, considering that newspapers were founded on middle-class, elitist principles,[2] and general levels of literacy were low, the print media were effectively unavailable to thousands. In the latter part of this century the community radio experiment was another democratic move. With the suppression of piracy, and with the institutionalised doors of the BBC only slightly ajar to minority groups, an experiment into community broadcasting was launched to help develop the medium into a more accessible, relevant resource.

4 *Competition*. Monopoly, if unchecked, can harbour corruption and complacency. While I am not suggesting that the BBC radio monopoly in Britain was corrupt or complacent there is something to be said for competition in that it can force a broadcaster to wake up, brush off the cobwebs and seriously examine its service. In the 1950s that is exactly what the introduction of television and the pirates did for BBC radio. Management and producers were forced to redesign structure, scheduling and programme genres and to innovate in a bid to keep listeners. Radio had become a secondary medium.

5 *Dissidence*. While comparing radio and television is akin to comparing apples and oranges, a comparison between BBC radio and the pirates is like oranges and lemons, both citrus but completely different tastes. The BBC had to be realistic about the threat posed by television: the battle was unfair and radio was forced to reinvent itself and offer a different kind of service. However, in relation to the pirates, the BBC was competing on a very similar playing field. The pirates, maverick broadcasters, were offering listeners a fresh, irreverent flavour and, in order to compete, the BBC had to revamp its image.

6 *Politicking*. Throughout history, no matter what the subject or circumstance, governments have been intimidated by the inability to 'govern'. In the 1980s, the Thatcher government was determined to break the monopoly of the impenetrable BBC by following the American philosophy of free enterprise. As a result, the radio airwaves were deregulated and the floodgates opened to commercial broadcasting.

Vision: *from point-to-point to mass communication*

Broadcasting could be seen as a social invention rather than a technical one. Its development was driven by a need for communication, entertainment and information on a mass scale. But what exactly is mass communication and how does the concept relate to the development of radio? The characteristics specific to radio communication can be more easily understood by comparing it with other modes of communication.

1 *Intra-personal communication.* Where the sender and receiver are one and the same, i.e., the way in which we communicate with ourselves.
2 *Inter-personal communication.* The sender of a message and the receiver are physically close to and within sight of each other. Contact is oral, visual and sometimes tactile. The primary code is linguistic but is aided by various presentational codes such as facial expressions, gestures and body language. The context of the message is generally understood because the sender and receiver share the same background or experience. Also, because of the close proximity of the sender and receiver the sender can check that her message is being received and can obtain feedback. Examples are *phatic* communication (routine communication): 'How are you'? Or *metalingual* communication (critical understanding of discourse): 'Do you understand me?'
3 *Mass communication.* Here the sender has the advantage of being able to communicate with multitudes of receivers simultaneously and at distances beyond those achievable through interpersonal communication. However, contact becomes impersonal and runs the risk of being ambiguous. Also, with mass communication it is often impossible for the sender to obtain simultaneous feedback to ensure that she is being understood. Examples of mass communication are literature, television, film and radio.

The first significant development in the history of radio was the transition from point-to-point communication to broadcasting. Point-to-point was a vital resource for the military and its potential was never more obvious than in its role during the war, but the key event which put the potential of radio communication on the world stage was the sinking of the *Titanic*. A young Marconi operator working in the telegraph office of a New York department store picked up the following message: *SS Titanic ran into iceberg. Sinking fast.* The operator immediately contacted the press and then established contact with the SS *Olympic*, some 1400 miles away. The telegraph operator aboard the *Olympic* informed him that the *Carpathia* was picking up survivors. All other radio stations were ordered off the air by the president, and the young Marconi operator remained at his desk for seventy-two hours, receiving the names of the survivors. By the time he left his post, crowds had gathered outside the store, including the families of passengers aboard the *Titanic* and journalists, all hungry for information. This episode did more than any other to alert the American people and the authorities to the life-saving potential of radio. It also made David Sarnoff, the young Marconi operator at the centre of this dramatic event, a household name. He rose quickly through the ranks at American Marconi, becoming commercial manager for the company in 1916. In November of that year, he sent a memo to the vice president of the company, detailing his ideas for the future of the radio industry. In it, he saw radio communication expanding to one day become a 'household utility' like the piano or phonograph. However, with the outbreak of the First World War he was forced to put his dreams temporarily on hold; all radio enthusiasts were forced off the air as part of the wartime effort.

The Westinghouse Electric & Manufacturing Company had begun to produce wireless sets before the First World War, but America's wartime ban on amateur radio from 1917 to 1919 effectively killed the demand for receiving equipment. After the war, RCA had cornered the market in wireless telegraphy. There seemed little direction for Westinghouse to proceed. However, virtually unknown to the management of the company, important developments were taking place under their noses. Two of the company's employees, Donald Little and Frank Conrad, were keen amateur radio enthusiasts. When their radio work at Westinghouse dried up after the war, they continued their own experiments at home. Together, they spent their weekends and evenings sending out signals, talking to other amateurs and even playing phonograph records over the air. It was not long before other radio amateurs got to hear about Conrad and Little's activities and began to regularly tune in to their signal, searching for the call letters 8XL. The station quickly evolved into KDKA and radio fever spread rapidly throughout the country.

Ethics: development of Public Service Broadcasting

> You have created one of the greatest organisations in the world which will continue on your lines for centuries.[3]

John Reith, the first Director General, governed the BBC with 'an iron fist' until his retirement in 1938. A deeply religious moral puritan, he took a position of high moral responsibility in his role as the instigator of a new and powerful medium capable of influencing public opinion and creating a sense of a national cultural identity.[4] In turn, Reith's conception of broadcasting as a public service drew heavily upon his own Calvinist upbringing, his public school education and his military training. Through him, the conservative traditions of duty, loyalty, obedience, sovereignty, patriotism, morality and Christianity would impose themselves on the developing character of the BBC. Reith was determined that the BBC would remain a public venture; he compared commercial radio to 'dog racing, small pox and the bubonic Plague'!

Reith's manifesto for Public Service Broadcasting (PSB)[5] was concerned predominantly with the maintenance of high standards (i.e. quality) and with 'unified control' over all decision-making whether in regard to policy or the programmes themselves (Scannell and Cardiff 1991). The service which Reith set out to create in 1923 drew heavily upon the Victorian ideal of service. Not only had nineteenth-century Britain created the civil service, in which public servants worked towards the common good of the nation as a whole, but the middle classes more generally had been gripped by a passion for improving the lot of the poor, particularly the industrial working classes. Reith's policies[6] developed the eight key principles of PSB that we recognise today.[7]

1 *Geographic universality.* Broadcast programmes should be available to the whole population, in much the same way as the postal service will deliver mail to even the remotest homes, so the broadcaster recognises a duty to provide programmes to everyone who wishes to receive them.

2 *Universality of payment.* One main instrument of broadcasting in a country should be directly funded by the corpus of users. This principle, embodied in Britain in the licence fee, a tax payable by every owner of a television set, is a kind of contract between the citizen and the broadcasting service. It ensures that an equally good service shall be made available to all and argues that the service would be undermined by any system that made reception of the broadcast signal dependent upon ability to pay, e.g., funding broadcasting on a pay-per-view or subscription basis.

3 *Competition in programming, not numbers.* Broadcasting should be structured so as to encourage competition in good programming rather than competition for numbers. Following on from the second principle, this statement proposes a system in which broadcasting organisations do not compete for the same source of revenue. Thus in Britain the BBC is funded by the licence fee and the commercial independent television (ITV) and local radio (ILR) companies by advertising. This arrangement allows the broadcasters to compete for audiences on the basis of the range and quality of their programme output.

4 *Universality of appeal.* PSB rejects the argument that it should appeal only to the mass audience and cater only for existing established tastes. It also rejects the argument that it should only produce educational and cultural fare for a minority audience. The audience as a whole has a right to expect the public service broadcasters to provide a range of programmes which will explore and extend the possibilities of the medium and stimulate new ideas and new talent. It should aim to make popular programmes good and good programmes popular.

5 *Provision for minorities.* While servicing the whole audience, PSB has a special regard for the needs and interests of minority groups. These are both minorities of taste and minorities that are in some way disadvantaged in wider society, such as the handicapped, the very old and the very young, the poor and those of a different culture or racial origin.

6 *National identity and community.* PSB has an important function in providing a forum in which all citizens can find an expression of national

concerns and communal interests. In its universality of appeal and geographic and social reach, broadcasting can help create a shared sense of national identity.

7 *Autonomy*. Broadcasting should be distanced from all vested interests and in particular from the government of the day. PSB should not be subservient either to governments or advertisers. The institutional arrangements in Britain and in particular the establishment of the BBC as a public corporation under royal charter are meant to be both symbolic and practical devices for ensuring broadcasting independence. In the commercial sector there are strict rules to keep responsibility for programme-making and responsibility for advertising clearly distinctive.

8 *Editorial freedom.*[8] Guidelines for broadcasting should be designed to liberate rather than restrict the programme makers. In addition to preserving the independence of broadcasters from vested interests, the public service system should create an arena in which broadcasters feel free to experiment and innovate. The aim is to attract people into broadcasting who are genuinely interested in the artistic and creative possibilities of the medium.

It is interesting to note that during the development of the BBC, with its mission to provide a service that would cater for its listeners at a local and national level and its public commitment to minority groups, the Welsh case stands out as a contradiction to the whole PSB philosophy. It could be argued that an English-language station in a region where English was considered the second language by the inhabitants was at the bottom of the barrel of priorities for the BBC. In South Wales, the Welsh language was seriously depleted through the widespread growth of the English-language media and by the immigration of non-Welsh-speaking workers attracted by employment in the mining and the Tiger Bay docklands industries. Ownership of those industries was in the hands of non-Welsh speakers (i.e., workers were required to speak English to their bosses). Welsh nationals had been fighting an uphill battle for the establishment of a Welsh-language broadcast in the already established BBC station at Cardiff.

In a 'United Britain', public radio first broadcast in Wales in 1923. At the time it was recognised that Welsh topics and events needed to be featured, but

> the company's officials were insistent that such recognition of Wales should be subservient to one of the primary aims of British broadcasting – the projection of the unity of the British nation. ... It was incomprehensible that the 922,000 Welsh speakers of Wales (37.1 per cent of the population), should be provided with programmes produced specifically for them in their own language.

> (Davies 1994: 31)

Davies goes on to cite another example of the serious objections that 'London' had to the proposal of Welsh programmes for Welsh speakers:

'The Principality of Wales', as a commentator put it in 1925, 'was an extinct palatinate'. 'The average Englishman', wrote an emissary from Head Office in 1935, 'who is perfectly prepared to regard the Scotch and the Irish as being essentially different in outlook and character from the English, is seldom prepared to believe that the Welsh are a different nation, in fact, if there is any general attitude towards the Welsh, it is that they are a nuisance.'

(Davies 1994: 32)

With so much resistance from the central headquarters of the BBC, it was surprising that by 1937 a campaign to enable Wales to acquire its own regional station was successful. However, despite Wales reaching its objective with the establishment of BBC Wales, the struggle for autonomy was far from over. Welsh-language announcers were required to speak RSP English (Received Southern Pronunciation). Few Welsh speakers had such accents and the applicants tested were expected to speak in a manner that was 'educated or cultured' (the implication being that the Welsh accent was neither educated nor cultured). The best applicant was a woman, but she was turned down because she could not 'swear or be sworn at by London when things go wrong' (Davies 1994: 71).

Davies points out that the BBC's treatment of the Welsh language and its general prejudices against the Welsh were not untypical of that time. With this in mind, he argues that the setting up of BBC Wales was a success in itself as well as a 'springboard for greater success in the future' and that 'the entire national debate in Wales, for fifty years and more after 1927, revolved around broadcasting, and that the other concessions to Welsh nationality won in those years were consequent upon the victories in the field of broadcasting' (Davies 1994: 50).

Democracy: the development of news and current affairs

News is information about important or interesting events. (*The Australian Concise Oxford Dictionary*)

Tidings, new or interesting information, fresh events reported. (*Concise Oxford Dictionary*)

The immediate, the important, the things that impact our lives. (Freda Morris, *NBC in Boyd*, 1994: 3)

The history of radio news is synonymous with the development of the BBC, but it was really nothing more than a soap box for government in the early 1920s and a propaganda machine during the Second World War. However, its importance and potential were recognised particularly by the newspapers, whose powerful and influential editors orchestrated a prohibition against the BBC broadcasting any news bulletins before 7 p.m. and any commentary on public events (Crisell 1994: 20). There were, however, isolated events which created opportunities for the first steps in the slow breakdown of the ban.

When war broke out, normal programmes were replaced by news bulletins interspersed with serious, appropriate music. But the news was initially only a repeat of what was in the papers. Also, the BBC was constantly at odds with the Ministry of Defence (MoD) and Ministry of Information (MoI), and it was only Reith's determination to block government interference which saw the service emerge as the nation's most preferred and trusted information service. Its information reached a wide foreign audience in neutral and occupied countries and broadcasts seemed to be an authoritative reflection of official policy and opinion. When the MoI tried to curb reports, the public's thirst for information created rumours, the only solution to which was judged to be comprehensive news coverage.

The Second World War was not the only event which helped establish BBC news. In 1926 the General Strike saw the beginning of a culture of radio news selection and presentation and the end of propaganda. It was thought that to suppress information would create chaos, so the BBC reported information provided by the TUC, strikers and strike-breakers, who had previously found it difficult to have their opinions broadcast. The same privilege, however, was not offered to government officials, a policy which gave the service a sense of impartiality which was not shared by the newspapers. During the 1930s the BBC quadrupled its staff, raised salaries and acquired vast buildings. It was seen as a non-partisan organisation that did not shy away from controversy, but it was not until the outbreak of the Second World War in 1939 that an independent news service really came into its own. Since then, the BBC's news service and World Service have developed a worldwide reputation for credibility and impartiality, a tradition that has been used as a model for commercial radio network news services (which developed in the 1950s and 1960s but did not really come to the fore until the 1970s) and other public service networks throughout the world.

Access to information was otherwise not always through legitimised news services and, for many, it was felt that the information obtained was not necessarily democratic. Many minority groups (such as Asian, Caribbean, women's groups, etc.) felt that information catered primarily for the majority and that the interests of smaller, less powerful communities were marginalised. To counteract the situation, in the mid-1970s a recently elected Labour Government announced its plans for an experiment into community radio. These plans, however, were half-hearted and it was not until 1983 that the Community Radio Association was formed after years of steady lobbying by ComCom (the Community Communications Group), seeking public access to the airwaves for minority groups. By 1985, under a

Conservative Government, community radio was regulated and was seen as a way of legitimising alternative radio and superseding the 'maverick' terrestrial pirates. According to Stephen Barnard, 'The announcement of the experiment seemed designed to undermine the position of the pirates by apparently giving the more serious operators a chance to prove themselves worthy of legislation' (Barnard 1989: 173). Two types of licence were on offer: one for small, neighbourhood stations, designed to serve the needs of a local community; the other to cover a larger catchment area (over 10 km) and provide cross-community programming.

The government received 245 applications, 64 of those in London alone, causing major headaches where selection was concerned, since only twenty-one licences were on offer. Then the government backtracked. Having received the applications, ministers feared that such groups broadcasting during an election period could hamper their prospects of re-election, given that the majority of applications came from ethnic and left-wing political groups. In June 1986, in an unexpected u-turn, the project was cancelled without a single licence being granted; the Tories justified the decision by claiming that they needed time to consider the feasibility of the experiment. Then, in yet another surprise about-face, the government agreed that the community radio project should operate within a free-market economy and that any station would be permissible so long as it kept within the bounds of decency and good taste and, most importantly, was self-financing.

Since 1987, the government has issued short-term community radio licences to a number of groups around the country. The maximum eight-week licence or RSL (Restricted Service Licence), means that broadcasters do not have enough time to attract sponsors and advertisers to keep their station viable, despite community needs. As a result, community radio, for the most part, can only afford to make programmes which replicate the tried and tested formulas of the successful commercial stations, therefore restricting the development of an 'alternative' voice in British radio, the central mission behind the campaign in the first place.

Competition: the impact of television

Television was first pioneered by John Logie Baird in the 1920s and some fifteen years later a few thousand viewers in London received a regular BBC transmission. These early experiments were thwarted by the Second World War and did not resume until 1946. At first, television was thought of as an extension of radio broadcasting (Crisell 1994); for example, the first television news transmissions were simply the radio news read behind the test-card image. This attitude continued until the 1950s when two events consolidated television's role as an important mass medium and, for the first time, suggested radio's 'blindness' as a disadvantage. The first of these events was the coronation of Elizabeth II in 1953, when more than half the population watched the live broadcast. Then, in 1955, the introduction of a *commercial* network, ITV, saw BBC television faced with a threat to its broadcast monopoly and BBC *radio* faced with a threat to its whole future.

With the advent of ITV, radio audiences plummeted by more than half, virtually overnight. It was impossible for radio to fight back; instead it had to reinvent itself and find its own niche. BBC radio now found itself competing not only with TV but with Radio Luxembourg, which was seen as more entertaining than the 'serious', 'highbrow' BBC. Various production changes and gimmicks were introduced to lift ratings, but with little success. By 1964 when the British pirates hit the airwaves and found a new generation of listeners, BBC radio was at its lowest ebb yet. Ironically, when the tide eventually turned in its favour, it was thanks to new technology: technology, in the form of television, had nearly destroyed radio culture; now technology became its saviour.

The first technological development was in stereo broadcasting. Stereo was unavailable to television viewers but for the radio listener it offered truer, richer sound which music enthusiasts in particular often preferred. The second and more important development was the invention of the transistor radio, which revolutionised the culture of radio listening. The first transistor was made in 1947/8, but it did not come into widespread use until the 1960s. By offering an alternative to the bulky, electricity-consuming valve wireless set, the transistor ensured that in a time of increasing popularity for television, the radio would still attract listeners. The new, smaller set was cheaper to run (it was powered by small, inexpensive batteries rather than by electricity); it was cheaper to buy, which meant that more people could own a radio receiver and that some households could afford more than one. Furthermore, the transistor was light and reliable and could be taken outside: to the park, the beach, the caravan, the garden. For the first time in its history, the radio had become portable. The first transistor was marketed in the USA in 1953, but the trend did not take off in Britain until the 1960s, when the 'trannie' became associated with youth culture and the small sets were practically regarded as a fashion item.

The next major technical development which contributed to radio's popularity began in the 1960s but was not consolidated until a decade later: the car radio. In 1960 only about 4 per cent of cars were fitted with a radio. The installation of car radios as standard grew through the 1970s and by the 1980s all new cars were automatically fitted with a radio. The new technology consolidated what many radiophiles had known for years, that in terms of portability, flexibility and immediacy radio was second to none. But the portability of radio did more than simply render the medium mobile – it revolutionised the way in which it was consumed.

Historically, listening to the radio had been primarily a sedentary, group (e.g., family) activity when listeners sat down to their favourite programmes at the end of the working day. During the 1950s, listening to the radio in this way was slowly superseded by watching telelvision. Radio listening as a secondary activity, meanwhile, became more widespread with the introduction of portable receivers, and there was a shift towards solitary listening: young people walked around holding their 'trannie' to their ear; commuters listened to their car radio on the way to work; and home-makers would take their transistor from room to room while doing the housework.

Dissidence: the rise of pirate radio

PIRACY: a person or organisation that broadcasts without official authorisation. Also, a person who infringes another's copyright or other business rights; a plagiarist.[9]

The culture of pirate radio was initiated in the 1930s in the form of Radio Normandy and Radio Luxembourg (although these broadcasters were legal), but *British* pirate radio stations, or the illegal pirates, did not eventuate until the 1960s. Ironically, it was a Briton who started the movement. In 1931 a Conservative MP called Leonard Plugge was selling British-made car radios in Europe. To promote his product he helped set up an English service in a small radio station in Normandy, an advertising move that was soon adopted by other British companies.[10] British audiences could receive the broadcast signals and those audiences, bored with the conservative BBC broadcasts, began to tune into the continental stations, particularly on Sundays, when the majority of BBC broadcasts were of a religious nature.

The popularity of the European stations, like that of the BBC, waxed and waned through the Second World War, the Suez conflict, times of crisis in Ireland, and times of celebration such as royal events. The pirates enjoyed initial success because they were not bound by the Reithian principle to 'inform, educate and entertain' but were free to broadcast popular culture in the form of music, soap opera and talent shows. In 1949, Radio Luxembourg broadcast the first ever 'Top 20' on commercial radio, and through the early years of the 1950s the pirates enjoyed their largest audiences.

However, 1954 saw the beginning of a decline in listeners for the pirates due to the growth of television. By the end of that decade television had captured the imagination of a nation. If BBC radio had a problem competing with the pirates, the problem was multiplied tenfold when it found itself competing with television. The BBC recognised that television was superseding radio as the most dominant broadcast medium. As a result, in 1957, radio was reorganised to complement television rather than compete with it. Greater emphasis was placed on daytime broadcasting, with the radio day beginning at 6.30 a.m. (rather than 9 a.m.). The daytime schedule on the Light Programme became a mix of music and magazine programmes, whilst evening and weekend schedules became increasingly specialist. Youth was seen as one key area for specialisation, so youth shows were slotted into evening and weekend programming.

The revamping of 'Pick of the Pops' in 1962 was perhaps the first real attempt to win over British youth, but it was not in itself a sufficient measure. The time for British-based illegal broadcasters was ripe, as listeners were restless not only with the BBC but also with the continental broadcasts. (Stations like Radio Luxembourg could only broadcast at night and the signal was weak.) Also around this time the culture of radio was changing with the introduction of the transistor. Radio Caroline was the first British pirate. It began broadcasting from a ship off the coast of Essex in March 1964 and by 1967 there were no fewer than nine ships and forts on the air. In her first week Caroline gained 7 million listeners from a potential audience of 20 million. Other pirate stations to hit the airwaves after Caroline were Radio London, Radio North Sea International, Radio Nord and Radio Atlanta. Between 1964 and 1968, twenty-one pirate stations were broadcasting. It was claimed that within a year the total daily audience for pirates was between 10 and 15 million, and by early 1966 the combined audience for the pirates and Radio Luxembourg was over 24 million.

However, opposition to the pirates was fierce. The BBC pushed for the abolition of the movement on the following grounds.

- Use of unauthorised wavelengths.
- The pirate ships posed a potential danger to shipping and interference with essential services.
- Non-payment of copyright to authorised bodies such as the Performing Rights Society (PRS) and Photographic Performances Ltd (PPL).
- Adverse effect on the livelihoods of members of the Songwriters' Guild and Musicians' Union. (The pirates had an unfair advantage over the Beeb in that the BBC had a long-standing agreement with the Musicians' Union over royalties and needle time, while the pirates could play what they wanted when they wanted without paying anything and could therefore target the prime audience of people under 25.)
- Adverse effect on record sales and newspaper advertising revenue.
- The qualitative questions of unethical and unprofessional broadcasting and the lowering of standards.
- Pirates were free to broadcast political propaganda, potentially even of a fascist or communist nature.

While the pirates' greatest opposition came from the BBC their greatest support came, ironically, from the government of the time. The Conservatives saw the growth of piracy as a way of breaking the monopoly of the autonomous BBC and developing free enterprise in the form of commercial radio.[11] In 1967 the Labour Government outlawed offshore pirates under the Marine Offences Act, but the Act was not enforced. With little action coming from government to wipe out the pirates, the BBC retaliated by putting forward competition in the form of Radio 1, launched in 1967.

Many of the pirate disc jockeys were poached to present on the new youth station.

It was nearly twenty years before the pirates again faced the threat of extinction with the development of legitimate commercial stations under the newly formed Radio Authority, whose job it was to promote the expansion of commercial radio. In 1970 the Tories were voted into power and under the Sound Broadcasting Act set up Independent Local Radio, i.e., commercial radio. In response, the new pirates set up on the mainland, becoming terrestrial and often city-based. Radio Invicta was the first, running from 1970 to 1984. During the 1980s growth in terrestrial pirates was so massive that at one stage illegal operators actually outnumbered legal broadcasters. 'This sudden growth in piracy came about partly when people realised how easily pioneering stations like Radios Jackie and Invicta were able to transmit, and consequently followed suit' (Hind and Mosco 1985: 17). A clause in the Wireless Telegraphy Act (1949) created an opening for the new breed of pirates by stipulating that 'any apparatus manufactured in this country cannot be seized until the case goes to court and the order is made'. Another small but significant factor contributing to the growth of piracy was the fact that community radio broadcasters flouted authority and stayed on the air despite a government-enforced end to the official community radio experiment.

The new pirates had something of a cult following. They attracted audiences among many marginalised communities, such as ethnic minorities and political dissidents, by playing musical genres largely ignored by the mainstream broadcasters (reggae, soul, hip-hop, funk, jazz, rhythm and blues) and providing an avenue for political debate. The 1980s pirates were: Invicta, JFM, Horizon, DBC (the Dread Broadcasting Corporation) and LWR (London Weekend Radio).

Over the next ten years the more successful urban pirates were legitimised, paving the way for a new but less radical breed of pirates on the popular FM band who identified themselves with the growing dance music and 'rave' culture. This form of enterprise was not without its problems, however. Between April 1994 and 1995, 600 raids saw 51 broadcasters prosecuted as unlicensed and fined a total of £14250.

Politicking: regulation to deregulation

The politics surrounding radio are inextricably linked with competition. Deregulation of the airwaves in the 1980s forced the public service broadcasting sector to compete with commercial broadcasters. However, before deregulation there was regulation.

The American and British experiences with regard to broadcasting regulation could not be more different. While both nations were deeply concerned that radio broadcasting should not interfere with military requirements, the similarity ended there. Within the philosophy of free enterprise, a 1912 law denied the US Government power to refuse any application for a broadcasting licence and as a result the airwaves became heavily congested. It took fifteen years for a new Broadcasting Law to be introduced, seeking to regulate the industry without violating the essential principles of free enterprise and government non-intervention. Under the new Act, every station across the United States had to reapply for a licence within sixty days or shut down. In March the Federal Radio Commission was formed to oversee developments in the burgeoning radio industry, but by this time there were over 700 stations broadcasting throughout the States, most of which (approximately 600) were independent rather than belonging to a network. The use of sponsorship and advertising to fund broadcasting ventures had been normal practice since 1922, so any attempt to remove the glut of broadcasters from the air by starving them of funds was doomed to fail.

Across the Atlantic, the British Government observed the American broadcasting experience with interest and resolved to ensure that similar airwave chaos did not eventuate in Britain by regulating the industry with a firm hand. The British Government had always had a tight control over wireless. As early as 1904, it established the Wireless Telegraphy Act (an extension of the Telegraphy Act of 1869), which gave the General Post Office sole right to transmit telegrams anywhere in the United Kingdom. A free market, with plenty of competition and hardly any limitations on the quality and quantity of broadcast output, funded by private companies and advertising, did not seem likely to produce a radio broadcasting service which appealed either to the Prime Minister or the Postmaster General. Instead, in 1922 a series of restrictions and recommendations was implemented.

1 That radio broadcasting should be confined to a small number of stations throughout England, Scotland and Wales.
2 That the hours of broadcasting be confined between 5 p.m. and 11 p.m. from Monday to Saturday (but all day Sunday was permissible).
3 That the wavelength for all broadcasting stations be restricted to a band of 350–400 m.
4 That transmission licences should cost £50 per station a year.
5 That all transmitting sites should be approved by the Post Office.
6 That receivers (listeners) should pay an annual licence fee of 10 shillings.

In May of that year, representatives from the major radio manufacturing companies met to consider these proposals. They included Marconi, Metropolitan-Vickers, Western Electric, the Radio Communication Company, General Electric (GEC) and the British Thomson-Houston Company. On 18 October, these manufacturers formed a new collective, the British Broadcasting Company, registered on 15 December 1922 and receiving its licence on 18 January 1923. Once born, the BBC thrived to monopolise radio broadcasting until the first steps towards deregulation in the 1970s.

Independent Local Radio (ILR), or commercial radio, began in 1973 under a Tory Government which decided that the BBC should not have sole responsibility for radio broadcasting in Britain. The government blocked the expansion of the BBC's local network and made local frequencies available to private companies in London (Capital Radio and LBC). It was a tough beginning, considering all the obstacles the new stations faced. First, commercial television (ITV) dominated the advertising market, which meant that local commercial radio stations had a hard time trying to sell airtime to advertisers, without whose money they would go under. Second, ILR stations faced tough competition in the form of national BBC radio services (most notably Radios 1 and 2). Third, ILR only had access to local resources, limiting the kinds of programme they could make. Fourth, ILRs had inevitably to recruit staff from the BBC, which meant paying them significantly higher wages in order to lure them away. Finally, the ILR stations had to comply with a set of BBC-like 'public service' requirements, such as providing a broad range of programme types and a mix of educational and informative programmes as well as the merely entertaining. The BBC had a guaranteed income from licence fees in order to do this.

The changes did not bring about a sudden 'opening up' of the British radio industry to free enterprise, but rather a cautious and highly regulated form of commercial radio under the watchful eye of the Independent Broadcasting Authority (IBA). Eventually, the IBA was forced to be pragmatic and amend some of its most restrictive regulations, but these amendments did not relieve the pressure immediately. By the early 1980s, ILR stations were facing tough competition, particularly from breakfast and daytime television and the pirate radio stations. In response to this, ILR managements used the Association of Independent Radio Contractors (AIRC) to lobby for deregulation in the early 1980s, calling for the further relaxation of restrictions on programme content and on the volume of advertising they were allowed to carry. Consequently, the ILR map was redrawn. Margaret Thatcher's Government did a great deal to free the ILRs, now called Independent Radio (IR), from the original regulations and set out radical proposals to deregulate the British radio industry as a whole. Whilst at the end of the 1980s, virtually everyone had been expecting government to propose the setting up of one national commercial channel, in fact it proposed to set up three (using two frequencies taken from the BBC and one additional VHF spectrum which was to become available due to international reallocation in the early 1990s). At the same time, several hundred small stations were proposed and no distinction was made between commercially orientated stations and genuine non-profit community stations. BBC local radio was to continue to provide a public service at a local level, whilst IR stations were to be freed from all such obligations. Three further surprises were announced. First, the government proposed to auction the national commercial channels to the highest bidder. Second, the IBA was to lose its commercial radio empire to a new Radio Authority. And, third, the three national channels would each be required to provide a diverse programme service calculated to appeal to a variety of tastes and interests and limited to a single format.

Today, Independent Radio accounts for almost 50 per cent of all radio listening in the United Kingdom. Commercial radio has never been so popular. Nor has it ever been so lucrative: in the early 1990s, radio expanded its share of advertising revenue faster than any other medium.

Things to do

Split the class into small groups of four or five students. Each group is allocated a particular period of history, for example 1950–5 or 1990–5 (the length of the period will depend on how many groups are available), and sets out to research that era of radio in depth, with particular reference to three significant developments or themes. For example, if your group sets out to look at the early part of the 1980s you could examine the growth of the terrestrial pirates, their popularity, their impact and the legacy they have left for the current radio industry. Each group's findings can be presented to the class in the form of a talk, enlivened with archival soundbites and illustrated with overheads. The results of the research as a whole might be gathered together and typed up in the form of a reader, which would provide an invaluable resource for the study of radio history. Also, using the time-line model in this chapter, make a time-line of your own, concentrating on your particular period of history.

Notes

1 This time-line has been put together from various sources: Briggs 1979; Crisell 1997; Curran and Seaton 1991; Ditingo 1995; Seymour-Ure 1991.
2 See R. Williams 1974.
3 Sir Maurice Hankey to John Reith on his retirement from the director-generalship of the BBC (MacCabe and Stewart 1986: 70).
4 The term *national* cultural identity is used loosely considering the cultural difference between the English, Welsh, Scottish and Irish. The whole issue of national identity was, at the time, centred on London and the Home Counties.
5 PSB is defined by MacCabe and Stewart (1986: 70) as 'a service that puts its programmes together according to certain principals or, for example, according to a mandate to "inform, educate & entertain". It also carries certain defined rules on how much of each there should be.' As defined by parliament in the BBC's licence and charter, PSB is 'the operation of a broadcasting service as a means of information, education & entertainment'.
6 These became known as the 'Rethian theory', much as the term 'Thatcherism' was coined for the methods and policies introduced by Margaret Thatcher's Government during her office as Prime Minister.

7 Taken from *Communication Research Trends* 8 (3/4) (1987), from the Centre for the Study of Communication and Culture.

8 This rather 'liberal' theory was somewhat contradictory considering that, at the same time, Reith insisted that 'his' presenters wear dinner jackets while they were presenting. Also, Reith was quoted as saying, 'it is occasionally indicated to us that we are apparently setting out to give the public what they need and not what they want – but few know what they want and very few what they need. In any case, it is better to overestimate the mentality of the public than to underestimate it' (Burns 1977: 36).

9 *Australian Concise Oxford Dictionary* (1992).

10 By 1934 companies such as Cadbury were advertising on Radio Normandy and Radio Luxembourg.

11 One of the BBC's most powerful opponents was Margaret Thatcher, who was frustrated by her lack of influence and control and wanted to see the institution privatised (Horrie and Clarke 1994).

|2|

Words, speech and voices

Where would radio be without words? If it could not actually speak to its audience, would anyone really want to listen? If all listeners could hear were noises, sound effects, music and silence, what would happen to radio's drama serials, comedies, plays, news, current affairs programmes, traffic bulletins, phone-ins, request shows, quiz and game shows? It's almost too extraordinary an idea to contemplate. The vast bulk of radio output would be obliterated in one fell swoop. Radio would become meaningless: literally insignificant. For of all the sounds which radio uses, speech is its most significant, its primary signifier. Without it, radio would be nothing. Wall-to-wall music and noise, expunged of all verbal information, would render radio inarticulate and uncommunicative. Its appeal for audiences, broadcasters and advertisers would vanish into thin air.

Radio's most significant code

Words, speech and voices are everywhere on radio. Some stations are almost nothing but words. Others are a more or less equal mixture of speech and music. Even music radio stations are liberally interspersed with DJ chat, news bulletins, time checks, weather forecasts and traffic news. Speech lends structure to the daily schedule and provides the context in which music operates as meaningful entertainment. Music is organised around the time checks, the news, traffic and weather bulletins, the interviews and the chatter of the disc jockeys. Without that structure, music radio would seem not only meaningless but formless. Radio shows and radio stations would lack distinct identities other than those determined by the musical output itself (e.g., classical, rock, country, jazz, etc.). One jazz station would sound like any other jazz station, be it national or local; one classical station like any other classical station. The broadcasting day would be the same from start to finish: jazz in the morning, the afternoon and the evening, with only changes of tempo to distinguish the times of day. Such a service might be seamless but it would also be senseless and soulless.

Speech has had an increasingly important role to play in radio broadcasting in recent years. Despite the fact that the rise of television in the 1950s and 1960s saw a drastic reduction in radio's speech-based output (e.g., drama, comedies, quiz and game shows), a major trend throughout the 1980s and 1990s has been the growth of speech-based programming, in particular the rise of talk-back radio shows and stations. Whilst music radio has proved increasingly costly, talk radio has been used more and more, mainly in the form of phone-ins. Partly this is to do with matters of economy: that is, the fact that phone-ins are one of the cheapest forms of radio since no royalties have to be paid to the callers. However, these programmes have also been adopted for reasons other than those of cost-cutting. For instance, it has been widely recognised within the radio industry as a whole that phone-ins enable stations to establish closer and more interactive relationships with their audience. At the same time, the voices of listeners repeatedly broadcast over the airwaves also allow radio stations (particularly local or regional stations) to establish distinct identities; identities that correspond to those of the communities they serve.

These developments come at a time when the numbers of broadcasters are expanding more rapidly than the radio audience itself, resulting in the need for radio stations to attract more and more specific audiences and, at the same time, establish stronger bonds between the station and its audience, achieving greater degrees of listener loyalty. These have become the primary objectives of many radio stations seeking to survive in an increasingly competitive market, and speech is seen to have a significant role to play here. Speech is a crucial part of a radio station's branding, its construction of a particular image. Speech can be (and is) used to articulate a station's identity, helping it to attract specific types of audience (in terms of class, age, regionality, gender, ethnicity, etc.). Listeners may select a particular station or channel for the type of music it plays (e.g., Classic FM for its diet of popular classical music or Virgin 1215 for its adult-orientated rock) but nevertheless the content and style of its speech will still be a significant factor in attracting listeners and gaining their loyalty. For instance, many people may choose to listen to Classic FM in Britain rather than the BBC's Radio 3 not just because it plays a more popular repertoire of classical music but also because its style of presenting (i.e., its use of speech in the DJ links) is more informal and light-hearted than that of the BBC's classical music service. In other words, the use of speech on Classic FM is more attractive, more friendly and more conducive to establishing a close rapport with listeners than BBC Radio 3.

The importance of speech in determining audience preferences has been recognised throughout the radio industry. Most station controllers today are acutely aware of the need to closely monitor the uses of broadcast speech and to make careful decisions about its content, style and delivery.

In particular, the content of radio talk raises serious concerns for producers and station managers. What is regarded as a suitable topic for discussion on a radio station will be determined by the nature of the audience and its values and beliefs. The decision to broadcast talks on such subjects as politics, religion, healthcare, crime, unemployment, race discrimination, abortion, sex or fashion will be determined largely by the (perceived) needs and interests of a station's listenership. Thus, whilst such topics as healthcare, gardening, age discrimination, legal and financial matters form the bulk of the subjects covered on BBC Radio 2 (with its mainly post-40-year-old audience), such subjects as body-piercing, AIDS, the club scene or police harassment are rarely mentioned. Moreover, the way in which these subjects are treated will again depend on the nature of the audience: for instance, what kinds of health matters to tackle (teenage acne or the menopause).

However, it's not simply a matter of what issues to talk about but also the style of the language used to describe or discuss particular subjects. The style of the language and vocabulary of radio speech are carefully scrutinised and form part of specific station policies. This may be a matter of adopting regional or ethnic dialects or even the vocabulary of certain subcultural groups for specific programmes. Youth programmes are clearly one instance where the use of specific words and phrases can win or lose the target audience. The same is true of programmes designed to appeal to certain 'interest groups' (e.g., blacks, gays and lesbians, people with disabilities, scientists, information technologists or business people). All of these groups have their own idioms and modes of speech which radio stations need to take into account when devising specialist programmes.

As radio moves into the business of catering for ever more specialised markets, its range of speech styles and the sophistication with which it communicates with its listeners seem set to increase. At the same time, this need for sophistication and caution in formalising policies on matters of speech style is being forced upon radio broadcasters in other ways. In particular, debates more generally regarding 'political correctness' have alerted broadcasters and listeners alike to the distinct (negative) connotations of specific words. This has produced an awareness (and wariness) of using particular words to describe certain things. For instance, the words 'black', 'coloured' and 'Negro' all carry different connotations and one or other of these may be deemed most appropriate to the specific character of a radio station or programme and its audience. Similarly, the words 'handicapped', 'spastic' or 'physically challenged' all signify distinct attitudes towards disability. A programme designed for a disabled audience, such as BBC Radio 4's 'Does He Take Sugar' (a programme, incidentally, whose title now seems implicitly sexist) may adopt a different policy on the acceptability or otherwise of using these words. Clearly, language has become an increasingly sensitive issue in recent times, and that sensitivity has to be recognised and reflected by both public service and commercial radio stations.

Finally, having determined the content and language of their speech broadcasts, a station must also consider the delivery of speech, paying particular attention to the appropriateness of specific modes of speech for particular types of programme. For instance, a news bulletin will ordinarily require a different mode of speaking than a rock music show, a phone-in or a cookery programme. Whilst each programme will obviously require a different mode of speech – different in terms of tone, pitch, pace and accent – the station will aim to establish an overall mode of speaking to which all its presenters will, to greater or lesser extent, conform whilst broadcasting on that station. Clearly, this is not the simplest of things to achieve with complete success. Presenters must somehow find ways of expressing their own unique personalities through their modes of speech whilst simultaneously adopting the corporate style of the station. Idiosyncratic speech styles are obviously permissible but only within the confines of the prescribed speech policies of the station which determine the content, style and delivery of all speech broadcast in its programmes.

In the end, a station's speech policy will be anything but uniform. In most cases, the policy will have to enable presenters to use their own idiosyncratic speech forms and, of course, allow callers on phone-ins to do the same. Speech styles will necessarily differ from programme to programme (i.e., news, music, phone-in, game show, etc.). Moreover, the station's speech policy will also have to take into account that certain forms of speech may be more or less permissible at certain times of day (e.g., the use of swear words in evening and late-night broadcasts). Thus, even with the most stringent policy on broadcast speech, a radio station is 'by no means confined to a singular and universal "radio voice" technique' (Wilby and Conroy 1994: 63). The desire of individual presenters to establish their own style, the need for different types of programme to adopt different modes of speech, and the need for individual radio stations to carve out their own particular niche within the market by attracting more specialised audiences, are all factors which contribute to the tremendous diversity of speech forms on radio today. What is clear is that modern radio broadcasting uses a wide variety of speech forms. Speech is, as Jonathan Raban has written, 'chaotically eclectic', ranging from the most elaborate and carefully scripted language through to what he describes as 'the most unofficial and unrehearsed grunts and squawks' (Raban 1981: 86–7). Radio speech can be informal, intimate, natural and gossipy or authoritative, public, preachy and artificial, with a huge range of possibilities between these two extremes. As such, there is no single form of speech that represents radio at its most pure or radiogenic. Given such diversity, it is difficult (and perhaps even misguided) to try and define comprehensively and conclusively such a thing as 'radio speech'. However, it would seem to be a useful exercise to consider some of the basic qualities underlying radio speech (whatever its specific form) and, although this will involve making generalisations, it may prove instructive to at least attempt to establish some general principles regarding radio's most significant (or primary) code.

Radio speech

Andrew Crisell, in his book *Understanding Radio*, suggests that much of the speech we hear on radio is scripted and, as such, it has a literary nature. Scripted speech, he points out, is (like literature) premeditated rather than spontaneous. As such, most radio speech lacks the vagaries of spontaneous speech: its rambling qualities, tangential asides (often leading to blind alleys, followed by abrupt returns to the subject), repetitions, hesitations and redundancies. Instead, radio speech tends to be 'more fluent, precise and orderly, less diffuse and tautological, than ordinary speech' (Crisell 1992: 58). However, Crisell notes that although much of radio speech is scripted, this is ordinarily disguised. Often, for instance, radio scripts employ figures of speech seldom used in written prose, using expressions such as 'come to think of it' (implying spontaneous thought). But why should it be necessary for radio broadcasters to disguise the fact that their words are scripted? According to Crisell the main reason is because the act of reading implies *absence*. What he means by this is that speech that is all too obviously scripted exposes the separation of addresser and addressee (the broadcaster and the listener). When words are evidently scripted, the speaker is replaced by the text itself, the speaker is simply the mediator between the script and the listener, which could also be thought of as a barrier between the broadcaster and her or his audience. Broadcasters must therefore become proficient in the art of writing and presenting their scripts in such a way as to sound natural and spontaneous, since the more natural and spontaneous it sounds the more informal and intimate will be the relationship with their audience.

We can pursue the significance of the gap between broadcaster and listener – and the implications of this gap for radio speech – further. Paddy Scannell, in his book *Broadcast Talk*, writes that 'the central fact of broadcasting is that it speaks from one place and is heard in another' (Scannell 1991: 2). Most talk on radio, he says, 'attempts to bridge the gap by simulating co-presence with its listeners' (Scannell 1991: 2). But how do broadcasters bridge the divide between themselves and their audience? According to Scannell, they have only one option and that is to adopt those modes of speech which are domestic, that conform to the ways in which most people communicate within their own homes.

One of the crucial problems which radio broadcasters have to face is that, although they can write their own scripts and determine the nature of their programmes, they have no control over the context in which their broadcasts are received. On the contrary, broadcasters have to adapt to the situation of their audience and adopt their audience's communicative behaviour within those circumstances. Broadcasters have first to understand the conditions of reception and express their understanding of these conditions in the language of their broadcasts. 'The voices of radio are heard in the context of household activities and other household voices' (Scannell

1991: 3). Because of this, the style of radio talk must be as informal and conversational as that of the ordinary 'interaction between people in the routine contexts of day-to-day life and especially in the places in which they live' (Scannell 1991: 4). It is for this reason that radio speech can be described as *mundane* as opposed to *institutional*. Distinguishing these two modes of speech, Ian Hutchby has written that 'mundane talk is designed, interactively, *explicitly for co-participants* and is differentiated from institutional talk by the fact that the latter is designed, and displays itself, as being designed, *explicitly for overhearers*' (Hutchby 1991: 119). What this means is that radio employs a form of speech typically reserved for private conversation in which both the speaker and the listener actively participate in the act of communication. The reality, of course, is that radio speech is a form of public speech: speech which is consciously intended to be heard by non-participants. There is clearly an element of contradiction in radio speech exhibiting the characteristics of mundane (private, informal, domestic and interactive) speech. Nevertheless, despite its status as a mass (and one-way) medium of communication, radio speech clearly strives to create the illusion of personal and intimate verbal interaction, implying not only intimacy but also participation and reciprocity.

Given this fundamental contradiction, the notion of radio speech being more mundane than institutional requires some qualification. Ian Hutchby has argued that the kinds of talk used on talk radio (i.e., radio interviews and phone-ins) reveal 'a variety of features which formally liken it to everyday or "mundane" conversation, on the one hand, and more "institutional" forms of verbal interaction (e.g. broadcast news, interviews, courtroom or classroom exchanges), on the other' (Hutchby 1991: 119). Therefore, since radio phone-ins provide forms of talk which fall between these two categories, we could in fact describe the speech used in talk radio as *intermediate*. As Hutchby writes, 'talk radio talk, which might in these terms be dubbed "intermediate" talk, can be seen as designedly an approximation of *mundane* talk, projected somehow into a *public* domain, and thus exhibiting features of institutional talk' (Hutchby 1991: 119–20).

The distinction between *institutional* and *mundane* talk proves useful in defining the speech conventions of radio broadcasting. The concept of *intermediate* talk, however, is the one which more accurately reflects the nature of radio speech as it enables us to recognise that, whilst in reality radio speech is institutional, more often than not it sounds mundane. In describing radio speech as intermediate, we can acknowledge the fact that, however mundane radio speech sounds, it is invariably self-conscious, performative and designed to be heard (publicly), offering few, if any, opportunities for listeners to participate in the communicative act.

Of course, the radio phone-in (talk radio) is only one form of radio speech, and different kinds of radio programmes tend to employ different forms of talk. News bulletins, for example, sound like institutional talk. Here, the speech is more obviously scripted and there seems little attempt to disguise the fact that the news is being read. In fact, the convention of news broadcasting is to emphasise this element (i.e., 'Here is the news read by Charlotte Green.') in order to stress that what is heard are neither the words nor the opinions of the news reader but accurate and impartial facts compiled by the news department. Nevertheless, even within news bulletins there is still scope for more informal types of speech to emerge, particularly in interviews and eye-witness reports. What is clear from even the slightest acquaintance with radio news broadcasts is the range of speech styles, from the impersonal, formal, precise (institutional) speech of the news readers, through to the personalised, informal, imperfect (mundane) speech of the 'man (or woman) in the street', with the speech of the experts, observers and correspondents coming somewhere between the two.

Whilst it is important to acknowledge the tremendous diversity of speech forms on radio, it would seem that we can establish some general and basic characteristics of radio speech. So far, for instance, we have noted that radio speech is predominantly scripted but disguised, and that it is, by and large, intermediate (i.e., a mix of institutional and mundane). One other important factor to be noted is the emphatic use of direct address on the radio. In the vast majority of cases, radio speech is spoken directly to the individual listener. The most obvious exception to this is, of course, drama. Here much of the dialogue is exchanged between characters (although narrators do appear quite frequently) and is therefore merely overheard by the listener in the role of an eavesdropper. Further exceptions would be programmes built around panel discussions (e.g., BBC Radio 4's 'Start the Week' and 'Midweek') or interview programmes (e.g., 'In the Psychiatrist's Chair' and 'Desert Island Discs'). In contrast, however, a greater proportion of radio broadcasting output is delivered directly to the listener by the disc jockey, the news reader, presenter or continuity announcer.

Informality and direct address are ordinarily combined in radio broadcasting to render radio speech a highly personalised speech: something many radio producers have long recognised as being an essential prerequisite for successful radio talk. Writing as an experienced radio producer and former head of the BBC's radio training section, Elwyn Evans has suggested that radio broadcasting requires a high degree of personalisation in the sense that speech needs to be made to sound as if it is directed personally to an individual listener with whom the broadcaster has an intimate acquaintance.

> It has been proved over and over again that the most effective speaker is the personal speaker. He may be reading a script but he *sounds* as though he's talking to me alone. My conscious mind may be aware that he isn't doing anything of the sort – but, as in the theatre, it's the subconscious impression that counts. If a radio speaker, thanks to the way his script is written, makes me *feel* he's talking to me personally, it becomes much harder to switch him off.
>
> (Evans 1977: 15)

Whilst Evans's statement suggests that the most effective radio speech is one which uses both direct address and informal language, it also implies that the experience of radio listening is one of collusion, one in which the listener is prepared to meet the broadcaster halfway. The notion of the listener colluding with the broadcaster in creating radio's illusion of spontaneity and intimacy seems to indicate that the process of disguising scripted speech and achieving an intimate and personal relationship with the listener is easily accomplished since the listener is so willing to be duped. Yet, as anyone who has attempted to broadcast from a script for the first time will testify, this is far from being the case. The skill of writing for radio and the ease of delivery required to make a script sound lively, natural, personal and intimate is an acquired skill. Writing for the ear is an entirely different matter than writing for the eye. Presentation (delivery) alone cannot disguise the scriptedness of radio speech. The naturalness, spontaneity and intimacy of the speech must be introduced into the script itself, requiring the writer to depart from many of the established conventions of written language in terms of both structure and vocabulary. This usually requires rigorous training and much practice in order to perfect one of the most important arts of radio broadcasting. The skill required to achieve this end is itself an indication of the fact that radio's use of the spoken word is much more complex than it appears. Beneath the apparently natural flow of radio speech lies something altogether more formal, more structured and pre-determined, enabling broadcasters to convey the maximum amount of information in the most cogent and economical manner, proceeding smoothly and logically from point to point and – perhaps most important of all – ensuring that they keep to time: i.e., reaching the end of their speech at precisely the moment they are due to go off air.

Given this situation, it would seem that radio speech is much more formal, unnatural and impersonal than it sounds. It would also seem that behind radio's apparently casual and spontaneous flow of words there often lurks a calculated and meticulously constructed text. Thus many speech-based radio programmes would seem to employ a deceptive simplicity which conceals what is in fact a much more sophisticated use of language. But, on the other hand, radio speech is hampered by complexity. Because radio is invisible, it cannot afford to be too sophisticated in its presentation of information. Long, complex sentence structures prove too much for radio listeners to comprehend, due to the difficulties and deficiencies of verbal memory. In most cases, radio broadcasters must express themselves in forms that are clear and concise: in a word, simple.

One of the things radio broadcasters must consider in writing and presenting their programmes is the ear's short-term memory; that is, the fact that it's harder to remember words and phrases than images. Radio, as it has often been noted, has an evanescent quality. This comes from the fact that its programmes exist solely in terms of time: that is, it's heard and then it's gone; and what has gone cannot be retrieved by the listener unless they have recorded the broadcast. Because of this, the listener must be constantly reminded of what is important. As a result, radio speech must not only be simple and to the point but also repetitive and predictable. This means that a great deal of radio speech is redundant: redundant in the sense of presenting information that has already been provided; information which must be presented again for the benefit of those who either failed to hear this information or have simply forgotten it as the discussion has moved on. Repetition is essential in radio broadcasting to ensure that listeners note and remember the key points of a discussion (or events in a radio drama). At the same time, the sign-posting of information (i.e., the signalling of important aspects of the discussion which will crop up later) helps to give the discussion as a whole a greater sense of structure from the outset and, by anticipating what is to follow, broadcasters have a better chance of maintaining their listeners' attention. The greater the complexity of radio talk, the greater the need for repetition and sign-posting to ensure that the listeners fully comprehend the significance of the discussion, the more redundant the information provided actually becomes. For this reason, simplicity makes for much more effective (because less redundant) radio.

Probably the most sophisticated and complex aspects of radio speech lie not so much in the way in which it is structured and organised as in the way in which it is spoken. The spoken word is inflected with meanings to a greater extent than the written word, enabling it to assume a multitude of different nuances. Thus the effect of speech often comes more from the way words are spoken than what the words themselves actually mean.

A great advantage of an aural medium over print lies in the sound of the human voice – the warmth, the compassion, the pain and the laughter. A voice is capable of conveying much more than reported speech. It has inflection and accent, hesitation and pause, a variety of emphasis and speed. The information which a speaker imparts is to do with his style of presentation as much as the content of what is said. The vitality of radio depends on the diversity of voices which it uses and the extent to which it allows the colourful turn of phrase and local idiom.

(McLeish 1994: 7)

As McLeish's statement suggests, the emotional content of radio speech (and the speaker's character and psychology) is conveyed less by their choice of specific words as by the manner in which their words are spoken.

The ways in which words are spoken, whether on the radio or in everyday conversation, introduce levels of connotative (i.e., suggestive, latent, implicit) meanings. In most cases this is a matter of stress. By stressing different words within the same sentence a range of different connotations can be produced. For instance, the statement 'I love you' could mean three different things according to which of the three words are stressed by the speaker: I love you (i.e., even if nobody else does); I love you (i.e., rather than hate you); I love you (i.e., rather than somebody else). At the same time, pitch can impose a range of emotional and psychological meanings upon this statement. So, for instance, 'I love you' in a high-pitched voice would no doubt suggest the speaker's desperation, vulnerability and nervousness, whilst a low-pitched expression of the very same words could imply a more calm, rational and reassuring affection, implying a greater depth of feeling and a more serious (and enduring) attachment. Speech also has other variables which can connote different meanings, such as tone, volume and speed. Thus, 'I love you' expressed in a hard, loud and rapid manner would imply one thing (e.g., desperation, jealousy or possessiveness) whilst the same words expressed softly, quietly and slowly would imply something quite different (i.e., reassurance or a deep, unshakeable devotion). And whilst variations in pitch, tone, volume and speed can imply different emotional intensities and emotional or psychological states, different accents can evoke particular social or cultural factors, such as class, education, regionality, nationality, etc. So, for instance, 'Ay lav yu' or 'Ah luv yoo' would say more about the social status of the speakers than the nature of their attachment. In all these ways then (stress, pitch, tone, volume, speed and accent) the spoken word can be seen to possess a greater expressivity than the written word.

Rudolf Arnheim, in one of the first serious studies of radio as an artistic medium, wrote that the sound of spoken words has a more powerful and direct effect than their meanings. In his book *Radio* (1936), Arnheim argued that on the radio the sound of a word is more 'elemental' and affects listeners more directly than the meaning of the word itself.

> In every art it is the most elemental and primitive means that achieve the most profound effects. The most elementary aural effects, however, do not consist in transmitting to us the meaning of the spoken word, or sounds which we know in actuality. The 'expressive characteristics' of sound affect us in a far more direct way, comprehensible without any experience by means of intensity, pitch, interval, rhythm and tempi, properties of sound which have very little to do with the objective meaning of the word or the sound.
>
> (Arnheim 1936: 29)

For Arnheim, one of the most crucial issues facing radio producers is how to exploit the expressivity of speech. The first step is to ensure that the expressivity of speech is not neglected by failing to modulate the voice, vary the tempo, volume and intonation of the speech. However, Arnheim realised that it wasn't just a matter of injecting words with dynamic expressivity, as this can seem as far removed from authentic speech (everyday conversations, non-scripted speech) as unmodulated and inexpressive speech. In other words, excessive or over-emphatic expression will seem as unnatural as no expression at all. For Arnheim it wasn't even just a question of too little or too much expression (of getting the balance right) but of avoiding false expression.

The falsifying of expression arises not altogether from the self-con-
sciousness of the speaker. If, at the microphone, the manuscript is reeled
off in a school-boy manner, there is a complete disappearance of the
few natural stresses and caesuras that the very driest voice will produce
if the speaker's thoughts are on his subject, if he is really thinking aloud,
instead of reading it off or 'delivering' it in the notorious public lecture
fashion, which gives to every sentence quite systematic and irrespective
of content an equal emotional emphasis.

(Arnheim 1936: 37)

The constant danger of scripted speech is that the natural stresses produced
by spontaneous speaking can all too easily be lost. Therefore, as Arnheim
recognised, the real issue is whether or not stress, pitch, tone, volume and
speed are used in the right places (as they would be in spontaneous speech).
This, as many radio broadcasters have realised, is one of the major difficulties of learning the art of speaking on the radio: how to capture and recre-
ate at the microphone the natural stresses and modulations of spontaneous
speech.

Elwyn Evans, having spent years training BBC broadcasters in the art of
radio presenting, tells readers of *Radio: A Guide to Broadcasting Technique*
that when they give their talk at the microphone they should avoid just reading out what they have written and 'converse, really converse, with someone
who isn't there' (Evans 1977: 16). And yet how exactly is this conversation
to be achieved on a one-way medium? Evans offers a number of basic dos
and don'ts:

Don't raise your voice at the end of a sentence; don't adopt an artificial
tone or special accent. Don't speak any louder or quieter, any lower,
any slower or quicker, than usual. In short, don't put on any sort of act:
your ordinary way of speaking is perfectly all right: if it weren't you
wouldn't have been asked to broadcast.

(Evans 1977: 20)

Meanwhile, the list of things to do includes, on the one hand, imagining that
the person you had in mind when writing the script is now listening and, on
the other, it also involves personifying the microphone (i.e., looking at it
when speaking, even gesturing towards it: in short, pretending it's a real person listening to what you have to say). Evans also notes that the speaker
should forget all the work that went into writing and rehearsing the script
and imagine that the talk is happening for the very first time. According to
Evans, minor departures from the script (such as changes of phraseology)
are permissible and even advantageous since they make the whole thing
more spontaneous and help the speaker concentrate on the subject in hand.
In this way, the presenter can avoid reeling off the script in an unnatural
declamatory way, placing equal stress on every word or, worse still, placing
the dramatic stresses on inappropriate words. Even if a few errors or hesita-

tions creep in as a result of departing from the script, Evans suggests that this will give the talk a 'psychological lift'. The script might best be thought of as only a reminder of what is to be said. In other words, what Evans advocates as the most effective form of radio speech is that which, whilst reliant upon a script, is actually more prepared than scripted.

If radio broadcasters generally use scripts in the manner advocated by Elwyn Evans then it would seem that the principal function of the radio script is merely to prompt the speaker rather than dictate their every utterance. Thus, in the same way that radio talk has been described as 'intermediate' (in the sense of being somewhere between mundane and institutional), we can also see radio speech as intermediate in the sense of being something between scripted and spontaneous. However, in order to distinguish this kind of intermediate speech from the former variety, we could define radio speech as *prepared*, understanding this term to mean a form of speech that uses a script but involves in the process of presentation a degree of spontaneity through improvised departures and 'ad libs'.

If, finally, we are to establish a model of radio speech then we could define it in terms of the following: (i) *prepared* rather than scripted or spontaneous; (ii) *intermediate* rather than institutional or mundane; (iii) *personal* (through the use of direct address); (iv) *simple* rather than complex in structure; (v) *highly connotative* due to the greater expressivity of the spoken rather than the written word. Clearly, these five qualities represent neither a comprehensive nor a particularly subtle framework for understanding radio speech, but they do alert us to some of the more basic and general aspects of radio's most significant code. The model of radio speech proposed here is provisional and is only intended as such. Rather than provide an exhaustive, conclusive or sophisticated notion of radio speech, these five basic points are designed simply to establish the framework upon which actual (and more specific) examples of speech on the radio can be articulated and understood (e.g., across its various genres). Indeed, the usefulness of the model may lie in the opportunities it offers us to demonstrate the ways in which various specific forms of radio depart from these rather simplistic and generalised conventions.

Radio voices

The radio voice seems to come to us as something established, something we take for granted, having characteristics which are easy to recognize. Generally, the dominant radio voice talks – its speech is clear, articulate, sometimes eloquent. Most of what it says is perceived by the listener as factual and informative, newsworthy, or at least dedicated to the betterment of life. It does not mutter or stutter, it pronounces full and meaningful sentences, it says something. As a voice, it is traditionally male, having a certain timbre and intonation that suggests a belief in what it is saying and a degree of authority in saying it.

(Dyson 1994: 167)

Frances Dyson, in her essay 'The genealogy of the radio voice' (1994), has drawn attention to the fact that the radio voice has not simply emerged from nowhere but, on the contrary, that it has a heritage (a tradition of public speaking and oration) and a set of conventions. In particular, Dyson has noted a number of salient features which the dominant voice of radio has acquired. At the same time she has also considered voices and vocal qualities which have traditionally been excluded from mainstream radio broadcasting. Her arguments are worth considering here in some detail, although it should once again be pointed out that this is not for the purpose of establishing a fixed and exhaustive definition of the 'radio voice' but rather to provide a model with which radio's various voices can be compared and understood: understood, in other words, in relation to a specified ideal or norm.

Dyson has written that the 'dominant radio voice is a purely technological construct, crafted from language and electronics, having undergone extensive shaping by elocution and electrocution' (Dyson 1994: 178). Whilst radio speakers have adopted specific modes of speech deemed to be the most suitable for broadcasting, their voices are commonly subject to amplification and editing in order to achieve those properties the radio voice is required to possess. Whilst amplification ensures that the radio voice is heard distinctly, editing produces what Dyson describes as 'an unlikely speech: faster, clearer, more audible' (Dyson 1994: 179). Speech, in other words, which is more perfect than natural speech since it makes a point of extracting the repetitions and hesitations, the coughs and wheezes of ordinary speech. Nevertheless, whilst editing renders radio speech unlikely, it is generally accepted by listeners. For Dyson, the credibility of the radio voice is assured by the audience's desire to believe in what they hear. It is not that audiences are ignorant of the 'mechanical and electronic mediation' of the radio voice but that they have a vested interest in believing that what they hear is authentic and live. (Dyson, 1994: 179) Dyson speaks of listeners' willingness to be 'seduced by the intimacy which the well-trained and well-microphoned voice can convey' (Dyson 1994: 179). The credibility of the radio voice rests with the listener and her or his faith that it is directed at them personally (the voice close up, whispering in their ear) and also that it is live, immediate and co-present. The irony is, of course, as Dyson notes, that 'the aura of liveness it projects is due less to its live, real time transmission, than the entirely constructed aliveness which the technology bestows' (Dyson 1994: 179).

Apparently spontaneous and live, much of the speech we hear on the radio is in fact pre-recorded and meticulously reconstructed. A great deal of the speech that is heard on the radio has been subjected to a process known as 'fine editing'. Basically this is the process of cleaning up voice pieces by removing individual sentences, words, coughs, sneezes, fluffs, etc. Its purpose is (ostensibly) to create a more succinct, clear, better-paced and more dynamic (even more stylish) speech. As Wilby and Conroy write, 'An interview may be transmitted word for word as it was recorded but given greater dynamism through faster pace, simply by editing out the gaps and pauses in the original dialogue' (Wilby and Conroy 1994: 121). They add that 'All this is achieved simply by cutting the tape with a sharp razor blade and splicing it with specially designed sticky tape' (Wilby and Conroy 1994: 121). Put this way, the process sounds simple and straightforward. However, the effects of such fine editing are more complex. As Dyson argues, it leads ultimately to the disembodiment of the radio voice since in removing the sounds of coughs and wheezes, etc., what is effectively being removed are all the sounds which evoke the physical and bodily presence of the speaker, rendering the radio voice virtually divine, lending it an almost God-like authority (Dyson 1994: 172–8). The radio voice aspires to this kind of authority. However, what it cannot afford to do is to draw its audience's attention to the fact that its speech is not live and spontaneous but a recorded reconstruction. As Pete Wilby and Andy Conroy point out to budding broadcasters in *The Radio Handbook*, the 'skill that a trainee in radio is encouraged to develop when editing the spoken word is in fact to create the illusion of spontaneity, such that the splices are undetectable to the listener' (Wilby and Conroy 1994: 122). The golden rule of editing is that the joins must be unnoticeable.

> From a professional broadcaster's point of view, evidence of editing reduces the impact of the recording and distracts the listener from the message that it is intended to convey. It betrays the act of manipulation that has occurred; the recording reveals its own process of production and is identified instead as an artificial construction.
>
> (Wilby and Conroy 1994: 171)

Clearly, the last thing broadcasters wish to convey to their listeners is the fact that the radio voice is an artificial construction. It is essential that listeners believe in the authenticity as well as the veracity of radio speech. Therefore, whilst the radio voice must use something more perfect than ordinary speech, it must simultaneously sound natural: live, spontaneous, unpremeditated and unmediated. For this reason much effort goes into enlivening what is in fact a premeditated and highly constructed way of talking. According to Frances Dyson, one way of achieving this is through the use of acoustics. She writes that 'the bare bones of the voice are … given life through the addition of the simulated spatiality offered by *reverb*', the effect of which is to give the voice depth; profiting by its associations with depth of character, sincerity and truth (Dyson 1994: 179). In other words, reverb implies that nothing is being concealed. This is essential if the radio voice is not to sound too good to be true whilst attaining the authority of the disembodied voice.

There is no doubt that the radio voice is an authoritative voice: powerful, knowledgeable, articulate, in control. As Frances Dyson has argued, even the most democratic forms of radio like phone-in or talk-back programmes ensure that the technology of the medium (namely, amplification and acoustics) is used to consolidate the authority (and the superiority) of the presenter.

> Listen to the presence of the host's voice compared to that of the callers as their voices (particularly those of women) crackle and cackle over the phone lines. Listen to their respective eloquence, and remember that there is always the seven-second delay and the dump button to silence any unwanted opinions.
>
> (Dyson 1994: 180)

The voices of the callers heard alongside and in contrast to those of the professional radio presenters demonstrate the extent to which the radio voice is a contrivance and a construction or, at the very least, a refinement of ordinary speech. National, regional and ethnic accents may have been widely adopted by the presenters on radio stations, along with more personal and idiosyncratic speech patterns, but still the radio voice remains more formal, more self-conscious and more authoritative than voices heard in everyday life. When set beside the untrained and untreated voices of callers on phone-in programmes, the voices of radio presenters seem anything but natural or mundane. Of course, few, if any, radio stations nowadays advocate the use of 'Received Pronunciation', requiring their announcers to speak with all the anonymity and formality of 'Standard English' (an essentially educated, upper-middle class, Home Counties accent). Now, in fact, the emphasis is very much on personality and informality (hence intimacy) with only few exceptions (e.g., news bulletins). Even the BBC's great mission to standardise spoken English has largely been sacrificed to the more urgent needs of reflecting, representing and articulating cultural diversity. (See Scannell and Cardiff 1991: 176.) Nevertheless, the traditions in which radio speech evolved in Britain have been dominated by the BBC's principles of Received Pronunciation and the desire to standardise and formalise spoken English. It might be argued that the legacy of these ideals can still be felt today across a broad spectrum of radio broadcasting.

The ideals which determined the evolution of radio speech in British Broadcasting were laid down by John Reith, the BBC's first Director General, in his book *Broadcast over Britain* (1924).

> It is certainly true that even the commonest and simplest of words are subjected to horrible and grotesque abuse. One hears the most appalling travesties of vowel pronunciation. This is a matter in which broadcasting may be of immense assistance. ... We have made a special effort to secure in our various stations men who, in the presentation of programme items, the reading of news bulletins and so on, can be relied upon to employ the correct pronunciation of the English tongue. ... No one would deny the great advantage of standard pronunciation of the language, not only in theory but in practice. Our

responsibilities in this matter are obvious, since in talking to so vast a multitude, mistakes are likely to be promulgated to a much greater extent than was ever possible before.

(Reith 1924: 161)

Received Pronunciation was designed to set the standard of spoken English in Great Britain in the late 1920s and 1930s. It was part and parcel of Reith's ambition to establish through broadcasting a distinct national identity beyond class and regionality. Whilst this ambition may have been shared by many of those working at the BBC at this time, not all agreed with Reith that the standardisation of spoken English was necessarily the best way of achieving a sense of British national identity (the sense of a shared or common culture). For instance, Reith's views on Standard English were contradicted by those of Hilda Matheson, Head of the Talks Department at the BBC between 1927 and 1932. Matheson, in her book *Broadcasting* (1933), questioned the very notion of Standard English as a concept, stating that 'there is no single pattern of Standard English which can be defined with complete phonetic exactitude' (Matheson 1933: 65–6). Matheson argued that the 'nearest approach to a definition which would be at all widely accepted is that Standard English – in the academic sense – is roughly the educated speech of southern England' (Matheson 1933: 66). However, she only noted this in order to challenge the appropriateness of adopting the speech of southern England as the standard for the nation as a whole: that is for all those living beyond the south of England. Matheson pointedly declared that many British people 'regard southern English as a backbone-less, affected and mincing form of speech' (Matheson 1933: 66). She also added that 'The BBC has been accused of popularising an effete, affected form of speech' and noted that '"Announcers' English" is in some quarters a term of disparagement'. (Matheson, 1933: 67) Matheson, in her discussion of the BBC's policy of announcing, argued that the BBC's speech policy was largely a matter of exclusion rather than inclusion.

It is a fact that Standard English and Received Pronunciation were achieved by excluding local dialects and regional accents, along with a variety of speech styles deemed exaggerated or affected (such as those of the working and upper classes). The justification for excluding so many forms of British speech was partly to avoid using announcers who would alienate (or be unintelligible to) the 'great British public'. It was also justified on the grounds of technology. It was argued, for instance, that clear and precise speech (hence formal and standardised speech) was necessary to overcome the poor quality of microphones and receivers during the 1920s and 1930s. The same argument was also used to favour the male voice over the female voice. The deeper register of the male voice was judged to have better definition. There was, however, more to it than this. For instance, women were banned from reading the news on the BBC for many years as it was widely believed within the corporation that the female voice was too closely associated with gossip and rumour to be appropriate for conveying information which required a maximum of veracity as well as clarity. Thus when Reith wrote that 'We have made a special effort to secure in our various stations men, who, in the presentation of programme items, the reading of news bulletins and so on, can be relied upon to employ the correct pronunciation of the English tongue', he really did mean men (Reith 1924: 161).

As Frances Dyson has pointed out it was not simply that the male voice had greater definition over the earliest microphones and receivers but that the technology was designed to lend the male voice greater definition, to enhance the voice which had already adapted itself to the purposes of oration and public speaking (e.g., the pulpit, the floor of the Houses of Parliament, Speaker's Corner in Hyde Park, concert and town halls, etc.). 'The most consistently excluded or derided voice is feminine. Not only has radio's mode of direct address developed from oratory, a traditionally masculine pursuit, but radio's fundamental technology, the microphone, was originally designed for the male vocal range' (Dyson 1994: 181). By the time radio emerged as a broadcast medium, the public voice was the male voice and the technology of radio was designed to consolidate this. Despite technological developments which drastically improved the sensitivity of microphones and receivers ('speakers'), female voices continued to be excluded from many key areas of radio broadcasting on the grounds that the qualities of the female voice were unsuitable for certain types of programming. This attitude has made a lasting impression upon the media industry and it would be naive to think that 'equal opportunities' has eradicated all trace of this. As David Graddol and Joan Swann point out in their book *Gender Voices*, 'TV and radio producers are notoriously circumspect about using women for "serious" work, such as news bulletins', noting that 'It was many years before female news readers and continuity announcers were heard, and when they were, only "suitable" voice qualities were selected' (Graddol and Swann 1989: 39).

As members of the Centre for Language and Communications in the School of Education at the Open University, Graddol and Swann have been actively involved in preparing sociolinguistic courses for television and have experienced first hand this kind of prejudice. They write, for instance, that 'We know how difficult it can be to persuade the BBC producers who make Open University programmes to let women provide commentaries or voiceovers' (Graddol and Swann 1989: 39). Whilst their experience of this prejudice against the female voice has been in relation to television, it is clear that this is something that pervades broadcasting as a whole and, if anything, is likely to be more endemic within radio than television. Yet how is this prejudice justified within an industry that has embraced an 'equal opportunities' policy? On what grounds do modern-day producers justify their preference for a male rather than a female voice?

Social psychology is one area of research which offers broadcasters some justification for using lower-pitched voices (hence male voices or masculine female voices) for serious educational, documentary or news programmes. The research of many social psychologists has shown that high and low voices are heard differently by listeners, with high-pitched voices being heard as less confident, less authoritative, less competent and less truthful than low-pitched voices (Graddol and Swann 1989: 31–5). However, you do not have to be a social psychologist to note the way in which high- and low-pitched voices lend different connotations to the same statement with the result that the listener's attitude towards the speaker (and their evaluation of the accuracy and veracity of the statement) is affected. Frances Dyson has noted that 'Higher pitch is associated with nervousness and a lack of confidence, suggesting that the speaker neither believes in themself nor what they are saying' (Dyson 1994: 181). She also points out that 'A rising pitch often produces a shrill voice, and is associated with hysteria and irrationality' (Dyson 1994: 181). It goes without saying that the implicit suggestion of hysteria and irrationality created by a rising pitch is hardly conducive to radio and television commentaries requiring a maximum of credibility and competency. If one of the qualities which distinguishes a female voice from a male voice is not only its higher register more generally but also a more frequent use of rising rather than descending pitch, then one can see why radio and television producers think twice before using a female voice to record the commentary of their educational and informational programmes. One can also see why many female presenters on radio and television (particularly news readers) self-consciously lower their voices and adopt a more monotonous tone in order to be taken seriously. As Dyson puts it, 'to be listened to or even heard on radio, women have to adopt the persona (from the Greek, meaning through sound) of the ideal male voice' (Dyson 1994: 181).

So is the ideal radio voice synonymous with the ideal male voice? According to the research of the American Communications analysts Carol Ann Valentine and Banisa Saint Damian, the answer would seem to be almost but not entirely. Their research, carried out in the 1980s, suggests that the ideal radio voice is composed of both male and female vocal qualities. They do, however, establish a preponderance of male qualities over female and, in addition, demonstrate that the actual composition of male and female qualities is subject to distinct cultural influences and, as such, varies from one culture to another. In their comparative analysis of Mexican and North American radio, Valentine and Saint Damian discovered that the ideal Mexican voice was composed of an almost equal mix of ideal male and ideal female vocal characteristics, whereas in the United States (more specifically, Arizona) the ideal voice seemed to be made up of predominantly male vocal qualities (Valentine and Saint Damian 1988).

Valentine and Saint Damian's project was basically concerned with understanding the extent to which the members of a particular national culture share a common perception of ideal voice types. Their project sought to reveal the ways in which ideal voice types in Mexico compared with (and differed from) those in the United States. In both contexts an ideal voice was considered in relation to an ideal female voice. In order to be able to do this a group of students at a university in Arizona were asked to describe an ideal voice, an ideal male voice and an ideal female voice (the students were, in fact, asked to consider these as ideal radio announcers). Valentine and Damian subsequently compared the descriptions of the ideal male voice with those of the ideal female voice and then compared both to the ideal voice itself. In this way they were able to assess the extent to which male and female vocal types corresponded with the notion of an ideal voice in the two different cultures. Amongst other things, their findings suggested that the ideal male voice in both Mexico and the United States was very similar, whereas the ideal Mexican female voice was quite different from that of the North American female voice (the Mexican ideal female voice being more delicate and sensuous than its North American counterpart). This seems to suggest that the female voice is more readily subject to cultural determinants. But perhaps the most significant finding was that despite the fact that the ideal female voice had more in common with the ideal male voice in the United States (i.e., in Mexico there seemed to be greater attempts to define/construct more distinct differences between male and female voices), nevertheless, the ideal voice in North America was more decidedly masculine than in Mexico. In the United States then, there seemed to be, on the one hand, a greater correlation and mutuality between male and female voices (suggesting a greater parity or equality between the sexes) and, on the other, a more marked exclusion of female characteristics from the model of the ideal voice (suggesting anything but sexual equality).

Considering the ideal North American voice in terms of pitch, volume, rate (speed) and diction, Valentine and Saint Damian discovered that:

1 the ideal voice is slightly higher in pitch than the ideal male voice and significantly lower in pitch than the ideal female voice. Hence, *the ideal voice is closer to the ideal male voice in terms of pitch*
2 the ideal voice is slightly softer in volume than the ideal male voice and significantly louder than the ideal female voice. Hence, *the ideal voice is closer in volume to the ideal male voice*
3 the ideal voice is paced at the rate of both the ideal male and female voice, both being somewhat slow. Hence, *the ideal voice is as close to the female voice as it is to the male*
4 the ideal voice is enunciated as carefully (precisely) as the ideal female voice and with much more precision than the ideal male voice. Hence, *the ideal voice is closer to the female voice than to the male voice in the way it enunciates.*

What this analysis reveals then is that, overall, the ideal voice (as it is popularly perceived in the United States) has more in common with the ideal male voice (in terms of pitch, volume and pace) than it does with the ideal female voice (with which it only corresponds in terms of pace and diction).

However, this is not to say that the ideal male voice and the ideal voice are equivalents. Clearly, they are not: *the ideal voice only approximates more to ideal male vocal qualities than female qualities.* At the same time, it is important to recognise that although this research suggests that the ideal North American voice is predominantly characterised by male vocal qualities, this is not a universal phenomenon. On the contrary, the gendering of the ideal voice is subject to specific cultural (national) factors and in some cultures (e.g., Mexico) the ideal voice may actually be a more or less equal mix of ideal male and female types. Of course, in neither of the two national cultures analysed by Valentine and Saint Damian did the characteristics of the ideal female voice constitute the defining qualities of the ideal voice (over and above male qualities).

Do we have a model then of the ideal radio voice? If we review briefly all that has been said so far in this section, we can (for the purposes of clarity and cogency) define the radio voice as: (i) refined, (ii) masculine, and (iii) authoritative. Just to specify what we mean by this we can summarise our examination of the radio voice by noting, first, that the radio voice is more refined than ordinary, everyday voices. It is amplified and edited, and although it sounds live, immediate and co-present, it is often recorded and reconstructed, using a process of fine editing to remove coughs and wheezes (and other bodily noises) as well as hesitations, fluffs and repetitions, producing not only a perfected but also a disembodied voice. At the same time, acoustics are used to lend depth – character, sincerity and veracity – to this otherwise artificial voice. Second, we can say that, whilst the radio voice possesses masculine and feminine characteristics, the ideal radio voice approximates more to male than female vocal qualities. Third, both of these factors – refinement and masculinity – can be seen to invest the radio voice with authority. The radio voice signifies knowledge and power. With its mistakes, hesitations and bodily noises extracted and with the majority of feminine vocal qualities excluded, the radio voice acquires for itself connotations of confidence, competence and truthfulness. It seems to have mastered and refined the art of speech, enhancing those qualities which connote authority and excluding those which do not. Given the importance of words on the radio, it would seem to be an essential requirement of the radio voice to speak with both precision and confidence. We, the listeners, must not only hear what the radio voice is saying but also believe it.

The points raised in this chapter alert us not only to the importance, indeed the primacy, of words on the radio but also to the complexities of their uses. Radio talk is extremely important (the medium's most significant code) but so are its ways of talking. Understanding this complexity is something of a challenge. Our purpose here has not been to present a comprehensive understanding of radio talk so much as to establish some basic guidelines for analysing forms of radio talk; whether it be in terms of its choice of words, the manner in which those words are spoken or, ultimately, the way in which those words are heard. Our points, and the research projects on which we have drawn, are not meant to be conclusive in their assessment of radio speech and radio voices. On the contrary, they are intended to provoke further thinking about and analysis of words, speech and voices on radio.

Things to do

1 Conduct a survey in which people are asked to list their ideal radio voices (citing their favourite radio DJs and presenters) and note the proportion of male and female voices chosen.
2 Analyse the vocal qualities of your favourite radio voices, defining these voices in terms of pitch, volume, speed, diction and modulation. Do your favourite voices share certain basic similarities in the way they use pitch, volume, speed, etc.?

|3|

Music, noise and silence

Speech may be the primary code of radio but, nevertheless, non-verbal codes, such as noise and music, are still integral to the medium. They evoke radio's moods, emotions, atmospheres and environments. They provide a fuller picture and a richer texture. Without words, radio would be seriously disadvantaged, rendered obscure, ambiguous and virtually meaningless. Nevertheless, without noises and music radio would lack depth and detail, making it seem sterile, flat and unrealistic. It is therefore necessary to combine verbal and non-verbal sounds in order to provide listeners with an experience that is both meaningful and evocative. Noise and music are powerfully evocative forms, operating on our imaginations and our emotions. They resonate with associations, triggering emotional responses in us that lie beyond words (which could not easily be put into words). But if they are to provoke specific and meaningful responses in us they require words to anchor them, to harness and direct their potential to stimulate ideas and feelings, to enhance their significance (i.e., their ability to signify).

But is this anchorage absolutely necessary? Do non-verbal sounds really need words to render them meaningful? Could a range of natural noises not provide meaningful entertainment? Some years ago the BBC commissioned a short radio play to explore this very issue. The results sounded something like this.

From silence there emerges the sound of birdsong and then a faint humming noise which could be running water somewhere in the distance. A siren wails, shattering the tranquillity of this pastoral scene and a man's breathing is simultaneously heard in close-up, panting and pained. Footfalls are heard moving over soft ground, accompanied by the rustle of clothing and the panting of breath. In the distance, along with the birdsong, men's voices are heard shouting inarticulately, accompanied by dogs barking. Close-up, the man's breathing is laboured with intermittent gasps of pain. Each breath is forced out. It's the sound of fear. Feet running, distant voices shouting, dogs barking and, in the foreground, the continuing struggle for breath. The footfalls and the breathing become faster, more determined, even desperate. Then the sound of footfalls change, becoming softer. They rustle upon leaves. Branches snap under foot. They slow down and stop. The man catches his breath and sighs heavily. The shouts and barks seem all around. Running water can be heard more distinctly now. The footfalls resume and change their sound once again. They squelch. Then they splash, moving through water, first shallow but with each step becoming deeper and more laboured. The man grunts as he wades into the watery depths. The water surges, bubbles and plops. The man pants, filling his lungs with air. Suddenly he takes a deep breath. There is a subdued splash followed by a bubbling noise and at that moment all the other sounds become strangely muffled and distorted. The dogs and the men's voices are now heard through the water, gradually diminishing and leaving only the sound of the water itself. The water ripples around us (in stereo) until there is a brutal burst of sound, immediately followed by the man gasping for air. Panting and splashing follow. The sound of the men and their dogs are now far off. The breathing slows, becomes more rhythmic. Footfalls sound, squelching upon a soft carpet of leaves, hesitantly at first but gathering into a steady pace. There is no longer any sound of men's voices or dogs barking. The man sighs. A bird sings. The steady breathing and footfalls fade to silence.

This is the first scene of *The Revenge*, a play without words, written and performed by Andrew Sachs in 1978. This play, about a man on the run (presumably having escaped from prison) who eludes his pursuers, steals a motorbike, breaks into a house in a remote rural location and there drowns another man in his bathtub, was produced with sound effects alone: no words, no music. It constructed its simple narrative through environmental sounds (e.g., birdsong, water, gravel pathways, traffic noises), through the sound of objects (e.g., doors, telephones, motorbike engines, sirens, cigarette lighters, breaking glass, clock chimes, ticking watches) and through bodily noises (e.g., sighs, panting, breathing, grunting, the rustle of clothing, footfalls, exclamations, humming, inarticulate shouting, meows). In so doing, the play sought to exploit the dramatic possibilities of non-verbal sounds (namely sound effects and acoustics) and prove that a story could be told and, more particularly, could be understood without using any recognisable words. Yet if it had not been called *The Revenge*, and if the announcer had not proclaimed it to be *The Revenge* before and after the play, would any of its listeners have had any clue that these actions were motivated by vengeance? As it stands, *The Revenge* demonstrates that audiences can recognise certain actions solely through their sound: e.g., the man being pursued across the countryside, his success in eluding the police, stealing a motorbike, breaking into a house, stealing up on and drowning another man in his bathtub. But what it also demonstrates is the limitation of non-verbal sound to evoke a drama: that whilst sound effects and acoustics can successfully convey something of the what, the where and the how, they are incapable of dealing with the why. By the end of the play, we know what has happened, how it happened and where it happened but have no sense of who the characters are, what their relationship is (or was) to each other nor what motivated this act of revenge. In other words, we have only half of a story.

Jonathan Raban, writer of many radio plays produced by the BBC, has called *The Revenge* a 'wordless sequence of noises' and denounced it as 'a well-puffed curiosity' (Raban 1981: 80). He has criticised the play on the grounds that its assemblage of grunts, thuds, crunches, gratings and footfalls is ambiguous and confusing. For him, it stands for all that is wrong in contemporary radio drama. He sees it as the fruition of a trend in radio drama which has increasingly been putting sound effects before dialogue and attempting to evoke the sounds of the real world over and above an articulation of ideas (reality before art). Raban sees such a project as the product of producers and technicians rather than writers, whose primary objective is to create something along the lines of a sound cinema. Opposed to this, Raban claims, is another (older) tradition of radio drama in which writers approach the radio play as if it were an audible version of the printed page. Raban describes the major difference between these two approaches in terms of icon and symbol. The producer-technician creation he calls *iconic*, since it is concerned with sounding real and using real sounds, and the writer's creation he calls *symbolic*, given that it is concerned with conveying ideas through a set of conventional practices and codes of representation that substitute for reality (rather than replicate reality). He points out that for a long time radio was a writer's medium in which words ruled and sound effects performed an essentially supportive role, as little more than an embellishment. Moreover, the sound effects that were used were themselves symbolic rather than realistic, requiring the listener to interpret artifical noises (e.g., coconut shells for horses' hooves, drumbeats for heartbeats or footsteps). But, according to Raban, all that changed with the advancements in radio technology, most notably the introduction of VHF and stereo, which saw radio begin to 'manufacture its own iconic version of reality' (Raban, 1981: 83). In other words, radio began to replicate the world of everyday (or natural) sounds rather than create an intelligible (but artificial) representation of it. In the shift from symbolic to iconic representation, noises and sound effects assumed a greater role than words or music.

Jonathan Raban's mourning of the writer's diminished (or diminishing) status within radio drama might be regarded as merely symptomatic of a legacy of privilege which the writer has held within western culture for the last few centuries, a status which has been increasingly challenged, partly as a consequence of increasing multi-media or audio-visual media literacy during the latter part of the twentieth century. Some may feel that the writer's sway over the arts and media has been justifiably challenged in more recent times and that Raban's comments represent little more than the reactionary ranting of the dispossessed. However, his arguments cannot be so easily dismissed for he has put his finger on one of the fundamentals of radio form. That is, that the non-verbal codes of radio perform an essentially secondary (and supportive) role in relation to speech and that the inversion of this relationship (the privileging of noise, music and silence over words) invariably leads to the listener's confusion and, as *The Revenge* demonstrates, to producers being restricted in terms of what they can successfully communicate.

In this chapter on the non-verbal codes of radio we shall be exploring in more depth the role of noise (most notably, sound effects) and music, examining the contribution they make to radio programmes, their relation to verbal codes, and the conventions which have emerged for using them. But first, we shall begin where most radio programmes start, with silence.

Silence: dead air and ambient noise ('atmos')

Silence must be radio's most underestimated and least understood code. Seemingly not a code at all, silence can actually be one of the medium's most evocative. Those who use it, recognise its power and its potential. Take, for instance, the following comments by Donald McWhinnie, one of the BBC's most acclaimed radio producers who numbers among his credits such landmark productions of radio drama as Dylan Thomas's *Under Milk Wood* (1954) and Samuel Beckett's *All That Fall* (1957):

> silence as a calculated device is one of the most potent imaginative stimuli; prepared for correctly, broken at the right moment, in the right context, it can be more expressive than words; it can echo with expectancy, atmosphere, suspense, emotional overtones, visual subtleties.
>
> (McWhinnie 1959: 88)

McWhinnie points out that there is a common misconception about radio broadcasting that the airwaves are to be filled at all times, that words and sounds must occupy every moment of airtime and that silence represents dead air. 'Dead air' is indeed absolute silence: it's the term broadcasters use to describe the airwaves devoid of all sound. Dead air occurs frequently on the radio but only for the briefest of moments. It is an important boundary demarcation, separating one programme from another or one item within a programme from another: for instance, marking the end of a scene in a play. In radio drama, the fade to dead air is the audio equivalent of the 'fade out' in the cinema, not only representing the end of a scene but also heralding a shift forward in time or a change of location. Moments of dead air can occur every few minutes, marking these shifts, from item to item, scene to scene, but they are used with caution. If prolonged they can be disturbing. 'Has the radio died? The batteries run out, the electricity gone off? Has the radio station been taken over by terrorists or (worse still) government censors? Have I gone deaf?' Dead air can raise disturbing questions in the minds of the listeners if it persists for more than the briefest of moments. Listeners seek reassurance by tuning to another station to make sure their radio is still working. Dead air must exist for less time than it takes the listener to reach for their dial.

But there is another kind of silence to be heard on the radio: silence which is not really silent at all. It is this silence which can be more expressive than words, which can echo with expectancy, atmosphere, suspense, emotional overtones and visual subtleties. It is the silence we think we hear when a speaker pauses for thought or when a character's dialogue is momentarily arrested. Such moments are pregnant pauses. As such, they fill our minds with anticipation, expectation and wonder. 'During silence,' writes Donald McWhinnie, 'things happen invisibly, in the minds of the players and in our imagination' (McWhinnie 1959: 88). When speech comes to a sudden halt, the listener is immediately alerted to the fact that something has happened. They must wait to be informed of what has occurred to interrupt the flow of words (e.g., a kiss, the sight of a monster or a gun, etc.). In the meantime, for little more than an instant, the listener's mind is filled with possibilities. As McWhinnie writes, 'it is in silence that the listener is at his most creative; if he does not depend on visual stimuli it is at these moments of pause that he will evolve, out of the creative act and his own experience and potential, the most compelling moments of insight and realization' (McWhinnie 1959: 90–1). Moments of invisible silence provoke extraordinary acts of imagination as a direct response to – and as compensation for – acute sensory depravation. But in these moments we are not really hearing silence at all. These brief snatches of interrupted sound are not silent: not dead silent. They are atmospheric or ambient noise. As such, they have their own distinct acoustic. What we take for silence is often a subtle and virtually unnoticeable range of atmospheric sounds which are essentially a background to prominent or significant sounds. The silence of a church, a field, a forest, the sea, a living room, a mountain top or a cave all sound different and, therefore, they all sound. We may not consciously perceive it but we still hear it. This kind of silence, which broadcasters usually refer to as 'atmos', is perhaps the most subtle noise we ever hear on the radio.

Noise: SFX, acoustics and perspectives

In speaking of noise on the radio we can make a number of distinctions between the kinds of sounds we are hearing. The term 'sound effects' (commonly abbreviated to SFX) is most often used to designate all those sounds other than speech, silence or music, such as doors creaking, clocks ticking, a person breathing, footsteps, birdsong, etc. The term 'sound effect' applies equally to natural and artificially produced sounds: whether what we are hearing is actually someone's head being sliced off or (more probably) a cabbage being sliced in half to represent the effect of a guillotine. The term 'acoustics' meanwhile is used to designate the various treatments of speech and noise which distort natural sounds for dramatic effect (e.g., fades and echoes). In addition to 'acoustics', we can also use the term 'perspectives' to designate the spatial qualities of sound: for instance, whether they are heard close-up or from a distance. The terms 'sound effects', 'acoustics' and 'perspectives' enable us to articulate the variety of types of noise and to describe the specific effects produced by non-verbal sounds on the radio. These terms enable us to understand and articulate the different ways in which sounds create distinct environments and atmospheres. They provide us with a means of exploring the subtleties and varieties of what is otherwise taken for meaningless background noise.

When we hear something, what we are actually hearing is movement or, more accurately, the vibrations of air caused by moving objects. But indirectly we can also hear space in two different ways: first, through the reverberation of sound upon walls and objects (in other words, by the amount of echo) and, second, by the distances between different sound sources. If sounds reverberate, resonate or echo noticeably then the sense of a vast enclosed space is created (e.g., a public hall or a church). If no reverberation, resonance or echo can be heard then this indicates either a small space (e.g., a living room) or an open space (e.g., outdoors). In both cases, space is created acoustically. Meanwhile, if all the sounds emanate from the same point then a lack of space is created. If, however, one sound is foregrounded before a background of other, distant noises then a sense of extensive space is produced. This is what is meant by 'perspectives'. Together, acoustics and perspectives indicate the spatial dimension of the environment occupied by sounds such as speech and sound effects (e.g., footsteps).

Acoustics have another important function, however. The amount of resonance a sound has (or is given) can tell us even more about an environment than simply its spatial dimension. If the sounds are produced in a studio and all resonance is deadened then these sounds seem to occupy the same space as that of the listener, replicating the acoustic qualities of most people's homes, where typically sounds are deadened by carpets, wallpaper, curtains and furniture. However, if the sounds on the radio are highly resonant (i.e., they have a noticeable echo) then these sounds seem to come from a quite distinct space beyond the listener's own environment. For this reason, resonant sounds offer radio broadcasters a means of creating environments that are distinct from the domestic, everyday and real spaces in which their audiences listen. Whilst most news, current affairs and chat programmes employ deadened sounds to replicate the acoustic qualities of the listener's home, radio dramas often use more resonant sounds to liberate their listeners from the confines of everyday life. Obviously this depends on the type of drama being produced. One would expect to hear more resonant sounds in a science-fiction fantasy than a drama-documentary striving for realism.

Robert McLeish, in his book *Radio Production* (1994) writes that there are four basic acoustics which radio uses, each created by the various combinations of the quantity and duration of reverberation. The first acoustic McLeish notes creates a sense of outdoor space by having no reverberation at all. The second acoustic creates a sense of a large, well-furnished interior (such as a library) by having a little reverberation for a long duration: that is, for more than the normal reverberation time of 0.2 seconds. The opposite effect – a small empty room (say, a bathroom) – is created by having much reverberation for a short duration. Finally, the effect of a large empty interior (such as a church, a palace or a concert hall) can be created by having much reverberation over a long duration. The creation of a sense of space which simultaneously conveys something of the setting itself (not only small or large but empty or furnished) is obviously of importance to radio producers. The acoustic properties of sounds can convey information which, on stage or screen, we could perceive at a glance. However, they are only a starting point for the creation of environments, locations and settings. Whilst 'acoustics' play a key role in establishing space on the radio, 'sound effects' (SFX) are the means of creating specific environments: for instance, a public library or a restaurant, a busy high street or a living room. The sounds of muted conversation and squeaking trolley-wheels evoke both the public library and the restaurant but the additional sounds of tinkling cutlery and crockery are sufficient to conjure up the unmistakable sound of a public dining room. The recognisable sounds of familiar everyday objects provide the 'props' of radio: the incidental details which distinguish one kind of room from another. As such, radio sound effects substitute for the setting of the theatre, its scenery and props.

Robert McLeish has pursued the analogy between the stage set and radio sound effects, drawing parallels between the theatrical backdrop and the atmospheric sounds on radio, and between stage 'props' and specific radio sound effects (which represent, or emanate from, objects). He writes that 'The equivalent of the theatre's "backdrop" are those sounds which run through a scene – for example, rain, conversation at a party, traffic noise or the sounds of battle' (McLeish 1994: 234). He also writes that 'The "incidental furniture" and "props" are those effects which are specially placed to suit the action – for instance dialling a telephone, pouring a drink, closing a door or firing a gun' (McLeish 1994: 234). There is, however, an important difference between stage sets/props and radio sound effects, between those details that can be seen and those which can only be heard. The most significant difference is that radio environments can more quickly become cluttered than stage sets. To put it another way, the same amount of detail would cause too many distractions for radio listeners than theatre audiences:

When the curtain rises on a theatre stage the scenery is immediately obvious and the audience is given all the contextual information it requires for the play to start. So it is with radio, except that to achieve an unambiguous impact the sounds must be refined and simplified to those few which really carry the message.

(McLeish 1994:234)

Robert McLeish points out that many radio producers new to drama are tempted to use too many sound effects. Similarly, Felix Felton, who worked in the BBC Drama Department in the 1930s and 1940s, wrote back in 1949 that 'one learns that the first rule in the use of sound effects is to use them with economy' (Felton 1949: 42). Felton, in his book on the radio play, pointed out that to establish a seaside background there is no point taking all the different noises heard on the beach (e.g., waves, children, rock sellers, Punch and Judy, donkeys, etc.) and lumping them all together, as the inevitable result would be confusion. 'The ear, unlike the eye, cannot assimilate a complex combination of impressions' (Felton 1949: 42). What listeners require is 'a few pointers' and the art of effective radio 'lies in choosing the effect which will most successfully set his visual imagination working' (Felton 1949: 42). This assertion indicates that a few selective sounds are capable of producing a vivid and recognisable sound environment whilst a cacophony of authentic noises simply causes aural chaos. On similar lines, Felix Felton also suggested that where more than one sound effect is used, they should be introduced successively rather than simultaneously. But, wherever possible, if the sound effects do not serve a specific dramatic function they should be dispensed with. If in doubt, Felton suggested, leave them out, particularly in the case of footsteps and doors for exits and entrances: 'A fussy succession of doors and footsteps is simply an irritation to the listener, and prevents their being dramatically significant when we want them to be. Effects should be effective; and the less they are used, the more effective they are' (Felton 1949: 44).

What this suggests is that the function of sound effects is not to make a radio programme more realistic but more dramatic, more expressive. Sound effects, therefore, when used selectively in this way have a symbolic rather than an iconic function. The comments of radio producers (particularly those working for the BBC in the 1930s, 1940s and 1950s) indicate that the conventions of using sound effects were seldom intended to present an authentic (iconic) sound environment. Moreover, the symbolic nature of the sound effects would appear to be two-fold. On the one hand, radio sound effects (both the atmospheric and the specific) tend to be produced artificially. On the other hand, the sounds we hear on the radio often signify something other than the thing itself which produces the noise.

The continuous 'backdrop' sounds which are used to establish the setting of a radio production are usually pre-recorded and reproduced from records, compact discs and tapes. Similarly, the intermittent noises accom-

panying various actions are ordinarily manufactured in the studio by technicians. Robert McLeish has described some of the techniques commonly
used, including the rustling of tape to represent undergrowth or jungle, and
the rustling of cellophane accompanied by the breaking of small sticks to
represent a burning building. These sound effects, in being artificially produced, are quite clearly symbolic. If iconic, the rustling of recording tape
would signify recording tape being rustled. It is much more likely, however,
that this sound would be used symbolically to signify a long-flowing gown
moving through a forest. Radio obviously gains from the fact that invisibility enables sound effects to evoke far more than what actually produces
them. Our ears can easily be deceived and our imaginations can transform a
most mundane noise into something quite fantastic.

Radio producers are less concerned with using real sounds than using
understandable sounds. Often the real sound of something (such as the sea)
sounds unrecognisable on radio, whilst a more immediate and intelligible
sound can be produced artificially by using computers, musical instruments
or a variety of curious objects, materials and substances. Yet even when the
sounds used in radio programmes are real sounds (recorded on location)
their function can still be more symbolic than iconic. For often sounds are
simply a shorthand and have attached to them a host of associations. Over
the years certain sounds have acquired specific sets of meanings. Some of the
most well-known and often-used radio sounds are described by McLeish.
These include such things as a clock ticking to signify time passing, seagulls
and sea wash to evoke the coast, the creaking of ropes to signify being on
board ship, a crowing cock for morning and birdsong for outdoors or the
countryside. Once again these sounds fulfil an essentially symbolic function:
for instance, the hooting of an owl is frequently used to symbolise night
(and is associated with mystery and the supernatural) rather than represent
literally an owl. The relationships between these sounds and their associations is largely a matter of convention; so, for instance, the crowing of crows
or rooks is widely used as a signifier of graveyards. This, of course, is by no
means specific to radio alone. Indeed, radio draws upon a range of noises
which have acquired specific meanings in film and television.

Most sounds, in having a host of associations attached to them, need
some form of qualification when used on the radio: that is, some additional
information to determine more precisely what they are intended to represent. For instance, the twittering of birds can be interpreted as morning in
the city or as the countryside at any time of day. Usually the precise meaning of such sounds is established by the words of a voice-over (a narrator)
or the dialogue of characters. This is not always necessary, however, as
additional sounds can also be used to determine the precise meaning of the
initial sounds. For instance, if the birdsong was followed by an alarm clock
the listener could deduce that it was morning rather than the countryside
that was being signified. If, on the other hand, the birdsong was followed by
cattle mooing then the listener would realise that the countryside was being

represented. Nevertheless, even though additional sound effects can be used to render noise more meaningful on the radio, the only real way of ensuring that listeners interpret sounds appropriately is through the use of additional words. Most sounds, other than the most general and familiar environmental noises, require words to establish narrative significance.

Elwyn Evans has written that although it comes as a painful surprise to each new generation of radio dramatists, the fact is 'that sound effects on their own usually signify very little' (Evans 1977: 115). In *Radio: A Guide to Broadcasting Technique* he points out that whilst we can instantly recognise certain sounds like telephones ringing, doors opening and shutting, and birds singing, there are many other sounds which we would find almost impossible to identify without being told what they are. He explains that one reason for this is because even real sounds (recorded at source) sound different on the radio. That is, the technology of microphones and speakers does not enable real sounds to be heard with absolute fidelity. Another reason is that in real life we seldom recognise sounds in isolation from other factors. This leads Evans to conclude that:

> Unaided, most effects can't set a scene: still less can they convey physical action. But once associate them with dialogue and they start to mean something. In an interesting mutuality the lines explain the effect and the effect adds richness and impact to the lines.
>
> (Evans 1977: 115)

Similar comments can be found in Donald McWhinnie's *The Art of Radio*. For instance, he writes that:

> natural sounds alone, divorced from the text, can rarely be effective. If they are to be even comprehensible, the text must demand them and, moreover, must give a fairly sure signpost to their nature; indeed they will hardly ever register at all unless the text provides a key.
>
> (McWhinnie 1959: 80)

McWhinnie has argued that such a key is essential given that natural sounds are extremely hard to identify when heard over a radio or when heard in isolation from other details, most notably visuals.

> The blade of an axe biting into a tree could just as well be a pencil tapping on a desk, a man snapping his fingers, a grandfather clock ticking. A clock ticking could be – and has been taken to be – a horse trotting. Indeed, there are so many possibilities of confusion that one wonders whether it would not be advisable to avoid this range of sounds altogether.
>
> (McWhinnie 1959: 79)

These sounds are used, of course, and for good reason: they provide richness and texture or sometimes just rhythm and punctuation. These sounds are seldom used, however, without words to accompany them: words which render them recognisable and meaningful. As McWhinnie has written, 'It follows that whenever a text needs the reinforcement of real sounds to achieve whatever purpose cannot be compressed by words alone, the words themselves must guide the mind towards an accurate apprehension of those sounds' (McWhinnie 1959: 80).

The comments of some of the most important British radio producers indicate that sound effects are considered a valuable means of enlivening and enriching narration and dialogue. Yet they also indicate a general consensus that radio's non-verbal codes cannot substitute for verbal ones and should not be made to carry the heavier burden of representation. 'In the average radio play', writes Elwyn Evans, sound effects 'are only intermittently important', their purpose being 'to make plays more convincing, or more atmospheric, or funnier, or just clearer' (Evans 1977: 117). In short, sound effects play second fiddle to words on the radio and it would be a mistake to have the second fiddle leading the orchestra.

Music: jingles, signature tunes and incidental

Music is undoubtedly one of radio's most important codes. Some radio stations are almost nothing else. Many others broadcast as much music as speech. And even speech-based radio stations have music within their features, dramas, comedies and game shows. Jingles repeatedly announce the name and wavelength of the station. Signature tunes herald the beginning and end of individual programmes. Incidental music forms a backdrop to dialogue and action, fills the gaps between one scene and another, and punctuates the emotional rise and fall of a drama. Music exists purely for its own sake, selected and played in the studio and transmitted directly into our homes, vehicles and workplaces. Recorded or live, classical or modern, serious or popular, radio is the principal means of disseminating music, of bringing it into our lives. Most of the music we hear in our lifetime may even be heard on the radio.

Music is eminently suited to radio broadcasting. This is primarily because it requires no visual accompaniment. In fact, the most important things that are lost are the distractions which can interfere with our experience of it. The sight of the musicians or singers performing music is often a distraction and a hindrance to the enjoyment and appreciation of music itself. Often at a concert we have to look away from the performers or, better still, close our eyes to really hear the music. One of the advantages of radio is that it closes our eyes for us, focusing our attention on the product rather than the process of musical performance. Radio renders music more important than the performers and, consequently, enhances its elemental power. Add visuals to music and music itself becomes the accompaniment. The sovereignty of the eye over the ear makes this an inevitability. Only a medium that caters to the ear alone can prevent the performance or the visual accompaniment from diverting attention from the music, of robbing it of its power and its purity.

Most radio stations use recorded music as their staple output (i.e., their major source of programme material) since it is both popular with audiences and one of the cheapest forms of programming. The music played by individual radio stations is ordinarily such a dominant feature of the overall output that the station's music policy can influence the size of the audience and, in the case of commercial stations, the sale of airtime and the overall profitability of the company. Very often the key factor in attracting audiences is music. When stations are faced with low audience ratings, the first thing they usually do is rethink their music policy. They may, for instance, decide to adopt an exclusive musical style, such as classical rather than rock, or 'adult-orientated rock' rather than pop. They may decide, on the other hand, to broaden the range of their musical output (broadcasting a greater diversity of musical styles) in order to attract a more general listenership. In the case of a pop music station, a decision will be made on whether or not to adopt a Top 40 format and whether to have a playlist (a list of records regularly featured throughout the daily schedule and chosen each week by a senior executive of the station's management team). The playlist creates a greater sense of continuity across the schedules and also enables the station managers to assume a greater degree of editorial control rather than simply leaving the choice of recorded plays entirely to individual presenters and disc jockeys. The choice of music is often considered too important to be left wholly to the idiosyncratic tastes of DJs, requiring a more objective and systematic approach to guarantee the station's popularity and profitability. The use of playlists on both public service and commercial radio stations throughout the world signals how important music is in attracting audiences and determining the overall identity of a station.

Different musical genres have specific social and cultural connotations attached to them. Opera, chamber, jazz, folk, country and western, brass band, pop, heavy metal, reggae and rap all evoke different social, cultural and political factors. Consequently, they tend to have a specific appeal for particular age groups, classes and races. Some of these musical forms appeal predominantly to young urban black audiences. Others appeal almost exclusively to middle-aged, white, rural audiences. Some of these musical forms tend to appeal to predominantly middle- and upper-class educated professionals whilst others have strong working-class associations. At least one of these musical forms is associated with the north of England. Therefore, music can be defined not only in terms of differences in age, class and race but even in terms of political radicalism, education, geographical location and professional status.

Because the various forms of music have acquired distinct social and cultural connotations, music has become a way of defining one's identity and of pledging allegiance to a specific group. 'What music do you like?' is a standard question when first getting to know someone. It's a convenient way of determining first impressions, of making assumptions about people we hardly know. It acts as a shorthand, telling us about other things we are less likely to feel comfortable asking on first acquaintance. A specific musical taste (to the virtual exclusion of all else) can suggest a great deal about a person. If someone likes only opera or only country and western or only reggae, we can swiftly form an opinion of their other likes and dislikes, their tastes, their beliefs, their values. Similarly, in professing to like a particular type of music we can present ourselves in a certain way, either as we would like to be seen or as we judge someone else would like to see us. For instance, if we want someone to identify with us, we would probably profess to share their taste in music. In doing this, we would be establishing a common ground: one in which we could hopefully find other, and more important, areas of mutual interest and belief. Music plays a key role in establishing communities of shared interests and values. Music may be an extremely personal thing (open to individual interpretation and redolent with personal associations, often of an intimate nature) but it is also a communal activity. Music brings large groups of people together to perform, to listen and to dance. All music is, in a sense, tribal music. Music on the radio offers listeners a sense of being part of a larger community: a community with, if nothing else, a shared taste in music. At the same time, it offers station managers an opportunity to determine their particular listening community. Radio station personnel are acutely aware of the fact that different types of music appeal to different kinds of people and they adopt a specific music policy with this in mind. In short, music forms a major part of a radio station's branding and is probably their most important marketing tool (Barnard 1989: 113–34).

Radio stations (local, regional and national) use music to create their own particular house style, to distinguish themselves from the competition. To be effective, a station's image needs to be easily identifiable for the purposes, if nothing else, of finding the station on the dial. Radio style is determined not only by the kind of music played (e.g., classical or rock) but also by a very specific form of radio music: the jingle. Jingles are the most radiogenic form of music to be heard on the radio. They are one of the few musical forms which radio has created. Jingles are far more than just short bursts of music and words detailing the name of the station and its wavelength or the name of a particular presenter. They are a highly condensed expression of all that the station stands for, capturing in seconds the essence of a station's character, style and output. The jingle's musical style (e.g., rock, techno, acoustic, orchestral, etc.) is intended to suggest the character of the station, its presenters and its target audience. They are designed not only to reflect but also to blend in with the station's total output of music and speech. Station jingles ('idents') will usually be interspersed with a presenter's own jingle (often a variation on the station's theme) defining their distinct persona and role. But the style of a presenter's jingle might be used more specifically to suggest the time of day at which their programme is broadcast, to evoke the mood most appropriate to the time of day. Jingles can establish a sense of time by varying the tempo, pace and instrumentation of the theme from morning to afternoon to evening. Jingles are also a useful way of effecting instant changes of mood, enabling presenters to shift between a range of programme items of contrasting mood and emotion (e.g., news, listeners' letters, timechecks, weather reports, advertisements, traffic news, etc.). They are a kind of aural punctuation, like commas, semicolons, colons and full stops, we hardly notice them after a while. Many stations are peppered with them and, as such, most of us take them for granted. Yet the vast amounts of money stations spend on their jingles each year (specialist companies being commissioned to design them) suggest that they are anything but incidental.

Another form of radio music regularly heard but seldom noticed is 'incidental' or theme music, which forms a background to most dramas and features. Incidental music is used by radio producers in much the same way as noise and silence. Like silence it can act as a boundary demarcation, only here it effects a smooth transition from one scene to another rather than marking the break between scenes (as silence does). Music seals over gaps whereas silence creates them. Like sound effects, music can create a sense of time and place, and is particularly adept at conjuring up the past. At the same time, music creates atmospheres and moods, alerting us to what characters are thinking and feeling. Music can both underline dialogue or provide a counterpoint to it, suggesting the feelings that words may disguise. Music can even substitute for sound effects, creating storms, battle scenes, raging seas and ocean depths. It can be used to represent the sound of an electrical storm more effectively than the actual recording of thunder and lightning, conveying the emotional effects that often accompany such an event.

Music can also be used literally, to signify the presence of music or musicians within a scene: for instance, a cafe orchestra, a busker on a city street or even a radio tuned in to a well-known music station. Such sounds evoke an acoustic world that exists for the characters in the programme. These are distinct from other forms of radio music in that they are 'diegetic': that is, they belong to the world of the drama and can therefore be heard by characters within the story. Voice-overs, incidental and theme music and musical sound-bridges (signifying changes of scene), on the other hand, cannot be heard by the characters themselves and are therefore designated 'non-diegetic'. Non-diegetic sounds are heard only by the audience and their function is to heighten the drama, provide pace and rhythm to the action and convey both objects and emotions that would otherwise be undetectable for the listening audience. These sounds (music and otherwise) are not to be met with in real life and are part of the conventions of film, television and radio drama. They are a very significant part of what makes drama dramatic. Listeners are accustomed to hearing them and, consequently, often hear them without really noticing them.

Despite the fact that most of us pay little attention to it, theme music or incidental music fulfils a range of functions and makes a significant contribution to the overall production of a radio drama or feature. Such music is carefully chosen in order to reflect and enhance the character and setting of the programme. Sometimes radio producers select pre-existing pieces of music to accompany speech and sound effects. Such music can provide an effective and economical way of establishing time (i.e., period, era) and location (i.e. country, region): for instance, Strauss for late nineteenth-century Austria or Elvis Presley for 1950s North America. Other forms of music are associated with particular states of mind, conditions and events: for instance, Rachmaninov's Piano Concerto No. 2 for romance, Purcell's 'Dido's Lament' (from *Dido and Aeneas*) for death, Wagner's 'Ride of the Valkyries' (from *Die Nibelungen*) for war. Alternatively, producers will commission original pieces of music in order to avoid such connotations (or clichés). Original music may be reminiscent of pre-existing music (e.g., Wagneresque) or can be a radical departure. The BBC Radiophonic Workshop has produced distinctive and radiogenic music to accompany such productions as Samuel Beckett's *All That Fall* and Douglas Adams's *The Hitch-hiker's Guide to the Galaxy*. The creation of original musical themes enables radio producers to employ forms of music most suitable to the medium itself. After all, music heard on the radio sounds very different to live music heard in a concert hall and, therefore, the arrangements of music designed for concert halls are rarely suited to the unique circumstances of the microphone and radio speaker.

As Donald McWhinnie points out in *The Art of Radio*, 'It is possible to achieve the subtlest variation, the finest nuance, when one is working microscopically – that is to say, focusing one's effects rather than projecting them – but it is not possible to reproduce the dynamic range of the concert hall' (McWhinnie 1959: 65). Consequently, the levels of live sound will be distorted and brought into a new relationship with other sounds. Contrasts of volume and acoustic texture are evened out and often lost. Effectively, music on the radio is flatter and more homogeneous than otherwise. To recapture the various levels and nuances of live music heard at source, music intended for radio broadcasting must be arranged differently, its details foregrounded. Inevitably, pizzicato is more effective than symphonic sound on radio. McWhinnie writes that the best radio composers are preoccupied with exploring 'new, more sensitive, tones and timbres' (McWhinnie 1959: 68). He also writes that 'what is required of the radio composer is understanding of the special qualities of the microphone rather than impeccable musical perfection' (McWhinnie 1959: 68). This is the reason many radio producers prefer to commission original pieces of music which take into account the peculiarities of the medium.

Whether pre-existing or original music is used in a radio programme, the producer and composer must decide on the appropriate tempo, rhythm, melody and instrumentation of the score intended to function as the musical theme of the programme. A romantic drama, a thriller, a comedy will all require different kinds of music, such as particular rhythms and specific instruments, to establish the appropriate mood (e.g., yearning, fear or humour). Through rhythm, music can be sombre or cheerful, up-beat or down-beat, soothing or jarring. Meanwhile, instrumentation can add significantly to such effects. Strings can create different effects from wind instruments (particularly brass), whilst harps create different effects from violins. There again, violins can be used for the most touching and tender scenes (i.e., when softly undulating) or for the most disturbing and terrifying (i.e., when screeching and piercing the air in rapid, jagged strokes). Phrasing and instrumentation must be considered simultaneously when creating the musical theme of a dramatic radio production.

Whilst a particular piece of music can establish the generic nature of a radio production and locate it in time and place, a particular melody or musical phrase can be associated with a specific setting or character, creating recognisable motifs that help listeners to recognise without otherwise being told which character is present or where they are. Many, if not most, radio productions use a variety of motifs and phrases. Productions very seldom use the same music (i.e., the same rhythm, instrumentation and melody) throughout the entire programme but rather establish a range of distinct musical themes. Individual characters can, and often do, have their own theme: the choice of instrument, tempo and melody being used to evoke their particular character-traits. For instance, the lugubrious tones of a double bass might be used for a morbid, overweight and rather pompous character, whereas a lilting tune played on a fiddle might be used for a sprightly and unpretentious character. Ordinarily, of course, musical themes for individual characters are much more subtle than this and one of the reasons for the subtlety is that they are intended to be registered subconsciously by the listener and are only really used as a secondary and supplementary means of indicating the presence of particular characters. If they are too obvious, musical passages will distract listeners from the more significant features of drama (i.e., the dialogue).

Incidental music rarely operates in isolation from dialogue or narration. Donald McWhinnie writes that 'words must always be predominant in radio and music subservient' (McWhinnie 1959: 71). He notes that long passages of music draw attention away from the real business of a radio programme and, therefore, incidental music should be concise and to the point. Most radio producers reserve music for moments of extreme emotional climax, precisely to convey the extremes of feeling overwhelming characters at certain moments and to manipulate the listeners' own feelings for characters: e.g., sympathy or dread. As such moments only appear intermittently, music is most often heard in a radio drama or feature between scenes. Here it functions as a link between one scene and another, signifying a change in location or an elapse of time. Music can make the artificial shifts from one location to another or the sudden leaps forward in time that are necessary for the development of the plot to seem smooth and seamless.

The BBC drama series *Journey into Space* offers a good example of music used effectively to enhance a radio production. Episode 1 of the first series, 'Operation Luna' (originally broadcast in September 1953, recorded in 1957 and released commercially on audio-tape cassette in 1989) is composed of six scenes and nine individual musical segments, three of which are diegetic (i.e., can be heard by the characters). The remaining six musical segments are boundary demarcations, marking the close of one scene or bridging the gap between one scene and another, and marking the opening and closing of the programme. An examination of where each musical segment occurs demonstrates that music is used only intermittently and for brief periods of time, primarily to fill the gap between scenes. Also, the music chosen for this drama series (particularly the non-diegetic music) is used to enhance its themes and moods.

The episode opens with the announcement '*Journey into Space*. BBC presents Jet Morgan in "Operation Luna"', followed by the sound of a space rocket taking off and then the signature tune. The music builds to a dramatic climax, ascending the scale (charting the trajectory of the rocket), growing ever faster and producing the effect of spiralling upwards until it reaches a point where it begins to fall, descending the scale and slowing down, becoming heavy and emphatic. A voice emerges towards the end of the signature tune, describing the launch of a rocket ship and introducing the crew: Jet, Mitch, Doc and Lemmy. Here, the action begins with the characters preparing themselves for the launch. Halfway through the scene, a brief burst of music (approximately three seconds of wavering, quivering strings) marks a dramatic climax as the spaceship fires its atomic motor to propel it through space. The next music to be heard comes a little later, at the end of Scene 1. This musical segment, which lasts for approximately twenty-five seconds, features a drum roll followed by wind and strings, growing louder but maintaining a steady rhythm (producing a chiming effect) which is followed by a spiralling upward to a high pitch (strings/violins) and ending on a very high note prolonged for several seconds, which then fades. As it fades, dialogue is introduced over it and Scene 2 begins, introducing an argument between Jet and Mitch. At the end of the argument, music once more heralds the close of the scene, lasting for just under twenty seconds, and producing a similar theme to that heard before: a hesitant ascending of the scale, a swell of strings, sweeping upwards to a higher pitch and ending on a prolonged high note (violins) which then fades away. This time there is a second or two of silence until Doc's voice signals the opening of Scene 3, which features Lemmy repairing the radio. As Lemmy operates the ship's radio, the crew hears strange music: a range of bizarre electronically produced sounds which includes deep echoing pulsations, a high-pitched wavering electronic noise and, briefly, a series of deeper notes which could almost be a voice, all of which is overlaid by intermittent noises reminiscent of submarine depth charges. Scene 3 ends with a fade-out rather than a musical sound-bridge, marking the halfway stage of the programme.

The next scene, Scene 4, ends with just over twenty seconds of music and the most dramatic so far: louder, deeper and heavier than before, with more percussion (drums and cymbals) and brass (trumpets). The effect is more bombastic (heralding danger ahead but the determination to go on). The mid-section of the musical segment features a swirling, whirlwind effect which swoops down to something softer and slower, fading abruptly to a second or two of silence before Lemmy's voice is heard, opening Scene 5. Scene 5 begins calmly inside the ship, with Lemmy playing a mouth organ. This is the second diegetic music of the drama. As he plays a rather doleful tune there is a sudden burst of noise (SFX) which shatters the tranquil atmosphere and represents a meteor hitting the ship. When the crew venture outside to investigate the damage, Lemmy (and this time only Lemmy) hears again the strange pulsating, echoing, electronic music heard in Scene 3. This (like Scene 3) ends with a fade-out rather than a musical sound-bridge and in the next and final scene we find ourselves back in the ship with the crew refusing to believe that Lemmy really heard the strange music. Scene 6 ends with a dramatic burst of music, a rapid ascension of the scale followed by an intermittent falling, which slows, deepens and fades. But rather than fading out completely, it hovers beneath the announcer's voice, which proclaims, 'You have been listening to Episode 1 of *Journey into Space* with Andrew Faulds as Jet Morgan ... '. After the announcer has named the members of the cast along with Van Phillips, who composed and conducted the music, and the author Charles Chilton, the music sweeps up to an extremely high-pitched wavering of strings before finally fading, signalling the end of the programme.

The first and most obvious thing to note about the music used in this episode is that it constitutes only a small percentage of the overall programme (little more than three minutes of the total running time of twenty-five minutes). Also, where music is used without any accompanying dialogue, it never exceeds twenty-five seconds. The other thing to note is that most of the music used is non-diegetic (i.e., cannot be heard by the characters) and is most often used to signal the end of a scene. Whilst a fade to silence is used on two occasions to demarcate the end of a scene, music is used four times, effecting a smooth transition from one scene to another. Moreover, it should be noted that on each occasion, whilst the musical segment reproduces the same basic theme tune, it is always varied slightly in order to capture the specific emotional tone of the preceding scene. For instance, the heavier, more bombastic music used at the end of Scene 4 takes its cue from the closing words of the scene in which Jet expresses his determination to go on with the mission despite the fact that the ship has used up too much of its fuel reserves. The use of more percussion and brass instruments here, along with a more emphatic rhythm, signals both the danger of continuing the mission and Jet's staunch resolution to go on in spite of the possible dangers.

The nature of the incidental music, which is established in the opening musical segment (i.e., the signature tune) and consistently repeated (with some degree of variation) throughout the programme, is clearly designed to reflect the nature of the drama itself. Broadly speaking, the music is dramatic and intense, exciting and adventurous. More specifically, the key features of the incidental music are: (i) the rapid ascending and descending of the scale (pitch); (ii) wavering, quivering and swirling; and (iii) the use, primarily, of strings. Each of these features can be seen to be directly related to the theme and content of the drama: that is, travelling through outer space. The rapid ascending and descending of the major musical theme is quite obviously determined by the launching and landing of the rocket ship. Ending each musical segment on a prolonged high note (one that often wavers uncertainly) captures the sense of the ship and its crew suspended far above the Earth. The wavering/quivering conveys both the heightened emotions of the characters in their strange environment and something of the character of outer space itself. Meanwhile, the swirling effect of the musical theme (the sense of spiralling upwards or downwards) creates the effect of being out of control, disorientated or lost, thereby emphasising what happens to the characters in the story. The use of strings as the key form of instrumentation would seem to be intended to enable the rapid climbs from deep tones (double bass and cello) to extreme high notes (violins) and to create the wavering, quivering, shimmering effects. The mix of rapidly ascending and descending, wavering and shimmering strings represents a musical interpretation of space travel, creating a distinctive musical signature to be used in each and every episode of *Journey into Space*.

Like *Journey into Space*, many radio programmes have their own distinctive musical signature to herald the beginning and end of the show. Signature tunes are used to establish and sign-post the character of a specific radio programme from the outset. They are also an attention-seeking device. What better way of alerting listeners to the start of another thrilling episode of *Dick Barton: Special Agent* than Charles Williams's 'Devil's Gallop'? What better way of alerting *Archers*' addicts to the start of another prosaic day in the life of Ambridge than a bucolic jig ('Barwick Green' by Arthur Woods)? In a matter of seconds, each piece of music captures and conveys the spirit of the programme itself. These are two of the best-known BBC radio signature tunes but there are hundreds of other short pieces of music which are closely associated with particular radio programmes: e.g., 'Hancock's Half Hour', 'Desert Island Discs' and 'In the Psychiatrist's Chair'. Words may be the most important sound heard on radio but every now and then we need a short burst of music to attract our attention and revive our interest. Words alone can only sustain our interest for so long. After a while we inevitably pay them only half a mind. At this point the notes of a familiar signature tune make us sit up and take notice and fill us with anticipation. It is our cue to rush to our radios, eager to hear a favourite show or reach for the dial and turn off a despised one. Either way, we are summoned to action by music. Music motivates. Not only does it get us moving but it also initiates programmes and moves them from one scene or item to another. In short, music sets radio in motion, charts its rises and falls, and moves it on to something new. Its key function is to stimulate and maintain momentum. The moment radio stops, it ceases to exist. Music, above all else, keeps it flowing.

Coda

Orchestral music takes us smoothly into a new scene, rising and then fading, allowing the voice of Jane Eyre to recount the period of her courtship and the anticipation of her marriage to Edward Rochester.[1] She speaks of her trunks, packed, locked, corded and waiting to be transported to London. She anticipates making the same journey herself in her new guise of Jane Rochester. Here a second voice is heard whispering 'Jane . . . Jane'. This is a female voice, lower than Jane's, reverberating with echo and closer to the microphone, rendering it both mysterious and disturbing. Jane continues, unheeding of the strange voice, telling of her disturbed night caused by bad dreams and of the arrival of her wedding dress. Low laughter is heard at this point and continues beneath Jane's description of her wedding costume, mingling with Jane's voice and the background music. Jane's voice becomes more earnest and excited as she stands before her mirror in her bridal gown. 'Is this real?' she asks. 'Am I to be a bride at last?' 'Bride' breathes the strange echoing voice. To the music is added now the dim sound of wind blowing. Jane wonders how long Edward has loved her. 'Loved me!' asserts the mysterious second voice, breaking into hysterical laughter, rising along with the sound of the wind. As this weird laughter continues, Jane screams that the dress is burning her. 'Take it off!' she cries, 'Take it off!' 'Off' echoes the strange voice. 'Take it off!' the voice repeats and breaks again into a manic and menacing laugh. Jane is heard gasping for breath. Her gasps mingle with the strange laughter, the squalling wind (which has been steadily rising) and the music. Jane takes a deep breath and the wind and music grow louder, marking a change of scene.

The sound of the wind and music continue and seem to struggle for supremacy until the music fades out leaving only the squalling wind, over which Jane's voice is reintroduced. Jane describes herself in the orchard, where she has come to seek shelter from the wind which has blown all day. Low laughter accompanies Jane's 'Oh I wish he would come! Edward, where can you be?' Jane describes herself running before the wind to the wreck of the chestnut tree. At the mention of the tree (under which Edward made his proposal to Jane in an earlier scene), the sound of a violin is heard playing a romantic air (Jane and

Edward's love song). Here she describes the moon buried beneath a deep drift of cloud and, as she does so, the sound of horses' hooves and men's voices shouting can be heard in the distance. 'Oh Edward! Jane cries, and horses are heard to snort and rattle their reins. 'My Jane!' answers a man's voice (Edward). Dogs bark excitedly in the background. Jane is over-wrought and seems, to Edward, feverish. As they are reunited, the violin grows ever louder and is joined by an orchestra. As Jane draws the scene to a close by accepting Edward's invitation to have supper with him later that evening, violin and orchestra rise over her voice and take us into the next scene where tea-cups will be heard clinking and logs spitting on the fire, signalling both a new location and an elapse of time.

Charlotte Brontë's love story takes on new life thanks to the voices of the actors Sophie Thompson, Ciaran Hinds and Vivienne Rochester, an orchestra and a violin, and the technicians responsible for the wind, the horses and dogs, the tea-cups and the log fire. The dialogue, written by Michelene Wandor, has the most vital role to play in this radio production of *Jane Eyre*. In the sequence described above, words are definitely the key component. They tell us what the characters are thinking and feeling, establish the events which have taken and are taking place, and establish the setting (e.g., the moonlit orchard). What role is left then for the non-verbal codes?

The non-verbal sounds operate in various ways and have a variety of functions in the two scenes described above. First, non-diegetic music establishes the fact that this is a classic romance through its use of classical orchestral music. The theme captures the dark, foreboding and yearning aspects of the story in its score and instrumentation. The musical theme also has a distinctive air performed as a violin solo which it reserves for the love scenes between Jane and Edward (heard in this sequence when she describes the chestnut tree and continued throughout the arrival of Edward and the reunion of the lovers). The music also has a key role to play in moving the narrative along by signalling the breaks between one scene and another, effecting a smooth transition between the two whilst taking us from one location to another and moving us forward through time.

Sound effects are heard less often than speech or music in the sequence from *Jane Eyre*. The most consistent is that of the wind, which is introduced during the bridal gown scene and heard throughout the scene in the orchard. The wind suggests a storm brewing, literally and figuratively. We hear it most clearly when Jane herself is at her most desolate and in her greatest turmoil. Other sound effects which stand out include the horses (hooves, snorting and reins jingling) and dogs, which herald Mr Rochester's return: the horses signifying the approach of someone, the snorting and reins signifying their arrival and the dog's excited barking signifying that the person in question is their master. Nevertheless, these sounds still require Jane to confirm the identity of the newcomer with her words 'Oh Edward!' Perhaps the other noise most worthy of note is the acoustic treatment of the second female voice, which has a greater reverberation than Jane's. The greater reverberation renders the voice mysterious by locating it in a different space to that of Jane's. The peculiar echo suggests the voice is either ghostly (comes from beyond the real world) or internal (comes from Jane's imagination). The acoustic properties of this voice alone do not make it seem strange (the repetition of Jane's words and the accompanying manic laughter do this), but they do enhance the effect of strangeness created by the actress's performance.

There is no question that in the scenes described above radio's verbal code is essential whilst the non-verbal codes are incidental. Without the accompaniment of music and noise we would still discover Jane in her bedroom with her trunks packed, the arrival and trying on of the wedding dress, her fears of becoming the new Mrs Rochester, her escape to the orchard and her reunion with her fiancé. Her voice alone would sketch in all the details of her surroundings and convey her various emotional states. Yet something would be lost. The drama would be less dramatic. The difference would be like that between a pencil sketch which presents all the details in outline and a painting which brings the scene to life. For words punctuated by silence are the figure and the ground, the aural equivalent of black and white. Words are the substance of radio. They solidify the air which would otherwise be abstract and ambiguous, giving it shape, form and structure. Yet, if words give radio its structure, noises (particularly sound effects) embellish and elaborate this structure, providing texture and detail, interest and nuance: the aural equivalent of colour and shading. Finally, music moves the whole thing along. It invigorates, energises, animates, bringing radio to life. Radio needs structure, detail and life. In the absence of any visual component these are provided by words and silence, noise and music.

Things to do

1 Produce an analysis of a range of jingles either from different types of radio station or from different programmes from the same station. What does the jingle tell you about the character of the station, programme or presenter? What kinds of audience is it likely to attract? On which types of programme or station are jingles most used? On which kinds of radio station or programme are they never used?
2 Analyse the signature tunes from a range of different programmes and consider the ways in which the musical themes and orchestration convey the nature of the programme itself.

Note

1 Michelene Wandor's four-part adaptation of Charlotte Brontë's *Jane Eyre*, produced by the BBC and broadcast as the 'Classic Serial' on Radio 4 in 1994.

|4|

The mind's eye

There is silence. There is silence until, very softly, a voice breathes the words 'To begin at the beginning'. From that moment on, a world is carved out of darkness, a world that is eventually rich in sounds, sights and smells, but a world that only comes to light slowly and cautiously, as though its foundations were too unreliable, too unpredictable to just appear before us fully formed and all-present. This is the world of Llareggub, a fictitious Welsh fishing village created by Dylan Thomas in his radio play *Under Milk Wood* (1954). It is a world of pure radio. Gently, even tentatively, Llareggub emerges from darkness and silence, the darkness and silence of night: the darkness and silence of the medium without its message; radio at rest.

> It is spring, moonless night in the small town, starless and bible-black, the cobblestreets silent and the hunched, courters'-and-rabbits' wood limping invisible down to the sloe-black, slow, black, crowblack fishingboat-bobbing sea. The houses are blind as moles (though moles see fine tonight in the snouting, velvet dingles) or blind as Captain Cat there in the muffled middle by the pump and the town clock, the shops in mourning, the Welfare Hall in widows' weeds. And all the people of the lulled and dumbfounded town are sleeping now.
>
> (Thomas 1995: 3)

This is how the stage of Llareggub is set: black upon black. The sky is bereft of moon and stars, the shops and houses are dark and silent: no light reflects upon the sea, no lights shine out from windows. Only the narrator, invisible and omniscient, breaks the silence of the town and alerts the audience to the scene so shrouded and still. Out of the blackness and silence the narrator enables the listeners to see the dark and empty sky overhead and, beneath it, the unreflecting sea with its boats. Lying between the black sky and the sea can be seen the invisible wood (inhabited by rabbits, moles and courting couples) and, under it, the town with its cobbled streets, its rows of darkened houses, shops and public buildings, their inhabitants sleeping. This is the manner in which Thomas chose to reveal Llareggub to radio listeners, each detail appearing momentarily, as if from the shadows (to which it quickly retreats). Light is shed cautiously and gradually and everything the listener sees is initially black or invisible. On stage or screen such a setting would remain invisible and the spectator would be conscious of their blindness (their inability to see in the dark). Radio, however, as *Under Milk Wood* demonstrates, can allow its audience to see in the dark, to see the invisible, to see the unseeable. As Thomas's narrator tells them, 'Only your eyes are unclosed, to see the black and folded town fast, and slow, asleep' (Thomas 1995: 3). If the listeners draw close and attend carefully, as they are told to do, they can not only 'hear the houses sleeping in the streets in the slow deep salt and silent black, bandaged night' but can also 'see, in the blinded bedrooms, the coms and petticoats over the chairs, the jugs and basins, the glasses of teeth, Thou Shalt Not on the wall, and the yellowing dickybird-watching pictures of the dead' (Thomas 1995: 4). In their mind's eye, the radio listeners can see all of this and possibly even more besides. And yet, ironically, radio is defined as a blind medium.

Radio is invariably described as blind. Take, for instance, the comment that 'it is from the sole fact of its blindness that all radio's other distinctive qualities – the nature of its language, its jokes, the way in which its audiences use it – ultimately derive' (Crisell 1992: 3). But why call an entirely auditory medium 'blind'? There is, after all, a significant difference between calling a medium 'entirely auditory' and 'blind', given that the latter implies that something crucial is lacking and that the medium is, therefore, inherently deficient. Why 'blind' and not 'invisible'? Why, in other words, define radio's status as a non-visual medium in terms connoting impairment, disability and lack rather than positive attributes such as power and magic? The repeated use of the words 'blind' and 'blindness' to describe radio would suggest that those writing about radio consider its lack of visuals to be a problem rather than a positive attribute: as something to be overcome rather than exploited. Perhaps what this reveals most strikingly is the extent to which sight is privileged over hearing and, this being the case, what is most notable about radio is what cannot be seen with the eye rather than what can be heard with the ear.

Sight is generally regarded as a more useful and comprehensive means of perceiving the world around us than sound, touch, taste and smell. The status of sight as the most important of all the human senses is even incorporated into the English language: for here, to 'see' something is the same as to behold or understand, to 'know' (if you see what I mean). In other words, so far as humans are concerned, sight is the one sense with which we believe we can most fully perceive something, whereas our hearing, taste, touch and smell merely enable us to experience certain qualities of a thing. Furthermore, we can see virtually any object (so long as there is sufficient light) whereas not everything is capable of being heard. Because what we hear are the vibrations of air created by an object rather than the object itself, we can only hear things that move or, more specifically, when they are moving. Thus, given that we can see so many things that cannot be heard and given that sight provides us with a greater understanding of something than hearing, it is perhaps not surprising that radio is almost invariably discussed negatively, in terms of what it lacks rather than what it possesses. Radio's great (and apparently unforgivable) failure is that it provides nothing for our eyes to look at and, in so doing, provides us with no opportunity to use our most important sense.

Radio is obviously set apart from other media by the fact that its form cannot be seen. Clearly, by not enabling its audience to use their primary sense, radio would seem to be, in a most obvious way, more defective and incomplete than other media. Whilst paintings, posters and photographs lack sound, their silence ordinarily goes unnoticed. Moreover, it is unnecessary for their images to attempt to compensate for their lack of sound. They are complete in themselves and thus prized (and praised) for the qualities they possess rather than for their ability to compensate for what they lack. However, judging by what has so often been said of radio, it would seem that the medium's lack of visuals rarely goes unnoticed and that listeners are virtually incapable of ignoring or forgetting its blindness. Unlike the visual arts, which require no justification or compensation for the fact that they may lack sound, radio would seem to be constantly striving to make amends for the fact that it has no visual dimension: its primary object being to disguise this fact by the substitution of sounds (mainly words) for the missing images. Hence radio would appear to be both a deficient (incomplete) medium and one obsessed by its own limitations and inadequacies. The notion of radio as blind and, in particular, the notion that all its formal characteristics are essentially compensatory devices for its blindness, perpetuates this view of an inadequate (even neurotic) medium, robbing it of any potential virtue or strength it may have as a purely auditory form.

There are those, however, who have argued against the notion of radio as, first and foremost, a blind medium. For instance, Jonathan Raban has written that 'Blindness has been cited far too frequently as radio's unique attribute' (Raban 1981: 80). He has also drawn attention to the unsuitability of using a word to define the medium which carries obvious implications of disease and affliction. Radio, he argues, rarely renders its listeners blind: rather, it reports 'from a world in full possession of its senses' and is received by 'a listening world equally well endowed' (Raban 1981: 81). This aspect of radio (whatever term we use to describe it), says Raban, 'should certainly not be thought of as the one quality distinguishing radio from all other media' since it is a feature which it shares with literature (Raban 1981: 80). Books may seem different from radio programmes in that they provide their readers with something to look at (i.e. the type, the printed words upon the page, the binding and possibly also illustrations), but the true images created by fiction exist not on the page itself but in the mind of the reader, whose task is to both decipher the meaning of the words and phrases *and* to visualise the characters and settings with the help of the information provided on the page. Similarly, radio's writers, producers and actors 'create a skein of sound – noises, voices, music – which exists in order to be unravelled in terms of our own memory and experience' (Raban 1981: 81). For Raban the sounds of radio are like the printed symbols of a book: they are there to be decoded and translated into sights, sounds, smells, tastes and textures. So, just as the written page can evoke strong visual impressions for its reader, radio's sounds, voices and music can similarly create vivid pictures in the mind of its listener.

Jonathan Raban is not alone in making this connection between radio and literature and in using this analogy to establish radio as anything but a blind medium. For instance, Robert McLeish, at the beginning of *Radio Production*, points out that radio may be a blind medium but it is also one that 'can stimulate the imagination so that as soon as a voice comes out of the loudspeaker, the listener attempts to visualise what he hears and to create in the mind's eye the owner of the voice' (McLeish 1994: 1). Later in his book, he tells those who aspire to write for the radio to 'remember that radio is an immensely visual medium' and instructs them to 'paint pictures, – and yes, in colour, and appeal to all the senses – the sense of smell, the sense of touch so we can all appreciate the roughly dimpled skin of this brilliant fresh orange that I have here in my hand – and the pungent smell and squirting juice as I cut it. Ah – and mm – the succulent sweetness of this first bite' (McLeish 1994: 70). 'Did you see something of that?' McLeish asks his readers, adding 'I hope so for it is the stuff of radio' (McLeish 1994: 70). In demonstrating the power of words to conjure mental images, a property of language exploited by both radio and the printed page (the written and spoken word), McLeish establishes radio as not only immensely visual but also aromatic and tactile. This ability, moreover, is seen by McLeish to be, as he says, 'the stuff of radio', confirming Raban's remarks about radio coming 'from a world in full possession of its senses' and received by 'a listening world equally well endowed' (Raban 1981: 81). For all those listeners familiar with oranges, the colour, texture, smell and taste can be vividly experienced on the radio by the judicious use of words, and particularly when those words are accompanied by the sounds of tearing peel and squirting juice. What so many have regarded as a sensorily deficient medium would therefore actually seem to be quite the reverse.

Radio: a visual medium

To say that radio is a visual medium when in one sense it is completely non-visual is to bring out the way in which radio encourages the listener's imagination to visualise what he is listening to, to create for himself the visual dimension he is apparently deprived of, to construct the settings and appearances of the characters from the clues that words and sounds provide.

(Lewis 1981a: 9)

Peter Lewis, in the above statement, not only points out the irony of calling radio a visual medium when it is so obviously lacking in visuals but, more importantly, suggests that one of the key features of radio is its propensity to stimulate its audience's visual imagination and (as with literature) to enable them to supply their own unique visuals: e.g., the appearance of the hero/ine or presenter, the decor of the location, be it a country house or a radio studio. Lewis, like Raban and McLeish, has pointed out that radio's visual dimension operates in a way similar to that of literature, where what readers see is not just the printed letters and words before their eyes but the characters and settings those letters and words represent. In both cases (radio and literature) the visuals exist not before the listeners'/readers' eyes as much as inside their heads and, as such, those visuals are the product equally of the producer/author and the listener/reader. In both cases, whilst the visuals are initially born out of the words and/or sounds of the programme/novel, they are realised (in the sense of made real or brought to fruition) by the imagination of the listener/reader. This feature of both radio and literature is, of course, absent from the 'visual arts' themselves, where the opportunity for the audience or viewer to actively participate in the creation of the images is denied. Here the viewer can only appreciate – rather than actually participate in the creation of – the images. So, for instance, as Peter Lewis says, 'Theatre, television and film give us little or no choice about what we see and prevent our visual imaginations from functioning: our eyes have plenty to keep them occupied' (Lewis 1981a: 9).

If all we want from the media is to give us something to occupy our eyes, no wonder film and television prove more popular and receive so much more in the way of critical (and academic) attention than radio. But what radio's lowly status within the arts seems to obscure is the fact that both the power and the pleasure of the medium derive in part from allowing, even encouraging, its audience to participate in the creation of its programmes, enabling them to create for themselves more personal and hence more affective, more meaningful images. This view of radio offers us an alternative way of understanding radio from the one which establishes it as a medium whose form is determined by an inherent need to disguise or compensate for its lack of visuals. This alternative view perceives radio as (despite appearances to the contrary) a visual medium: one that is informed by the visual world and speaks to (in most cases) an audience that is both visually aware and has a large stock of visual experiences and memories which can be drawn upon to make sense of radio programmes. What this conception of radio reveals is the extent to which visuals are actually the most dispensable element of any artistic, dramatic or communicative medium (because audiences can supply these themselves). What it also reveals is that the notion that radio is the most deficient medium is quite mistaken.

Martin Esslin, former Head of the BBC's Sound Drama Department, made the point at the beginning of his essay 'The mind as a stage' (1971) that 'There is, on the surface a striking analogy between radio and silent cinema – both dramatic media which lack one vital element of drama: the silent film words, sounds and music; the radio the whole gamut of visual information' (Esslin 1971: 5). However, as he went on to write, this analogy soon breaks down. 'The eye', he wrote, 'certainly is as powerful an organ as the ear. Yet it is through the ear that *words* are primarily communicated; and words communicate concepts, thought, information on a more abstract level than the images of the world the eye takes in' (Esslin 1971: 5). For this reason, Esslin argued that silent cinema always had to rely on the written word, in the form of intertitles, to convey anything more precise than the appearances of the characters, the settings and landscapes of the drama. Narrative information and character motivation were heavily dependent upon the written caption which constantly interrupted the flow of cinematic images. In contrast, Esslin pointed out that radio 'can evoke the visual element by suggestion alone. The dialogue can carry the scenery and the costume within it and the human voice can powerfully suggest human appearance' (Esslin 1971: 5). He argued that this is possible 'due to the fact that man is above all, a creature of the eye and that our minds automatically translate most information we receive into visual terms' (Esslin 1971: 5). This fact enabled him to establish a fundamental difference between silent cinema and radio when he stated that 'Seeing the lip movements of the characters in the silent cinema could not stimulate the audience to great feats of imaginative effort in reconstructing what the dialogue they were missing might have sounded like; in radio drama the slightest verbal, musical or sound hint *does* powerfully activate the visual imagination' (Esslin 1971: 5). This was presented by Esslin as one of radio's major assets: a point emphasised when he commented that 'as imagined pictures may be more beautiful and powerful than actual ones, the absence of the visual component in this form of drama may well be a considerable asset' (Esslin 1971: 5). To reaffirm the point further still he also wrote, and it is worth noting here, that some things (such as battle scenes) tend to be 'wholly unsatisfactory' when rendered visually, whereas 'In radio each listener will automatically see *his* ideal before his mind's eye and thus be satisfied' (Esslin 1971: 5).

We shall see in a later section of this chapter how many of the BBC's radio dramatists have in the past exploited the medium's so-called blindness for dramatic effect. However, before we get completely carried away by the notion of radio as 'an immensely visual medium' and as superior to the 'visual arts' such as theatre, film and television, it is important to qualify these arguments and acknowledge a number of drawbacks for a medium which cannot be seen other than inside the minds of its audience. First, it is all well and good to say that radio is visual in the sense that it allows and encourages listeners to use their stock of visual experiences and memories, but what happens when radio's sounds fall outside of the listener's experience? One potential problem for radio producers and writers is surely the need to deal only with those things which are universally known and familiar to all, otherwise they must resort to lengthy descriptions (often in minute detail) in order to convey the qualities of the unfamiliar. In contrast, such information could in many circumstances be conveyed in a fraction of the time by an image: a picture, it is said, paints a thousand words.

Second, we should not overlook the powers and pleasures of pure spectacle. Whilst Esslin's comment about silent cinema's dependency upon the written word to convey ideas and dialogue may suggest the inadequacies of the moving image alone, we should not forget that many of the great and truly thrilling moments of silent cinema were entirely visual: the slapstick antics of the Keystone Cops, Charlie Chaplin, Buster Keaton and Harold Lloyd; the sheer beauty of Rudolf Valentino and Greta Garbo; the terrifying and mesmerising ghastliness of Max Schreck as *Nosferatu*; and the thrill of D.W. Griffith's race-to-the-rescue endings or, perhaps one of the most famous silent movie scenes, *Ben Hur*'s breathtaking chariot race. Deriving pleasure from the purely visual, whether in terms of humour, beauty, erotica, fear or simply the thrill of action, should not be underestimated as one of the reasons why film and television are so popular and, to state the obvious, in this respect radio can in no way compete.

Another thing to note is that whilst drama and fiction may be able to adapt well to radio by exploiting the imaginative potential of the listeners to create for themselves more realistic and satisfying images than those ordinarily presented by actors, costumes, make-up and sets, some types of broadcasting – say, for instance, documentaries or news and current affairs programmes – may often require a more precise and objective presentation of visual information. Those programmes which require specific, even graphic, details of things and events to be accurately conveyed to their audience would obviously have difficulty if they had to rely upon listeners' subjective and imaginative reconstruction of verbal and aural information. Some subjects (technology, medicine, science, etc.) that rely heavily upon the accurate and objective presentation of facts are clearly much more difficult to translate into words than fiction.

This, of course, is not to say that only drama succeeds on radio, since a long history of making factual radio programmes exists, particularly in the field of news and current affairs, documentaries ('features') and even medicine and science, all of which are well represented on the BBC's Radio 4. Radio's lack of visuals has shown itself to be anything but a problem across the entire range of broadcast output and is indeed one of the principal factors in the continued success of radio since the loss of its evening and weekend family audience to television in the 1950s. Generally speaking, the medium's lack of visuals has proved attractive (and even liberating) for listeners in a number of ways. First, to enjoy radio programmes, listeners seldom have to give them their full and abiding attention. Radio's invisibility enables its audience to do other things whilst listening, such as driving, housework, gardening – virtually any activity that requires less than full concentration. As such, it can make long journeys or tedious manual jobs bearable, allowing audiences to be entertained and/or informed whilst getting on with their lives.

Another advantage of there being nothing to see when listening to radio is that this circumstance has often contributed directly to listeners being able to establish more intimate relationships with radio personalities and programmes, undisturbed by the constructedness and artificiality of their production values. In effect, blindness conceals the fact that radio personalities and their programmes are fabrications, and listeners have been able to achieve more intimate, companionable and lasting relationships with something or someone that appears to be authentic. As Pete Wilby and Andy Conroy write in *The Radio Handbook*, 'in terms of reinforcing a discourse of companionship through chat, banter, jokes, trivia and gossip, the absence of visual codes serves as a strength rather than a weakness in the communicative effectiveness of radio' (Wilby and Conroy 1994: 28). Whereas in film and television the viewer can all too easily be made aware of the sheer constructedness of the text, with radio there often seems to be no text at all. Whilst television personalities and film stars can seem as fabricated as their costumes and sets, again radio helps to disguise the synthetic nature of the mass-media personality. On the radio there is no artificial lighting or make-up to disturb the sense of one real human being (the presenter) talking to another (the listener). Similarly, there appears to be little in the way of equipment and technology mediating this relationship. Thus, seeing a chat-show host on the television, with a noticeably immaculate hair-do and outfit, missing (albeit momentarily) their cue or camera is quite a different experience to hearing that same person talking to their guests on the radio. On the latter, they will seem altogether more human, less contrived, less glamorous and less artificial, entering into our daily lives (usually our kitchens), seeming more ordinary, everyday, familiar and natural: more like us, in fact. Of course, they are much the same on television or radio, but only on the latter are we less aware of the mechanics of their work as a presenter or media personality. Here we can not only identify more closely with them but can also concentrate more carefully on what they are saying, without being distracted by their impeccable – too good to be true – image and by the all too obvious presence of the technology that brings them into our homes (i.e., the cameras, microphones, etc.).

Radio's lack of visuals clearly has both advantages and disadvantages, producing for its listeners both positive and negative effects. It would be quite mistaken to assume that the medium is any more deficient than any other media form, but it would be equally misguided to assert radio's superiority over the 'visual arts'. If we are to fully understand radio as an exclusively auditory medium we must examine both the benefits and the drawbacks of invisibility. In short, we have to accept that there are problems involved in not providing audiences with something to look at and yet, at the same time, we should not let these problems blind us to the fact that invisibility can be a positive asset for producers, writers, actors and listeners. In the following section, we shall be examining some of the drawbacks of radio's failure to cater for the human eye: drawbacks for both broadcasters and listeners. Here we shall be considering some of the compensatory devices which have been adopted in order to minimise the side-effects of invisibility. In the final section, however, we shall turn our attention to the positive advantages which invisibility has to offer by exploring instances where invisibility has been instrumental in the creation of powerful, original and pleasurable entertainment. This is intended to provide a balanced account of radio's invisibility and an understanding of the way in which the codes and conventions of the medium have evolved so as to minimise the drawbacks and maximise the advantages of catering solely for the ear.

Side-effects

Radio's invisibility is certainly less of an affliction than is implied by the term 'blindness'. In many ways, invisibility is radio's great strength and offers writers, producers and performers distinct advantages over the visual arts. Nevertheless, it also produces a number of negative side-effects: namely, audience confusion, distraction, boredom and forgetfulness. Without a visual element to engage their attention, radio listeners are easily distracted and most radio producers are aware that their audience is more inattentive than theatre-goers, film spectators and even television viewers. Moreover, without a visual element to both illustrate its messages and confirm the source of its sounds, the radio audience is also more easily prone to confusion. Most radio producers recognise that radio listeners, by using their ears alone, are only capable of deciphering so much information at any one time and will only retain that information for so long. It is not that radio listeners are any less intelligent or have worse memories than theatre, cinema or television audiences but that, by relying solely upon their ears to perceive radio programmes, listeners invariably succumb to the frailties of human hearing.

Most radio producers recognise that it is much more problematic for radio to handle a varied range of details simultaneously than for the visual media. On stage and screen, of course, objects and characters continue to exist side by side, the audience's attention directed to significant details by movement, looks, gestures and dialogue or, in the case of film and television, by the camera (e.g., close-ups). A multitude of characters and objects can co-exist without a serious loss of cogency or clarity other than relatively minor distractions. However, unlike the eye, which can take in a multitude of visual details simultaneously, the ear is only capable of distinguishing a

limited range of simultaneous sounds. We can, for instance, quite successfully comprehend a voice talking with music in the background and sound
effects, such as footsteps and a door opening. But more than this, more
voices or sound effects all operating at the same time, would simply cause
confusion. On the whole, therefore, most radio productions minimise their
use of voices, noises and music and often use these devices in succession
rather than simultaneously. So, for instance, characters seldom speak over
each other (other than short overlaps at the start or end of their lines), and
speeches are seldom interrupted by sound effects such as a door opening.

This need for simplification also influences the kinds of narratives used
by radio programmes and, in particular, radio dramas. One of the essential
deficiencies caused by radio's invisibility is, as noted above, that of memory.
Memory often works visually or, at least, we have a tendency to remember
images better than words (for instance, faces better than names).
Consequently, the events of a radio narrative tend to be more difficult to
recall than those of a stage-play or film, where key incidents of physical
action and spectacle can often imprint themselves firmly on to the audience's consciousness and memory ('once seen never forgotten'). Given that
sounds, particularly words, are less likely to be remembered as readily or as
accurately as images, radio producers have to accept a basic principle of
radio drama: that is, that the overall storyline needs to be stripped down to
a basic and easily comprehensible structure. This does not preclude the use
of sub-plots or flashbacks or any other narrative device familiar to writers
of novels, plays and films. Nevertheless, most writers of radio drama ordinarily recognise that they have less scope for departing from basic narrative
structures when writing for the ear alone. Few radio plays consist of a single storyline proceeding in chronological order but, in general, they do have
fewer storylines, fewer characters and less convoluted plots than those written for the page, the stage and the screen.

Another basic principle of writing for radio is that of repetition. As far as
radio drama is concerned it is necessary to constantly remind listeners of
important narrative events which have yet to be resolved. In other words,
key events need to be repeated or referred back to in order to keep them
alive in the minds of the audience. Obviously, the more events that take
place, the harder it is for listeners to remember what has actually happened.
This makes the multiple sub-plots of many novels difficult to adapt faith-
fully as radio plays or serials. As a rule, the more sub-plots, the more likely
it is that the listener will lose track of what is happening in the various narrative strands. In such cases there is, more than ever, a need to constantly
remind the audience of what has happened (to whom, and why) with each
return to a separate strand of the narrative. Such a strategy would mean that
much of the information being conveyed in a radio drama is actually redundant: redundant in the sense of adding little that is new rather than simply
restating what is already known (but is likely to be in the process of being
forgotten by the listener). The only way to avoid such redundancy would

seem to be to adopt the most straightforward linear narrative that moves one basic storyline rapidly through a sequence of events towards a resolution before beginning a new one. As this would eradicate any element of suspense from the drama, make adaptations of novels and stage-plays virtually impossible and also make for rather tedious listening, most radio producers and their listeners are prepared to tolerate a significant degree of redundant narrative information in their radio productions.

If repetition and redundancy are vital elements of radio narratives, then sign-posting is equally important. Not only is it necessary to remind listeners of what has already happened in order for subsequent events to be meaningful, but forthcoming events must also be sign-posted along the way, enabling listeners to anticipate (to some extent) what will happen next. The sign-posting of future narrative events helps to retain listeners' attention and ensure that they will follow the programme through to its conclusion. Obviously, if listeners can tell that something exciting or interesting is about to happen they are more likely to keep listening. But sign-posting is also important in that it helps to create a sense of continuity from beginning to end. By enabling the listener to anticipate later narrative events, a radio drama will be that much clearer. Sign-posting adds significantly, therefore, to both the cogency and consistency of a radio programme.

The necessity of being consistent and making continual references to the significant themes and events of a drama is directly born out of radio's invisibility: it is a consequence of memory being more visual than aural. One direct result of this is that once a character stops speaking on radio they virtually cease to exist in the mind of the listener. If they say nothing for a long time, when they do speak again it is often difficult for the audience to remember who they are and what their significance is within the plot. Therefore, to avoid such problems, radio plays tend to have individual characters speak as often as possible. Again, this can lead to redundancy if the characters speak solely for the purpose of reminding listeners that they still exist. One way round this is, in the case of original radio plays, to use a small cast of characters and, in the case of adaptations of novels and stage-plays, to reduce the number of leading characters, retaining only the most important. Any choice lines of dialogue originally spoken by characters omitted from the radio production can always by given to those characters that have been retained and thus enable them to speak with greater regularity. As a rule, a small ensemble of talkative characters tends to make for more lucid and entertaining radio.

Simplicity, repetition, redundancy and consistency are all vital qualities if radio is to off-set the deficiencies of human hearing. In a sense, they are forced on the radio writer and producer, who ignore listeners' propensity towards inattention, distraction, confusion and forgetfulness at their peril (or, at least, at their listeners' peril). Of them all, simplicity would seem to be the key to effective radio, since complexity only gives rise to an ever greater need for repetitiveness, redundancy and consistency. The more simple a radio programme is – in terms of the deployment of its codes (voices, sounds, music and silence) and the structure of its narrative – the less it needs to sign-post or repeat basic narrative information. Complexity not only gives rise to increasing quantities of redundant information but is itself redundant (in the sense of being unnecessary). Radio can achieve a great deal with relatively little. More is generally less on the radio, in the sense of being less effective and less meaningful. Few sound codes (speech, sound effects, acoustics, music and silence) are needed in order to strike a responsive chord with the listener. It is in this sense that radio can be considered one of the more economical arts. Radio has little need of multiple plots, a cast of thousands and long complicated monologues in order to be effective or exciting. It can achieve a great deal with a bit of cellophane and a few broken match-sticks. Radio has no need to aspire to the status of an epic by being longer, wider, larger and more colourful. Radio's scale is epic by virtue of being (largely) imaginary. Unlike the visual arts, it can be simple and uncomplicated without appearing cheap or low-budget. Simplicity is indeed one of its great strengths, its power lying chiefly in the purity of its codes. To put it simply, on radio, less is more.

The side-effects of radio's invisibility therefore have their remedies. Repetition, sign-posting and simplicity can all be used to counter the listener's propensity towards confusion, inattention and forgetfulness. However, there is another problem which radio producers must consider when working with an entirely auditory medium. All that would ordinarily be seen by the eye must be perceived by the ear, and this is problematic given that not everything can be heard and not every sound clearly denotes its source. On the radio, the visual elements which are such a fundamental part of drama – scenery, lighting, props, costume, make-up, facial expressions, bodily action and gestures – need to be made audible. Listeners need to be informed of what on stage or screen they would be able to see for themselves. There are essentially two ways of doing this. First, some things can be signified directly by their sound. So, for instance, a clock can be made perceptible by ticking or chimes; a character by footsteps, breathing or speech. But not everything can be perceived solely by sound. Not everything makes a sound (e.g., a mirror) and even those things that do make a specific and identifiable noise only do so at certain times; for instance, although a door can be heard when it is opening or closing and a clock can be heard when it is striking or ticking, once the door has closed and the clock has stopped they cease to exist on the radio. Therefore, mute objects will need to be referred to (either by a voice-over narrator or by the characters themselves) if all the elements of a radio drama are to be intelligible for an audience. Thus, the second way of making perceptible what cannot be shown on the radio is to replace visual codes with auditory ones: dialogue or narration.

This situation brings with it a variety of problems for the radio writer and producer. Chief among them is the fact that substituting visual information with verbal references can all too easily result in stilted and unnatural dialogue, with characters continually referring to things which would ordinarily go unspoken: the classic example being the statement 'Is that a gun in your hand?' Yet if, at a crucial moment in a radio play, one character suddenly pulls out a gun and aims it at another character, how does the radio producer indicate the gun to the audience when a gun only exists on the radio when it's being fired? Clearly, having the victim enquire 'Is that a gun in your hand?' is not a very sophisticated device since it both sounds contrived and unnatural and also exposes the medium's inability to show the gun itself. 'Put that gun away, you fool!' might seem rather more convincing but it hardly captures the sense of shock and fear that the character may be supposed to feel at that moment in the narrative. Obviously, the silent gun needs to be referred to verbally rather than represented by its sound. Any number of phrases could be employed by either the character facing the gun or the one pointing the gun; or, as a last resort, the scriptwriter could fall back on the services of an omniscient narrator to describe the event – on condition, of course, that this narrator was a consistent feature of the drama (i.e., used as a narrational device from beginning to end).

This is clearly one instance where the adaptation of a novel or play may run into problems, suggesting that certain actions which may work well on the page or on stage and screen are less suited to radio. However, fortunately for the producers of radio plays, drama is all about movement and change and, since movement and change generate sound, radio is able to capture and present most dramatic events. If drama consisted of characters sitting motionless and not speaking for two hours, radio would have a real problem presenting this inactivity to its audience. For the eye, of course, everything continues to exist whether it moves or not. This would therefore enable stage, film and television producers to present two hours of characters sitting motionless without speaking, should they wish to do so. This also means, however, that on stage and screen static objects are to be seen irrespective of their importance within the developing drama: for instance, a clock will still be seen sitting on the mantelpiece even though it has absolutely no significance for what is going on in front of it. Although in some ways this gives theatre, film and television directors certain advantages over radio producers, such details could be said to have the disadvantage of distracting the viewer's attention from the most significant moments of the drama, whilst on the radio the clock will only appear when it has a specific plot function. On radio an object would never impress itself upon the consciousness of the audience unless it had some narrative or dramatic significance. In this sense, everything that is heard in a radio drama is highly motivated: that is, it has a good reason (or even several reasons) for being there. Nothing is extraneous. Every sound has a specific function every time it is heard. The radio producer has complete control over the information conveyed to listeners at all times. On stage and screen it is often all too easy for the viewer's attention to wander or be distracted by incidental or even irrelevant details, such as furnishings, costumes, hairstyles, make-up, or maybe even the fact that the actor or actress is looking older or has put on weight since their previous play or movie. On the radio, there are fewer distractions and there is, consequently, an opportunity to focus attention much more thoroughly on the essentials of the action.

This feature of radio led Rudolf Arnheim in 1936 to conclude that sound was more inherently dramatic in nature than vision. In *Radio* he wrote that what is essential to certain moments of drama 'is not so much the existence of the inactive "being", but rather that which is just changing, just happening' (Arnheim 1936: 152–3). It was precisely this feature of drama (always something changing, something happening) which Arnheim believed was best captured by radio rather than stage or screen. For whilst theatre and cinema offer the viewer a very clear idea of what is happening at any moment of a drama (with the benefit of gestures and facial expression), both media are equally concerned with what Arnheim called the inactive or unalterable state of being. Radio's exclusive concern, on the other hand, is with action: the always evolving, always happening. On the radio, nothing static exists and neither does anything that is not vital to the action at the precise moment that it is heard. For this reason, Arnheim regarded radio as a more dramatic medium than screen or stage. Action is the essence of radio, as it is of drama itself.

To some extent, theatre, film and television can be thought of as less dramatic than radio because they are less active, less immediate and not solely the purveyors of action. As such, stage and screen could even be said to be hampered by their insistence on presenting the past: that is, showing objects and characters which have become, as the action has continued to unfold, superfluous and redundant. As Arnheim wrote, 'Much of what is placed before the eye on stage or screen for the sake of naturalistic completeness is only there so that the lack of it should not disturb one; it is not used positively' (Arnheim 1936: 153–4). So far as the stage or screen are concerned, to have objects and characters vanish immediately after they have fulfilled their narrative function would, in most cases, be more disturbing than having them remain even at the cost of becoming distractions from the action. Of course, in cinema, camera framing (e.g., close shots and close-ups) can direct the spectator's attention to the essential features of the action and, simultaneously, position incidental and irrelevant objects and characters outside of the frame; but this can only be achieved temporarily, for in the subsequent shots (i.e., long and medium shots) those same objects and characters reappear. To avoid this the film would have to be shot entirely in close-up. The advantage for the radio producer then lies in the fact that for radio everything is lacking and the task of the producer is to rule extraneous details out but to rule significant details in. Similarly, the difficulty of creating a cogent radio drama is not how to avoid distracting or superfluous background details but how to make perceptible static items that are important to the plot: a task which, whilst sometimes difficult, is generally easier to accomplish than ruling out all superfluous visible details on stage and screen.

What all of this demonstrates is that the notion that radio has a problem representing things unambiguously by their sound or by naturalistic and unobtrusive dialogue obscures the fact that radio is in some ways more effective as a dramatic medium than the visual arts. It is important to acknowledge that there are also disadvantages in visibility which, by being invisible, radio can circumvent. In other words, the perceived 'blindness' of radio has not only blinded some critics to the advantages of radio but has also blinded them to the disadvantages of visual media such as theatre, film and television.

Invisible assets

No doubt many radio producers have been (and are) blind to the advantages of invisibility. However, for every radio producer who sees their task as being essentially that of overcoming the disadvantages of blindness there is another who embraces invisibility as a positive asset and seeks to exploit some of the advantages radio has over stage and screen. In what remains of this chapter we shall be considering these advantages and examining some of the ways in which a variety of radio dramas have exploited the benefits of blindness.

Perhaps the most obvious and fundamental advantage of radio having no visible codes is that radio broadcasts are easier, cheaper and quicker to produce than stage-plays, movies and television programmes. Because there is no need to design and build sets or to design and make costumes, the production costs are considerably lower. Similarly, there is no need to hire such people as lighting technicians or dressers and make-up artists, which again makes radio one of the most economical means of staging drama. Time (and, hence, money) can also be saved by not having to rehearse the physical movements of the actors. Moreover, radio dramas require, and work better with, smaller casts than theatre, cinema and television. Not only are extras rarely needed but also the cast members of a radio play can, and often do, perform several parts. It is the very blindness of radio, the fact that the audience cannot see that the same actor is performing several parts, that makes this possible.

But the benefits of blindness are not only those of economy. Radio's invisibility also offers writers and producers a range of artistic advantages. For instance, radio can, as Peter Lewis has written, 'make rapid transitions in time and space, between speech and unspoken thoughts, and from consciousness to subconsciousness or dream, in an effortless way' (Lewis 1981b: 104). Such an ability is perhaps the key to the power and pleasure of radio drama: its ability, on the one hand, to speak from various realms of the mind and, on the other, to transcend the natural laws of time and space. We can perhaps begin to more fully comprehend radio's significance as a dramatic medium by concentrating on two main areas of its artistic strength: (i) its spatial and temporal flexibility, and (ii) its access to the inner recesses of the mind; both of which are the direct result of being invisible.

Radio dramas often transcend and defy the natural laws of time and space, creating vantage points which would be impossible in either the theatre or in life. In so doing, radio dramas can provide listeners not only with new perspectives but also with new insights. In this respect radio is more like cinema and television than theatre. Film, television and radio can all construct narratives which cut between scenes that have no actual physical (geographical) or temporal connection: between, say, a prehistoric cave-dwelling one moment and a twenty-first-century space station the next. However, radio can defy the laws of time and space to a much greater extent and with much less effort and expense than cinema and television. As Frances Gray has written, 'In radio, the author can set his play in Ancient Greece or on Mars without the need for sets or costumes; he can move between the two in seconds; his characters can age years in minutes; there is nothing, in fact, that words can do which he cannot, swiftly and cheaply' (Gray 1981a: 140).

Radio can shift from one place to another and one time to another with greater ease (i.e., more seamlessly) than film since there is no visible discontinuity between the disparate times or places. Moreover, sounds which signify distinct historical moments and geographical spaces can easily co-exist on the radio, as Tyrone Guthrie demonstrated back in 1930 in his play of a drowning clergyman whose past life is heard alongside that of his present (the waves and his heartbeats). In *These Flowers Are Not For You To Pick*, Guthrie capitalised not only on radio's ability to move effortlessly backwards and forwards in time and from place to place but also on the medium's ability to present the co-existence of different times and spaces. Throughout the play we move repeatedly between, and witness the blending of, adulthood and childhood, from the sea in which the young man is drowning to, among other places, his nursery, a moonlit lake and a Belfast parish, capturing the drowning man's 'stream of consciousness', his life flashing before him. It is, in fact, a simple task for radio to accomplish this transcendence of time and space, precisely because it exists not upon a screen in front of the audience but inside their heads, a space in which times and places are in a virtually constant state of shifting and co-existence (i.e., memory and dreaming).

Frances Gray, in her essay 'Giles Cooper: the medium as moralist', has noted how a tradition of British radio drama quickly emerged which sought not only to maximise the intimacy with the listener but also to exploit the opportunities of transcending time and space to an extent which neither the theatre nor the cinema could compete. According to Gray, the pioneering radio dramatists of the 1930s and 1940s located the strengths of radio drama in two qualities – intimacy and flexibility. She argues that Tyrone Guthrie's description of his first ever play for radio, *The Squirrel's Cage* (1929), as 'A rush through time and space', can equally be used to describe many of the BBC radio dramas which succeeded it. Gray writes, for instance, that 'every radio writer since has been aware of the medium's temporal and spatial capabilities' (Gray 1981a: 140). Certainly, the greater part of the BBC's most outstanding radio plays (i.e., plays written specifically for the radio) have exploited the positive advantages of the medium's invisibility rather than simply compensated for what would appear to be missing. Indeed, the first play ever to be specially commissioned for radio by the BBC back in 1924 exploited the medium's blindness by setting the action in a coalmine. Richard Hughes's *Danger* (January 1924) capitalised on the dramatic possibilities of being trapped in the dark and having to rely completely on sound in order to survive. So, from the start, writers commissioned by the BBC approached blindness as one of radio's dramatic distinctions which could produce thrilling, comic and fantastic effects.

There is, however, nothing peculiarly British about this and, indeed, there are many instances where writers and producers of radio drama around the world have exploited the dramatic potential of invisibility. For example, in the United States one of the earliest and most original radio drama serials on CBS made invisibility the basis of its hero's supernatural powers. In Walter Gibson's long-running radio thriller *The Shadow* (CBS, 1930), Lamont Cranston had the power to cloud people's minds so that he became invisible to them. In demonstrating week after week that crime does not pay, Lamont Cranston (a.k.a. 'the Shadow') outwitted one dastardly villain after another by using his powers of invisibility and, in episode after episode throughout the 1930s and 1940s, Americans were thrilled by the sounds of evil brought to justice by an invisible super-hero. Needless to say, the presentation of Lamont Cranston transforming himself into his alter ego and vanishing into thin air was something that radio proved it could do far more easily and convincingly than the stage or screen. By using macabre voices (and laughter) along with bizarre sound effects, acoustics and music, *The Shadow* capitalised on the medium's invisibility to produce one of American radio's most original, successful and fantastic characters.

Throughout its history, the radio play has consistently exploited the medium's blindness to delight and fascinate its listeners. For instance, Samuel Beckett's first radio play, *All That Fall* (January 1957) contains a marvellous moment when its central character suddenly realises that if she stops speaking she will cease to exist (as she is on the radio). Maddy Rooney, a sick, elderly and overweight Irish woman, has just struggled up a steep flight of steps in order to meet her blind husband from his train. At the top of the steps she finds herself temporarily silenced by the greetings of those around her, the mutual exchanges of 'Good morning', ignoring her and her sufferings. Suddenly she interrupts their conversation to declare (to the listening audience more than the other characters) that just because she is silent this does not mean that she is no longer present or aware of what is going on (Beckett 1990: 185). This is the playwright's self-conscious play on one of the major side-effects of blindness (that silence – and silent characters – cannot be perceived), transforming this problem into a positive asset. Similarly, Harold Pinter, in his first radio play, *A Slight Ache* (1959), exploited the potential ambiguity of silence through the character of the mute match-seller who is invited into the home of Edward and Flora. But because the match-seller never actually speaks throughout the play (is only spoken of, and to, by the other characters) the audience is left with the tantalising suspicion that this enigmatic character does not really exist other than in the minds of Edward and Flora. In this way, Pinter exposes the ambiguity of silence for a blind listener and teases his listeners by inviting them to visualise a character who may be nothing more than a figment of the imagination. But if the match-seller only exists in the imagination then so do all the other characters and so does the greater part of the drama.

As Pinter's play suggests, anything can exist in the mind and, in being invisible, radio has privileged access to the mind and all that exists there. Thus when Arthur Dent and Ford Prefect are unceremoniously expelled from a Vogon space-ship (which has recently demolished the planet earth to make way for a new hyper-space bypass) and are rescued from certain death (yet again) by being picked up by a passing craft with an Infinite Improbability Drive, radio has no problem in conveying their bizarre visual experiences to listeners of Douglas Adams's *The Hitch-hiker's Guide to the Galaxy* (1978–9). The sight of the sea front at Southend with the sea as steady as a rock and buildings washing up and down presents no problem for the producer (Geoffrey Perkins) or his special-effects team. Neither does the moment when Arthur's limbs begin to detach themselves from his body or when Ford turns into a penguin. Even the sudden appearance of an infinite number of monkeys (who want to talk about a script they have worked out for *Hamlet*) is possible on radio or, at least, within the imagination of the radio listener.

'The stage of radio is darkness and silence, the darkness of the listener's skull', writes Frances Gray in her essay 'The nature of radio drama' (Gray 1981b: 49). In other words, radio dramas are staged not in a broadcasting or recording studio but in the minds of the listening audience. Here is a stage of infinite proportions and possibilities, on which absolutely anything can be built. Its sets may be simple or complex, huge or minute; either way they are the simplest to build. As Gray writes, 'words are spoken, and we [the listeners] become designers, producers, scene shifters, and the theatre itself' (Gray 1981b: 49). As such, anything is possible as the only real limitations lie within the listeners' imaginations. Radio, more than any other medium apart from literature, involves the listener in the creative process and makes them do much of the creative work for themselves: particularly in terms of creating the *mise-en-scène* (i.e., the sets, lighting, costume and make-up, the physical appearance and movements of the actors). One of the reasons why this is a strength rather than a weakness is precisely because it is something most of us are able to do (and enjoy doing) from an early age. As Frances Gray suggests, 'The willingness of the audience to participate in a creative act is largely owing to the second major fact about radio – its intimacy. Like a bedtime story, it whispers in our ear' (Gray 1981b: 51).

If radio is to involve its audience in the creation of its *mise-en-scène* it must not only draw its listeners in close to their radio sets but be granted access to the inner recesses of their minds. There, its dramas can be played out within almost any setting imaginable, ever-changing, expanding and contracting, moving swiftly and imperceptibly from one scene to another, from the most mundane to the most fantastic, just as we learnt to (or discovered we could do) as children on our parents' knees or tucked up in our beds. Gray's analogy between radio and the bedtime story is a fascinating one: one which alerts us to the fact that from our earliest and formative years our minds have been filled with stories which required us to supply our own images. If radio is capable of recalling the same pleasures and satisfactions those childhood stories once evoked, no wonder radio has continued to thrive despite the rise of television during the 1950s. If radio truly is like the bedtime story – the story that is read aloud to the subject (rather than read by the subject in bed), heard directly before sleep or whilst succumbing to sleep, a story which induces both sleep and pleasurable dreams – then it is clearly one of the most satisfying forms of entertainment designed to relax the body whilst stimulating the mind.

In listening to a bedtime story, we allow ideas to be put into our minds, ideas that can then pervade our dreams and affect our night's sleep. As such, there is considerable trust placed upon the reader (not to disturb our peace of mind). If we are to let radio invade our minds and use our imaginations it must first, like the person we allow to tell us a bedtime story (often, quite an honour), gain that same kind of trust. One of the primary pleasures associated with the bedtime story is, of course, comfort and the very process of being comforted. Even when the story is (as most bedtime stories are) frightening, it is still comforting to be tucked up in bed and, of course, we know that it will all come out right in the end. But that sense of comfort is still heavily reliant on our faith in the person reading to us. This analogy therefore tells us something about the relationship between the listener and the broadcaster: it has to be one of absolute trust.

Finally, just to pursue this analogy a little further, we can perhaps see similarities in the way that both radio and the bedtime story are at their best when actively engaging their listeners' imaginations in order to take liberties with their sense of reality. Because the imagination is so flexible in allowing bizarre transformations to occur, the most pleasurable bedtime stories are undoubtedly the most fantastic. In bedtime stories, everything is pushed to an extreme otherwise unobtainable in life: giants truly are enormous, heroines are beautiful and heroes handsome, monsters are terrifying and magical things really do happen. As such, these stories, however fantastic, are credible: they have a credibility that the theatre, cinema and television find difficult to match since all too often their giants are just big, their heroines and heroes just good-looking, their monsters vaguely ridiculous and their magic just tricks. Only radio can match the credibility of the bedtime story's fantasy and, therefore, it is no wonder that many of radio's most successful dramas have indeed been fantastic: e.g., Charles Chilton's *Journey into Space* and Douglas Adams's *The Hitch-hiker's Guide to the Galaxy*. This is simply because both the bedtime story and the radio play are staged within the mind. These plays may be heard by the ear but that is merely the beginning of their existence: to be fully realised they must be seen by the mind.

Inside the listener's mind the drama is necessarily more intense than when simply before their eyes. This means that radio is doubly internalised. First, the sound is, as Frances Gray points out, 'literally inside us' (Gray 1981b: 51). Second, the realisation of the drama takes place inside our heads, as our imaginations set to work on picturing the scene. The relationship between the medium and its audience is therefore unusually intimate (for a mass medium). Not only is it intimate but it is also participatory to the extent that we, as listeners, allow our imaginations to be guided by what we hear and work with the medium to complete the fantasy it has set out to construct for us. Our pleasure lies in being able to participate in the process and what we derive from this participation is the sense that radio's representations, far from being partial or incomplete (because lacking in visuals), are actually more authentic, more credible, more realistic because they conform exactly to the way in which we see the world.

In many respects we have moved a long way from regarding radio as blind: as deficient or defective. Partly, this is because we have questioned the suitability of the term 'blindness' (a term imbued with notions of affliction and disability) and often replaced it with the term 'invisibility' which has more positive (even magical) connotations. It is also, however, because we have recognised that visibility itself can have certain drawbacks and deficiences – something seldom considered in accounts of radio. Clearly, it is important in any assessment of a particular media form to acknowledge both its positive and negative attributes and what we have tried to do here is not to set radio above the visual arts for any reason other than to redress a perceived imbalance whereby radio has been established as one of the lesser arts simply because of its lack of visuals. In this chapter we have attempted to reconsider radio in terms of its own merits rather than in terms of what it lacks and, in so doing, it has been important to challenge the view that visibility is always necessarily an advantage over invisibility. Of course, one of the things that has emerged from our account is the notion that radio may be seen to offer more authentic and credible representations of reality than the visual media (e.g., theatre, film and television). Obviously, it is all too easy to get carried away with defending and ultimately valorising a particular medium at the expense of others. The notion that radio is a more realistic medium than the visual arts is quite probably the result of such an impulse. Therefore, as we move towards claiming radio as more real than theatre, film and television it is important to acknowledge that this perceived realism results largely from the fact that its invisibility conceals the constructedness of its texts and that, in fact, radio authenticity is often not what it seems.

Things to do

1 In the film *Dial M for Murder*, a young woman answers the telephone and as she does so a man emerges from behind a curtain and attempts to strangle her with a stocking. In self defence, the woman stabs the strangler with a pair of scissors. How could this scene be adapted to radio without destroying the suspense and yet still managing to clearly convey the actions of the characters and the objects they use?
2 Listen to a short extract of a radio drama or comedy (about three minutes). Note all the visual details which you can see in your mind whilst listening. How much of this detail is signified by the production itself (as noise, music or dialogue/narration) and how much is your own invention?

5

Truth claims

Edit: *v & n -v.tr.* (**edited, editing**) **1 a** assemble, prepare, or modify (written material, esp. the work of another or others) for publication. **b** prepare an edition of (an author's work). **2** be in overall charge of the content and arrangement of (a newspaper, journal, etc.) **3** take extracts from and collate (films, tape-recordings, etc.) **4 a** prepare (data) for processing by a computer. **b** alter (a text entered in a word processor etc.) **5 a** reword to correct, or to alter the emphasis. **b** (foll. by *out*) remove (part) from a text etc. *-n.* **a** piece of editing. **b** an edited item. **2 a** facility for editing.

(Australian Concise Oxford Dictionary, 1992)

The west has been preoccupied with proof and evidence since Plato. Before the advent of the camera (1839), and fingerprinting, western society found it difficult to ascertain reality and, as a result, was preoccupied with contracts and signatures; an obsession which still exists today despite sophisticated communication technology and DNA science. Following the collapse of religion and the full emergence of capitalism came humankind's search for reality and proof. With that search came the tools which could deliver: the ultimate instrument being the camera. However, audio recording devices also have played a major role in this search and distribution of truth, particularly in the areas of news and current affairs.

In the pioneering days of radio, news was not a priority; in fact, news was controlled by the print media which resented the potential competition radio posed. Newspaper bosses attempted to ban the broadcasting of news on the new medium, but this objection only succeeded in delaying the introduction of a radio news service. However, the early days of radio news were none the less fraught with problems; the service was only permitted to, at best, merely repeat those stories already covered in the day's newspapers or, at worst, it was a soapbox for big business and government. It was not until the advent of war that broadcast journalism come into its own as an authoritative, non-fictional medium, when journalists sent home information dispelling the romantic, heroic myth that enveloped war by bringing friends and families of fighting soldiers face to face with the stark, violent, horrific images of war. This material is part of our *audio socialisation,* or the historical role that radio has played in our social development.

As adults, we can choose what we wish to hear; but if we think back to our childhood, some may be reminded that it was parents and grandparents who controlled the dials, at least until we received our own radio for a birthday or Christmas. As children and teenagers, the portable radio offered sanctuary in bedrooms or excursions away from authority and represented a form of self-identification, forging musical tastes and political agendas taken into adulthood. However, not all memories of radio listening are those of solitude. Friends and family also partook in outings in which the radio may have played a major role, particularly in the late 1970s with the advent of the car radio. All these memories, as well as those passed down by family and friends, books and films, have played a major role in our audio socialisation, and that socialisation has built for radio a reputation of truth and honesty, simply because of the length of time it has been in our past and present, and the important functions it has played in our development. For older relatives, the radio was a link to information during times of war, political upheaval, world tragedy and celebration; and these memories and experiences have been passed down to younger listeners through family stories, literature and television. Radio is 'an old friend' that has provided entertainment, information and education for five generations. Admittedly, print has been with us for much longer but it does not have the element of the human voice, the intimacy and friendship which comes only through humanity. Television does, of course, play a major role in our daily lives, but I would argue that 'Hollywood', and the television news producer's search for images that will shock and (unfortunately) in turn attract audiences, have desensitised viewers and developed in them a strong cynicism. In fact, we listen to many more hours of radio in a week than we realise. It's almost an unconscious reflex; radio is just there, it always has been; through our lives and the lives of our parents, grandparents and great-grandparents. The way in which we use it has certainly changed through the decades, but it has always played a vital role as a source of entertainment, information and companionship, and with this history and socialisation has developed an almost unquestioning belief in radio: why would a friend lie? This question will be examined further in this chapter as we examine more closely the contradictory and often problematic areas of editing and live broadcasting.

But, why believe?

Radio's history is not the only element which gives the medium a cloak of trust and accountability; it emits a sense of honesty by its very nature, its technology. Next to the telephone, radio is the most intimate form of broadcasting, an intimacy that one cannot attain from TV or print. In many homes, radio is the first thing we wake up to in the morning, whether it be to a speech/news-based format, to the more dulcet tones of soft, classical or easy-listening music or to the more 'in your face' youth, morning crew, playing rock music and loud jokes, and it will usually remain with us through breakfast and the commute to and from work. It puts us in touch with the world by informing us of events, at a local and international level, that have happened while we have been sleeping. It informs us about the state of the roads, which will determine how we may choose to travel to work, and may remain as a companion during that journey. Radio is the only medium that we actually *wear* on our bodies, e.g., the walkman, or take into our personal space immediately surrounding our body in our most intimate room, the bedroom; our clock radio is placed only inches away from us on our bedside table. The radio is what we may listen to when working in the house or garden, driving in our cars, as background music while we are eating or even making love, all of which makes the process of radio listening an active and flexible pass-time, i.e., we can do other things when we are listening (we cannot read the paper while we are taking a shower!). Radio is also portable, i.e., a medium we can take with us when we walk or drive. It is also a very affordable medium: it does not cost anything to tune in every day, radios are inexpensive to buy and listeners are not obliged to pay a licence fee.

The 'radio personality' is another factor that contributes to radio's 'trustability'. The familiar personality is one we 'invite' into our homes. They would not be a guest if not liked or believed by the listener. And, ironically, it is the *lack* of personality in the production of news that offers the same benefits, i.e., one news reader is exactly the same as the next, presentation style is standard and language is simple and colloquial, written for the lowest common denominator (although that denominator may vary from service to service). Also, radio does not have the element of vision to sway public opinion, and it is less likely to go for the shock treatment we see in the almost cinematic images of TV news. Radio is also considered more non-partisan than print because it does not include editorials. Pictures and editorials give us more of an opportunity to scrutinise and challenge. Radio is simply the first port of call for the majority of people, who turn to it, particularly when they wake, to receive information. We are less outraged, less confronted and less challenged.

So, the advantages of radio news are its *flexibility*; we can listen to it in the car, in any room in the house or office, even while we are walking or jogging. It is easily *affordable* because the radio service carries no licence fee and radio sets are inexpensive. Radio news is easily *accessible* to listeners, i.e., it is easily comprehended and information can be delivered quickly. Radio has a sense of now: it is *immediate*, current, topical and therefore generally carries a sense of urgency. For example, in the area of news and current affairs, part of a journalist's mission is to *break*[1] a story. Radio news stories, by their very nature, can be turned around far more quickly than television.[2] Radio does not rely on visuals to impact or colour the story. Interviews can be done by telephone, whereas television journalists prefer to be face to face.[3] Radio news services are more frequent than television and can be broadcast easily outside regular bulletins, whereas in television, cutting into a programme will only be done in times of extreme importance and often will be in the form of teletext. Radio journalists can also go to air 'live' and from any location; television is more selective due to technological constraints. Print, on the other hand, can only deal with a story in its next edition. If a story breaks after the last edition then it will be the following morning before the story is printed, and in many cases it will generally be presented in the past tense. (I do not wish, however, to marginalise the extraordinary technical feats possible on television; just consider 'Live Aid' for a moment. But I do wish to stress radio's simplicity and 'personability'; after all, it is not often we see a pedestrian with a television strapped to their head!)

However, has this history of trust and practicality almost made the listener take radio for granted? Has the listener become complacent and unquestioning? Does the listener automatically believe everything s/he hears and, knowing this, do producers manipulate and exploit that sense of trust?

Get me a murder a day'[4]

Editing must not be used to alter the sense of what has been said or to place the material within an unintended context (McLeish 1994: 32). However, the line between presenting a story or issue *exactly* how it develops and packaging the piece for broadcast is extremely fine. So much of the process of editing is subjective, e.g., what is the producer's agenda, time frame (in which to turn around the feature), airtime, ideology, gender, culture (which impact upon the producer's interpretation of events) and budget. Very few 'raw' interviews are broadcast without some editorial intervention. The justification for intervention could merely be to remove intrusive background noises like a phone ringing, a banging door or a passing car. Another reason could be to 'tone down' a severe stutter (see case study, pp. 139–40) or to remove lengthy hesitations, reasons which seem perfectly acceptable but when examined more closely do highlight the power that exists in the hands of the producer. A stutter for the stutterer can be an excruciating moment, and to remove it renders the feature broadcastable and alleviates any embarrassment for the talent; but is it ethical to *completely* polish the characteristic? What is wrong with preserving some of the true characteristic of the voice and the human being behind it, at the same time educating the listener? The more one hears a stutter on the air, the more 'normalised' it becomes and, hopefully, eventually simply a characteristic rather than a 'disability'. That very situation has evolved with regional accents. Not too many years ago a regional accent was almost regarded as a 'disability'. Presenter-hopefuls were forced to adopt RP or forget about a career as a presenter. Today, the regional voice is perfectly acceptable, almost 'trendy', and almost always preferred by the listener in that region, who identifies with a voice not unlike her own.

Hesitations and pauses are another area of editing that, at face value, seem innocent and in many cases are. However, the pause is often loaded with heavy connotation and can create drama, as when a grieving parent takes a moment to speak of their dead child. Hesitation at such moments is intentionally left in; indeed such is the over-use of these moments that any grieving relation who does *not* pause or catch their breath seems uncaring or possibly guilty.[5] The use of pauses and hesitation is never more prominent than in the reporting of political events. Here the producer can use such moments to suggest uncertainty, incompetence or, particularly, dishonesty. So much is this the case that politicians are trained and groomed for the media and often rely on spin doctors for guidance. However, no amount of training can control the outcome of a story if a producer has a particular agenda in mind; as long as no laws are broken the producer can present a story as s/he wishes. This is particularly true in the case of the tabloid press: one would not expect the same of credible, ethical reporters. Politicians have learned to deal with this by mastering the 'seven-second grab' that is, they have acquired the art of getting their point across in as few words as possible.

> In many cases a journalist will wait for 'the grab' and then cut the interview and use the press release to write the rest of the story. There is very little investigative journalism around now. Commercial television chases dodgy dry cleaners and TV repair men, because everybody has got a TV.[6]

However, in some cases, the 'grab' is not conducive to the story and an interviewee will find that they have to speak at length about a particular issue. In such cases the interviewee will try to speak without taking a break, thereby making it harder for the editor to 'cut' their speech. Listeners may sometimes notice when a 'grab' sounds incomplete. This occurs when the editor cuts in the middle of a sentence regardless of intonation, i.e., the grab does not incorporate the complete sentence, but rather just the words that the editor requires to make a point. Interviewees are vulnerable to such editing and although such edits are noticeable, they are so commonly used that listeners are inclined to accept or overlook them.

But not all edits are noticeable. Listeners should be aware how easily edits are disguised, particularly in radio. A good editor will take into account voice intonation, background sound and sense (order of issues during interview); when all these things are considered, programmes can be edited without any evidence of the process. The same cannot be said for television, where edits have to be disguised with vision, two shots and noddies,[7] rendering the broadcast smooth. The listener (or in the case of television, the viewer) must also be aware that editing does not only take place after material has been recorded, but also *before* recording starts. A field reporter will often ignore certain material happening off mike, or off camera, or events leading up to and following a story. Selective editing is not always ethical (particularly if it is simply for effect), but in many cases producers justify such edits by claiming time constraints, i.e. that they have only thirty or forty seconds for their report and are working under the pressure of deadlines. A good journalist, however, will never present a story out of context, but will instead present enough material in their introduction or conclusion to give a fair representation of the soundbite (see case study, pp. 138–9).

Another interesting area, when considering news editing in particular, is 'file' copy. In television news, the editor has at her fingertips a catalogue of general vision, i.e., shopping centres, motorway chaos, school children playing, and so on. This vision, known as file vision, is available to use at any time for any relevant story when vision peculiar to that story is unavailable. This system, although not considered unethical, does raise questions about authenticity. Could this vision be unrepresentative or misleading? Radio does not face the same dilemma with regard to vision but it still requires sound. The use of file audio does occur but to a much lesser degree and possibly raises less sinister questions; after all, reporters do not use file interviews. However, the question of file audio enters the scenario in the case of feature and documentary making. SFX are used to 'colour' a piece of audio, e.g., sounds of the country, beach, motorway, church bells, etc., but is this as misleading as vision? For example, a viewer watching a TV story about an outbreak of meningitis in a university's halls of residence which has been packaged using file vision of university students could be forgiven for panicking unduly if s/he recognises a student or the institution; in radio, such instances are near impossible. This example highlights the advantage radio has with regard to simplicity when 'turning around' a story. A story that can be produced and broadcast within the hour for a radio journalist could take her television colleague half a day. Whatever the situation, or medium, editors need to take great care that the use of file vision/audio does not deflect from the story or misrepresent its context in any way.

Another key area that concerns the radio producer/editor is time constraints. Listeners can absorb more material through print than the electronic media. Signs which exist in *time* are rather less efficient than those which exist in *space*: it is quicker to read copy than to listen to it (Crisell 1994). Television is restricted also, but it has two mediums for the dissemination of information: sound *and* vision. Radio broadcasters therefore must be extremely selective and creative about what material is broadcast, which in turn accounts for the high level of editing required by the genre. While radio news offers up-to-the-minute information, it can be seen as being less comprehensive. The average news reader utters 160–180 words per minute, which means that a ten-minute bulletin is equal to only one-and-a-half columns of print news copy, and a newspaper can carry thirty or forty columns of news. Therefore, when considering time, producers must become very selective.

News selection is extremely important. If a news service is only three to five or even ten minutes long, then the producer must be very particular as to which stories are included and which are dropped. Such editorial decisions may be determined by the availability of an interview or soundbite/effects, relevance to listener and scale of the story. An event in Sydney may not be particularly relevant to a listener in Manchester, and vice versa, but if the story is about a plane crash in Australia carrying British passengers then it becomes relevant. Also the number of deaths in the plane crash determines the scale of the story.

The *order* of these stories, however, is less straightforward. The order of items in a news bulletin does not necessarily correspond to order of importance. Up to 98 per cent of the time, the lead story will be the most important according to its scale or relevancy to the audience, but the stories that follow in the rundown do not necessarily follow the same rule, i.e., the second and third story are not necessarily of second and third importance. Why not? Producers talk about 'light and shade'. Sometimes the listener needs a moment to ponder, or reflect, or to simply take in the information that is so rapidly delivered. In some cases, a light-hearted story, or one that does not have the same primary impact on the reader as the previous one, will follow to give the listener 'breathing space'. Also, the listener needs variety to keep her stimulated and interested – again, the issue of 'light and shade' – and the availability of good sound or grabs (and, in the case of television, vision) can determine the importance given to a story. Finally, another point that impacts the running order of a news bulletin is that the listener cannot pick and choose what she will listen to. Although a bulletin will often have headlines, it is almost impossible to select what you do or do not want to hear, or to retrieve or 're-hear' a story (that is why radio news is kept simple and concise) in the same way that one can re-read a newspaper story.

What is editing?[8]

Perhaps the issue of ethics and editing, particularly in radio, arises so often because it is so easy to conceal an edit and because the process of editing itself is easily mastered. A good edit will reveal no audio signs that the material has been manipulated; as Boyd (1994) so humorously puts it, 'A good edit should be like a good wig. The join should be invisible.'

There are several different formats on to which audio can be recorded. First there is analogue audio-tape, a polyester ribbon coated in magnetic ferric-oxide, commonly known as quarter-inch tape, stored on a reel. Audio can be recorded at various speeds on to this tape (using a recording machine such as a Uher, Tascam or Reevox); the higher the speed, the better the quality and the easier the editing. Speed is measured in inches per second, the rate at which the tape passes across the recording head of the machine. Speech programmes are usually recorded at 7.5 inches per second and music and drama at 15 inches per second. During the mid-1980s, DAT (Digital Audio Tape), became a popular recording format. The tape used is very similar to quarter-inch tape but is stored more like a cassette tape (see below). During the 1990s, audio found its way on to computer disc, a format similar to a floppy disc. Finally, mini disc, a very small CD, is another format which has become a very popular way of recording and editing audio.

Editing has several purposes.

1 *It helps to compress and summarise information to suit time constraints and scheduling.* Radio broadcasters therefore must be extremely selective and creative about what material is broadcast, which in turn accounts for the high level of editing required by the genre (see pp. 141–2 in this chapter). Producers are constantly grappling with time constraints: the time they have in which to produce their product (particularly in radio news, which generally works within hourly bulletins) and, second, the time which is allocated to each item. In a three-minute news bulletin, for example, each item may only be thirty to forty seconds in duration, so journalists need to become expert at conveying as much information as possible with as few words as possible; less is more. Some stories may be allocated two minutes while other stories may have only thirty seconds. In television, the viewer has the added dimension of vision; a great deal more can be said in a short amount of time with the clever use of visuals to complement the narration.

2 *To remove flawed, repetitive, superfluous or uninteresting material.* This process may be as innocent as removing the sound of a passing lorry or a slamming door. Information that is not necessarily relevant to the item is regarded as 'fodder', superfluous or unnecessary, and will be removed. The more sinister aspect of this function is when material that can impact the context of the item, such as background information, is edited out as boring, unnecessary or too complex. If a producer has limited time to broadcast a story then she will spend as little time as possible on the background and rather use the time to get immediately to the latest angle on the story, assuming that the listener already has a good understanding of the 'big picture'. However, for those listeners who do not have this assumed insight, the story may be misrepresented. The Bosnian/Serbian war is a classic example of a complex issue that required in-depth information. Producers did their best to keep listeners informed and up to date, but it was an extremely contentious and historically complex conflict and it was impossible for journalists to go over the history again and again.

3 *Legality.* Court reporting is a very complex function and journalists must take great care to report *exactly* what has been said in court and not to make assumptions. Any journalist who reports hearings out of context or

reports information that a judge or magistrate has embargoed could find themselves 'in the dock'. Journalists must also take great care that their reports could not, at some stage, be considered detrimental to a fair trial or hearing and lead them to be charged with contempt of court.⁹ When presenting court stories journalists will use discourse such as 'The court heard' and 'It was said in court'.

4 To *arrange material into a logical sequence*. In many cases an interviewer may record far more material than it is possible to broadcast; for example, a seven-minute feature may be the product of more than an hour of recorded material which is not necessarily linear: some interviewees can jump from thought to thought and back again. In such cases, it is the editor's job to arrange relevant material into an understandable sequence. Editors are also often required to assume the role of translator. Interviews about complicated subjects, for example, science, economics, politics, must be packaged into a product that the listener can comprehend.

5 To *create an impact or particular atmosphere by the use of SFX, music, speech, etc.* Human beings love drama and unfortunately, in our busy, high-tech society, many of us have lost the ability to concentrate on one item for more than a few minutes. Radio does not have the aspect of vision which so often provides the dramatic, enthralling images to capture the viewer's imagination. Instead radio relies on sound and therefore must be very creative with that sound to hold the listener's attention. Catchy tunes, either one-offs or others that listeners recognise and identify with (sig-tune), spectacular sound effects and memorable or controversial phrases can achieve this. Realism also plays an important part. For example, one could never accuse programmes such as the BBC's long-running *The Archers* of holding the listener's attention through spectacular dramatic sound effects, but with its realistic atmosphere and familiarisation it does manage to retain a loyal audience. Other programmes, however, such as a seven-minute feature or a thirty-minute documentary, must use creative sound to first grab, and then sustain, the listener's attention and concentration.

There are several different types of editing.

1 *Electronic, dump* or *dub editing*. Here the producer uses one playback machine and one recording machine. The editor simply cues the beginning of the edit on the playback machine and presses play while the other machine is recording. The editor merely stops and re-cues the playback machine or 'master' and gradually constructs an edited feature.

2 *Splice or cut editing*. Here an editor will cut and paste using a blade and chinagraph pencil to mark where the incisions should go, in much the same way as in film editing. The editor simply cuts out or moves unwanted material. The advantage of splice editing over electronic editing is that the 'master' copy of an interview is broadcast rather than losing a generation and, with that, possible quality.

3 *DAT editing.* This revolutionised the editing process with technology similar to that of video recording. However, on DAT, the final source is recorded on to a small cassette (about a third of the size of a regular audio cassette). Editing is carried out on the record/playback machine and audio quality will not degrade with successive copies.[10]

4 *Computer editing.* This digital editing method is done with a computer and is gradually superseding older methods as more and more stations buy the technology. The computer has the same function as a recorder, but with this remarkable technology the editor actually 'sees' the audio on the computer screen and is always working on the master without actually 'damaging' the master copy as is the case with splice editing. Edits can be done time and time again by simply 'un-doing' a poor or wrong edit, much the same way as one could delete a spelling error when word processing. Material is stored on hard disk, making it infinitely accessible, and audio quality is excellent, i.e., successive copies will not degenerate sound quality. Most radio studios naturally prefer computer technology because of its efficiency, speed and audio quality; however, such editing is not particularly transportable or affordable. A producer who is on location in the middle of the Sahara desert or the Amazon jungle, may find it a little difficult to haul and then 'plug in' their technology and will, in many cases, fall back on the old but reliable Uher, which allows for good-quality recording and on-the-spot editing or, more than likely, a DAT machine which also does not necessarily rely on electricity.

Live, as in contrive!

So, with the technology mastered, a producer can deliver a self-contained, entertaining, informative item that is technically excellent; one where any signs of manipulation through editing are concealed. Producers will almost always try to present 'live' interviews and features, believing that 'liveness' has an edge, an adrenaline rush that is felt by the presenter and therefore transferred to the listener. One needs only to listen to the chilling live broadcast of the Hindenburg disaster in 1937 to acknowledge the truth of this claim. 'It can't be fresher than looking into the future.'[11]

So, if the element of live broadcasting is so dynamic and important, how many producers will advise the listener that s/he is listening to an edited pre-recorded item? Many pre-recorded features are obviously pre-recorded, such as a location piece in a market, at a crime scene, etc. But if the feature has been recorded earlier in a studio, who is to know the difference? Radio, unlike television, is a far simpler medium in which to 'hide' manipulation. What is the harm in passing off an interview that was recorded and edited in a studio several hours before its eventual broadcast? Or, more importantly, why bother?

The race for liveness has raised many ethical issues, because producers sometimes 'trick' the listener by presenting a pre-recorded programme as live. For example, it is very common for the listener to hear: 'Good afternoon and welcome to the programme. *Today* I'm *speaking* with',[12] rather than: 'Good afternoon and welcome to the programme. *Earlier* today I *spoke* with'. This practice is also very common in television, particularly in game shows where daily or nightly programmes, such as *Countdown* (Channel 4) are presented as live when in fact a whole week's programmes are recorded in one day. Another example is *Wheel of Fortune* (ITV), where one month's programming is recorded across ten days. In radio, a producer may desire a live studio guest but may find that due to busy schedules s/he is unable to attend an interview at the preferred time and is only available earlier that day. In such a case the talent will come to the studio at the earlier time and the presenter will often record the interview as if it were live. For example, the presenter could start recording the interview by saying: 'Mary, thanks for joining us today,' and finish it by saying, 'Thanks for giving us your time and the best of luck with your new film.' This interview can be played immediately after an advertisement, the news or some music – i.e., without a link – and when it is finished the presenter can play another piece of music without even opening her microphone, leaving the listener none the wiser. Or, 'It's Christmas, you'll be going away for the holidays and inevitably the garden will suffer. What type of plants should you be looking to plant now that will be hardy enough to withstand the cold but also attractive enough to give the house a lift on those grey days? Jim Marshall is from Greenfingers Nursery . . . '. At this point, Jim Marshall's advice is heard, although his interview was recorded the week before. The presenter has not exactly told the listener this fact, but neither has she said that the guest is in the studio.

Radio producers have argued over the question of ethics for decades, one side claiming that the 'trickery' is harmless and is merely offering the listener good radio, which in turn attracts listeners and consequently sponsorship and funding, which in turn offers the opportunity for excellence. It's thought by many that to explain to the listener that the programme is pre-recorded is distracting: the programme is about plants (or whatever), not about how radio is made. In fact, it could be said that so-called live radio is more important to the producer than it is to the consumer, who wants information and entertainment, and considers the question of how s/he receives it to be irrelevant. There are exceptions, of course. For example, in cases of drama and disaster (the death and funeral procession of the Princess of Wales, the 1997 ski-resort landslide in Threadbo, Australia, the sinking of the Zeebrugge ferry, the O.J. Simpson car chase or the Oklahoma bombing), people want up-to-the-minute news. However, for day-to-day stories it generally will make little difference to a listener whether the prime minister was speaking at ten in the morning or six in the evening. But evidence that producers will disguise pre-recorded interviews where possible indicates the importance live broadcasting has within the industry; perhaps 'radio hacks' want to preserve a sense of mystery and wonder about the nature of radio or even their own skills. Others, however, claim that the listener is not so easily fooled. Their argument is that the listener understands the nature of the medium and will therefore readily accept the pre-recorded programme.

There is also the question of 'gremlins'. Technology, no matter how sophisticated, sometimes falters, be it through simple human error (such as pushing the wrong button) or power breakdown. What impression lingers when a promised live interview turns out to be a washing-powder advertisement played backwards?! Or how does the interviewer explain away an incident where a 'live' interview breaks down halfway through? Where then does the element of trust and respect that the listener has for her favourite station go? Does she feel misled and patronised or is she philosophical about the nature of radio?

There are many different types of pre-recorded programmes and a radio station will broadcast a variety of pre-recorded and live programmes during the course of twenty-four hours. Some pre-recorded programmes are obviously so – for example, drama and location interviews (those that have been recorded outside a studio). Feature programming, talk shows and news and current affairs, however, often broadcast items that, unless told otherwise, the listener could be excused for believing to be live. Those working in the industry are aware of this, whether it be at a conscious or sub-conscious level. Producers of news, documentary and magazine features have many techniques at their fingertips to create a sense of reality. While edits are easily disguised on radio, those rough joins, poor audio quality or background noises that slip through are readily accepted by listeners because of our audio socialisation and in some cases are intentionally used to give the piece a 'grainy' historical atmosphere. The sound of the faint human voice being sent by cable across land and sea, and today through space via satellite, is reminiscent of some of the earliest and most historic transmissions: Churchill announcing the end of the Second World War, the news of J.F. Kennedy's assassination, sounds of the cultural revolution in China, Armstrong's message from the moon. It is true that technology made these broadcasts possible but it was not the technology that created the 'reality' that was achieved by human manipulation.

Producers set out with an agenda, and that agenda is achieved through interviews, soundbites, actuality and voice-over, all pieced together at the producer's discretion. The choice of material is influenced by availability, convenience, finance, ethics, ideology, topicality, audience profile and scheduling of the broadcast. The final piece is cut, mixed and edited together into a product in much the same way as a cake is baked; i.e., the chef chooses what type of cake s/he desires and simply follows a recipe to deliver; it is a process. The average listener, however, is ignorant of this process and has no idea how much of a feature/story ends up 'on the cutting-room floor'. Producers today take advantage of our audio socialisation and use their

audio tools and discourse to authenticate their work and seduce the listener
into a sense of belief. News producers use background 'disturbance' (rifle
fire, bomb noises, crowd sounds) to authenticate their reports.

The representation of truth and/or reality is an area fraught with difficulties, contradictions and subjectivity. One would assume that the closest a
producer can come to presenting the truth is through 'live' radio, i.e., where
the interview/feature is broadcast as the interviewer and talent are speaking,
unedited, something like a fly-on-the-wall[13] broadcast. However, this is also
the area where the question of ethics is most prominent.

Competition inside the medium is fierce; basically it is a ratings war, with
all services fighting tooth and nail for the lion's share of their demographic.
(Public service is of course a different animal, but competition is still very
much to the fore: how else can the industry justify licence fees?) Stations, in
particular news services, pride themselves on being the first to bring you the
story and on their ability to present that story live. The element of liveness
in a station's profile demonstrates an ability to have its proverbial finger 'on
the pulse' of the community to which it broadcasts. Liveness also offers
immediacy, vitality, spontaneity and flexibility. It says to a listener, 'We are
working hard to bring you up-to-the-minute information and entertainment.' A listener tuning into a live broadcast can feel that they too are part
of the process of 'life', that they are part of history *as* it is being made, rather
than being consumers of the past, whether that past is one minute or one
week ago. An example of this was the death in 1997 of Diana, Princess of
Wales, which shocked the world. Millions of listeners and viewers were
glued to their radios and televisions, hungry for the latest update; public
interest in the incident can only be compared with international occurrences
such as the assassinations of former US president John Kennedy and civil
rights activist Martin Luther King: all three were world celebrities and their
deaths were all untimely, i.e., an unexpected tragedy rather than a death
that the world had been prepared for through a lengthy illness or old age, as
was the case with the death, also in 1997, of Mother Theresa. In the case of
Diana, however, there was the added dimension of technology, which has
improved ten-fold since the 1960s in the way that it can offer up-to-the-
minute reports simultaneously to tens of millions of people world-wide. In
no other context is the chasm between the nature of the mediums of radio,
television and print so powerfully illustrated. How would a motorist stuck
in a three-hour traffic jam on the M6 receive such news if not for the radio?
Print may have been the first source, for many,[14] in Britain, to offer the news
that the Princess had been *involved and injured* in an accident, but no
sooner had this story broken than it was found to be wrong: Diana was in
fact dead.

As we now understand, the process of 'live' broadcasting and editing is
far more complex than it appears at face value. It means much more than
someone sitting down in a studio or being approached by a microphone-
wielding journalist out on the street. Programming is contrived, con-

structed, processed, manipulated, 'nipped and tucked', to offer the listener an entertaining, informative, focused, topical product. To believe most of what we hear is very common, if somewhat naive, but when we consider the way we have related to radio since the turn of the twentieth century, and the technology available to practitioners to 'create' good radio, it is little wonder. To suggest that radio is contrived and perhaps a little delusive does not for one moment suggest malice or duplicity on the part of producers. Radio, like all forms of popular culture, is merely a public service and a mirror to public taste and curiosity. But after reading this chapter, readers may now have a greater understanding of the nature of the medium, its strengths and weaknesses, and may possibly listen with wiser, more questioning ears.

Things to do

1 To what extent do you and your family rely on the radio for news? How do radio news reports compare with television and newspapers? Monitor various news reports on the radio during the day and compare them with how the same stories are presented on the main evening television news. For example, are the same stories covered? Is the same angle or lead used? (This is particularly important; note if the 'message' is the same.) Where is the story placed on the running order and how does that relate to the availability of vision or soundbites? (Often if a story is without good vision or soundbites it will not be the lead story; the opposite circumstance can see a story placed at the top of a bulletin.) Which medium covered the story first? What stories were available on one source but not on another? Why? Compare your findings with those of other students.
2 Listen very carefully to the language used when radio features/interviews are presented. Is the language ambiguous, i.e., neither indicating that the story is live, nor that it is pre-recorded? What percentage of output is offered as 'live'? In cases where you, the listener, know that the story is pre-recorded, take note of how you consume the story, i.e., is the presentation of the story credible? Entertaining? Dynamic?

Notes

1 A term which means to be the first to broadcast or release a new news story, i.e., topical stories such as high-profile resignations or paramilitary bombings. If a news service has the reputation for being 'the first with the news' then listeners will be encouraged to tune into its bulletins.
2 The technology necessary to produce a radio news story is more simple, therefore the process from the moment the story 'breaks' to when it is broadcast is much quicker than with television. Television relies predominantly on vision. News

selection and scheduling will depend on availability of vision, availability of face-to-face interviews and turn-around time. If the story has been carried by both radio and print for some time then it will change the nature of how it is handled on TV (e.g. top story, buried or dropped).

3 Television bulletins will use phone interviews where vision is impossible to use. In many cases 'file' vision (dated, nondescript footage stored and used when current vision is unavailable and therefore often giving a sense of the story being contrived or dated) can be used. However, television will use file vision as a last resort.

4 This famous phrase was coined by Lord Northcliffe, founder of the *Daily Mail*, which first went to print in May 1986. The *Mail* thrived on a diet of small features, adventure and human interest stories, readers' letters and a great deal of crime (hence the slogan). The *Daily Mail* was also seen as the catalyst that sparked the 'Fleet Street Revolution' (Williams 1998: 56).

5 On the 17 August 1980, in Australia, a woman called Lindy Chamberlain claimed that her baby Azaria was taken by a dingo. The story hit the world news and the mother, who the press insinuated was guilty because of her composure and control in front of the camera and behind the microphone, was hence 'tried by the media'. She was found guilty of murdering her baby and sent to jail. Her innocence has since been proved. The opposite was witnessed in Britain in 1997 when Tracy Andrews was found guilty of murdering her fiancé. Initially, a distraught Ms Andrews was seen giving an emotional press conference explaining how Lee Harvey was murdered during a 'road rage' attack, a phenomenon which had been recent front-page news.

6 Face-to-face interview by the author with Gerry Gannon, 6 p.m., Tuesday 27 February 1998, Perth, Australia.

7 'Two shots' are when the camera operator records the interviewer and talent in one shot, speaking off mike. A noddy is a head shot of the interviewer nodding. These shots are recorded before or after the interview and in some cases, if the talent has had to leave, the reporter may have noddy shots taken when s/he is nodding at no one! Noddies are supposed to give the impression of the interviewer listening to an answer to a question and are used to cover edits, as is the two shot or wild vision taken at the scene of the interview, e.g. photographs on a nearby table, the hands of the talent or images of the subject of the story.

8 All editing terminology used in this section can be found in the glossary.

9 This point becomes extremely contentious when considering 'Court TV' in the United States. Here, one could argue that the broadcasting of trials in a 'liberal' democracy such as the USA turns justice into a spectator sport. However, others claim, as was seen in the trial of British nanny Louise Woodward in the autumn of 1997 or O.J. Simpson in 1995, that the voyeuristic camera keeps the courts honest.

10 'Successive copies' can be explained by comparison to carbon paper or a blank audio cassette. The more copies made from the original source, the weaker the final product. In audio, each copy is called a generation, i.e., the third copy made of a programme is called third generation.

11 Face-to-face interview by the author with Rosemary Greenham, 3 p.m., Tuesday 27 January 1998, Perth, Australia.

12 Wherever possible, journalists/presenters will use the present tense, e.g., *has* instead of *had* or *says* instead of *said*, to give the item or programme a sense of immediacy and topicality.

13 A style of recording (video, film or audio) where the microphone or camera simply observes and should remain unobtrusive: operators must refrain from contriving scenes to record.

14 This information was available to report via radio immediately, but many people

in Britain were asleep at this time and instead woke to the news through early-morning radio reports or newspapers. In conversations with people about the event, many have claimed that they heard the news first on radio but needed to turn on the television for confirmation, indicating that the news was so shocking that they needed more than one source of information and perhaps pictures to confirm what they found so hard to believe.

|6|

Listening and talking back

Paul Donovan, in the introduction to his book *The Radio Companion* (1992), describes his childhood, adolescence and adulthood accompanied by radio, recounting, amongst other things, his first radio memory and his first ever radio set. More particularly, he writes that, since leaving home to attend university in the late 1960s, 'I have always had a radio close at hand and it has continued to provide unrivalled companionship both at home and ... abroad' (Donovan 1992: xi). This comment illustrates perhaps more clearly than any other the extent to which radio is, for many of its audience, a life-long friend and constant companion. The comment draws our attention to the fact that Donovan's choice of title for his A–Z guide of radio programmes and personalities, past and present, not only denotes that his book is a useful accompanying text for dedicated radio listening but also pinpoints one of the medium's most important functions: that of being a companion or friend. No other medium has been able to match radio on this score and it is not for nothing that radio has long been called the 'friend in the corner'. Since the 1930s, many millions of people all over the world made the radio an integral part of their daily lives, turning to it the moment they awake and, from that point on, relying on it to accompany them through the day, providing not just company in periods of solitude but also an organising structure and timetable. For many of us, radio is part of our daily routines (particularly our domestic routines). It is part of our history (as Paul Donovan indicates by his own example). It is virtually a member of the family, part of the fabric of our private lives. Radio is, therefore, much more than a technological device for receiving the transmitted signals of a local or national broadcasting station. Rather, it is the most personal and intimate 'mass medium': an unrivalled companion and one of the most interesting, reliable and useful of friends.

A one-sided conversation

The Broadcasting Standards Council (BSC), in its annual review of 1994, concluded that 'the audience enjoys a more personal and individual relationship with radio than with television' (Hargrave (ed.) 1994: 27). The BSC, having conducted its research and drawn its conclusions, ultimately confirmed what had long been claimed about the specific nature of radio listening and of what sets radio apart from other mass media forms. Personal accounts of radio listening have invariably captured the intensely personal dimension of this experience, the private and solitary nature of listening, the devotion to particular stations and programmes, even the sense of being able to interact with radio as though it were not a one-way system of communication at all. Take, for instance, the following statement by a dedicated radio listener included in the BSC's 1994 annual review.

> My best moments of radio happen in the car because I am stuck with it. Television and printed materials are out of the question and unless I want to listen to tapes, radio becomes the central focus of my attention. It becomes very personal and interactive: I jabber away with the guests, telling them to shut up (or worse with politicians) or cheering in agreement. More often than not, with my ancient AM/MW only equipment, I don't even know what I'm listening to. Detached from my preconceived ideas of station loyalty I leap from programme to programme, actively seeking someone to converse with or unfamiliar regional broadcasts to make pious judgements about. If anyone has ever seen a red Fiesta with the driver permanently leaning forwards and to the left, talking to himself, you know why.
>
> (Logan 1994: 53–4)

Tim Logan, the author of this statement, is one of the few avid radio listeners prepared to admit to responding to the medium as if it were a two-way system of communication; in his case, 'actively seeking someone to converse with' when making solitary car journeys. There is more than a hint of eccentricity here and a consciousness of admitting to some irrational, idiosyncratic or even prohibited behaviour. And yet there is also a note of defiance and even a tinge of bravery in being able to admit what others would be at pains to deny. The statement is something of a challenge for the rest of us to come out of this particular closet and admit that talking back to our radio sets is anything but a minority activity. Just how many of us do in fact regularly find ourselves talking back? It might be worth keeping an eye out in future for other drivers to see just how many people appear to be talking to themselves (leaning forwards and to the left). I have a strong suspicion that for most of us talking back to the radio is part of our everyday experience of what is otherwise called 'radio listening': a phrase that admits of no part for answering back and thus obscures perhaps a significant part of the pleasure of a mass medium that is consumed largely by a multitude of solitary listeners in need of companionship and a chat.

Radio is, of course, to all intents and purposes, a system of one-way communication. As a broadcast medium its messages are, by definition, transmitted from one source to an infinite number of possible destinations where they can only be received. Radio sets (or 'receivers' as they were once more widely called) provide no facility for the listener to directly interact on air. Listeners may indeed talk back, but only they themselves (or others in their vicinity) will hear their words. The radio discussion will continue unaffected by the listener's running commentary, reactions and criticisms and we would be struck dumb if suddenly, whilst ranting our way down the motorway, the host of a radio discussion suddenly responded directly to our own remarks or asked us what we meant by our last comment. The fact that this does not (and apparently could not) happen is in one way comforting, enabling us to vent all manner of opinions without being held to account. But the fact that their views and opinions cannot be heard in response to radio discussions might equally be a source of anxiety for radio audiences, drawing attention to their own alienation and helplessness. The last thing radio broadcasters want to do is make their listeners feel alienated or helpless; indeed, their intention is often quite the contrary. In general, radio broadcasters go out of their way to provide their listeners with a sense that they are part of the radio discussion, that their own personal cares, needs and attitudes are being catered for, that their presence is felt: in short, giving listeners a sense of power and participation. Radio has learnt over the years that to engage its audience it should, at every step, gain the listener's tacit compliance, creating a sense that the listener's response indeed affects the progress of the programme by some intangible form of osmosis. This may only be an illusion (designed to reassure the listener of their importance) but it is none the less a most convincing one, and has to be now that radio is little more than a one-sided conversation of which the listener is merely the dumb recipient.

This, however, has not always been the case. Prior to and throughout the First World War, radio was used almost entirely as a system of two-way or point-to-point communication, mainly as a form of wireless telegraphy (sending messages in Morse dots and dashes) and occasionally as wireless telephony (using the airwaves as a wireless telephone). In fact it was only during the 1920s that radio gradually came to be used more and more as a means of receiving one-way signals from broadcasting stations and radio users became simply radio listeners. It was, of course, only then that radio became truly public in the sense of becoming available to everyone, irrespective of class and wealth. By 1930, millions of people throughout the world were regularly tuning in to a diet of speech and music-based programmes on commercially bought and mass-produced radio receivers (i.e., radio sets which could only receive rather than send or transmit signals). It was around this time that the occasional voice was heard calling for radio to remain a two-way communication system. In 1932, for instance, the German playwright Bertolt Brecht made a forceful argument against radio being used simply as a means of supplying the public with in-house entertainment and information. Brecht, in his essay 'The radio as an apparatus of communication', argued against radio being used exclusively as a one-way means of communication (Brecht 1932). He argued against using radio merely as an apparatus for distribution and suggested that the medium would be better used if listeners could transmit as well as receive, if they could speak as well as hear, and if they could be brought into a relationship instead of being isolated. Brecht's conception of radio as a public service was one which involved listeners not just as consumers but also as producers (suppliers) of its material. This, he argued, would make radio a truly social or public medium. But radio did not proceed in this direction. With the exception of the brief popularity of Citizen's Band radio in the 1970s, people have preferred to be supplied with entertainment and information in their own homes and vehicles rather than assume the responsibility for supplying them. Nevertheless, the two-way system advocated by Brecht has become, to some extent, a part of the image which radio has assumed: that is, the sense of its being interactive and reciprocal when (in most cases) it is not. Thus, although radio involves its listeners in a one-way conversation, they are ordinarily made to feel more engaged than this, as though they really were involved in an interactive and reciprocal act of communication.

Of course, one clear exception to one-way communication in modern radio broadcasting is the phone-in programme, a staple of both commercial and public service radio. Here reciprocity is more than just an illusion and listeners indeed get to have their say on air, participating in radio discussion. Brian Hayes, the presenter of numerous talk radio programmes on both commercial radio in Britain and the BBC, has written that those who phone in to their local radio station and air their views over the airwaves have become an increasingly important part of modern radio broadcasting. 'Today', he writes, 'there is nothing special about hearing the voice of the public on the radio', adding that, 'The ordinary voice of the ordinary citizen is everywhere on radio, BBC, commercial and the occasional pirate' (Hayes 1994: 41). Hayes sees the appeal of these programmes lying mainly in the fact that they are the most personal form of radio: people like them because they 'like to hear fellow human beings talking, even if they talk a load of rubbish' (Hayes 1994: 43). He regards the increasing use of radio phone-ins over the last twenty years as the medium's maturation and he looks forward to a time when 'a talk radio station ... goes all the way and has a format which consists of nothing more than members of the public both presenting and contributing to a continuous debate using studio discussion and 'phone calls' (Hayes 1994: 44). With this, it might seem that Bertolt Brecht's conception of radio as a two-way system of public communication would at last be realised, the listeners becoming both the suppliers and consumers of broadcast material. With its ever-increasing reliance upon the phone-in, modern broadcast radio would seem to be moving steadily in this direction.

However, this utopian conception of radio is still rather a long way off. Whilst it is true that the phone-in is one of the few radio programme forms which actually allows listeners to interact, the vast majority of the audience of such programmes are content to remain listeners rather than become callers. Therefore, it would be more true to say that, for the majority of the audience listening to phone-ins, such programmes simply represent the possibility or potential of engaging directly in the programme: they could engage directly and participate in the discussion if they wanted to. Only a small minority of the listeners who regularly tune in to certain radio phone-in programmes will actually avail themselves of this opportunity (and only a few of those who try will actually get through and on to the airwaves). Therefore, the appeal of these programmes for the majority of the phone-in audience comes from listening to others participating in radio talk (on behalf of, or as representatives of, the listening community as a whole). This, for most of the radio audience, is participation and reciprocation, at best, by proxy.

The ubiquity of the phone-in on today's radio lends a certain credence to the reciprocity of the medium more generally. But, in fact, many types of radio programme produce a sense of reciprocity even without actually allowing listeners to engage in live broadcast debate via their telephones. Interview programmes, panel games, news and current affairs, music programmes and many more often create a semblance of reciprocity which is, perhaps, the reason why many listeners have a compulsion to talk back regardless of the fact that whatever they say will not be heard by anyone but themselves. Despite their ubiquity, phone-ins merely form part of contemporary radio's attempts to create an active, responsive and even (occasionally) interactive audience. Radio makes numerous ways for its listeners to have access (or, at least, a sense that they can have access) to the medium to a degree above and beyond that usually associated with the mass media. Radio listeners are repeatedly asked to telephone in or write in with their comments and criticisms, to use their fax machines and e-mail, or to telephone the station's various helplines for more information. There is a new kind of feedback now pervading radio broadcasting, one that is designed to give the audience an ever greater sense of being actively involved in the processes of broadcasting. For most listeners, however, particularly those who tune in to radio for entertainment and information because they are too busy to devote time to television viewing or newspaper reading, their only opportunity to interact – given their limited time – is to talk back spontaneously in the manner described by Tim Logan: a somewhat strange phenomenon to the uninitiated perhaps, but, in other ways, a quite natural and inevitable reaction to this particular medium.

If the phone-in is indicative of the natural desire of the listener to talk back then talking back to the unheeding radio perhaps indicates the unusual intimacy between radio and its audience. Even before the rise of the phone-in programme, radio had acquired a reputation as an intimate medium; the phone-in has consolidated rather than created this. Intimacy has long been regarded as one of the defining characteristics of the medium and is exploited by broadcasters across a broad range of programme output. Radio dramas, for instance, are staged inside listeners' minds, enabling them to participate in the creative process by producing their own visuals. Music on the radio works (in a way that only music can) to evoke personal associations for listeners, particularly in the form of romantic memories. These are just two instances where radio can be seen to establish intimate and participatory relations with its audience without them actually telephoning, writing, faxing or e-mailing in. They are mentioned here in order to indicate something of the extent to which the twin concerns of intimacy and reciprocity lie at the heart of successful radio broadcasting. Exploiting the medium's natural ability to establish intimate relations with its audience has undoubtedly been one of the most important lessons learned by radio broadcasters since it became a mass medium and certainly since radio lost its family audience to television and found its main audience in a multitude of solitary listeners. Since that time, radio broadcasters have been trained to create an even stronger sense of intimacy and reciprocity than otherwise existed and to bring these qualities to bear on almost every aspect of their work.

Elwyn Evans, former head of the BBC's Radio Training Section, has described some of the basic (and most fundamental) principles by which radio broadcasters can achieve intimacy and a sense of reciprocity. In *Radio: A Guide to Broadcasting Technique*, he instructs his readers (and, given the nature of his book, potential broadcasters) to approach their audience not as a mass but as an audience of one. 'In radio', he writes, 'the audience to be aimed at is *an audience of one* (infinitely repeated)' (Evans 1977: 16). He goes on to state that it is always useful when drafting a radio script 'to *imagine* that audience of one, pretend you're explaining a point or telling a story to him or her, and then put down on paper what you've said – not immediately, but after you've tried to phrase your message in different ways and settled on the best' (Evans 1977: 16). Evans's instruction here to budding radio broadcasters is one that has dominated much thinking behind the preparation of radio scripts and their presentation and it is echoed in many other publications aimed at introducing potential and trainee broadcasters to some of the basic radio broadcasting techniques. For instance, Robert McLeish, in *Radio Production*, writes that radio broadcasters should not regard the microphone as 'an input into a public address system, but rather a means of talking directly to the individual listener' (McLeish 1994: 3).

Like Elwyn Evans, Robert McLeish has advised aspiring broadcasters to write and present their scripts to an audience of one and to visualise a particular listener throughout the processes of both writing and presenting. McLeish argues that despite radio being one of the mass media and thus heard by thousands, even millions of people, its messages ultimately end up in the mind of an individual listener. This being the case, it would be a mistake 'to think of radio as a group experience – like an audience in a hall – or to treat it as a massive public address system reaching out across the housetops and countryside' (McLeish 1994: 65). Most of the thousands or millions of people listening do so on their own, and even when they listen with others radio remains an intensely personal activity, operating in the mind of each listener. Not surprisingly, then, McLeish cautions his readers to avoid phrases like 'listeners may like to know …' or 'some of you will have seen …', explaining that the act of communication should be between the broadcaster and 'the listener with his own thoughts' (McLeish 1994: 65). McLeish instructs budding broadcasters, therefore, to 'write for the individual, he'll feel that you're talking just to him and your words'll have much more impact' (McLeish 1994: 65). Such advice as this would appear to have been universally heeded and adopted as standard practice. The sense of one individual listener being directly spoken to can be detected across the full spectrum of radio these days. It is perhaps one of the distinguishing features of both the consummate professional and the natural-born broadcaster. Take, for instance, the following extracts from the beginning, middle and end of a short talk by Rabbi Lionel Blue, a regular contributor to BBC Radio 4's 'Thought for the day' slot within the 'Today' programme.

> You wake up on a Monday morning, switch on the radio and wonder what sort of world you're in. You've got your own personal problems: there's the tax falling through the letter-box; an awkward interview with your boss and what's more there's no marg left in the fridge. You feel gruff and growly already. And when you turn on the radio you shoot bolt upright and whimper because there's been yet another plane disaster, this time on the M1, which you've driven up and down so many times. Death is very very close. You need a cup of tea fast.
>
> I think things go wrong and disasters happen because the world is an incomplete sort of place. Like you and me, it's struggling to its own perfection, but hasn't got there. It's still going through its birth pangs.
>
> So don't dive back under your duvet as you hear the news this morning. … Get up quickly, have your cup of tea and work out what you can do. Can you comfort someone on the plane or give something to a disaster fund? It's a dreadful Monday morning, that's true, but that's why you're here. You might look and feel a mess but you're God's representatives, His hands on Earth, working to complete His creation. It's what you were created for. So come on, get up, get on with it! [1]

As one of the finest, most natural and best-loved speakers on BBC radio, Rabbi Lionel Blue is exemplary in the way he writes and presents his talks to Radio 4 listeners. First, he addresses his audience as an audience of one: so, for instance, he says 'don't dive back under your duvet' and not 'don't all of you dive back under your duvets'. Second, his language is informal and colloquial, e.g., *you've* and *you're* rather than *you have* and *you are*, *marg* rather than *margarine*. Third, he speaks in relaxed and familiar tones, assuming an air of mutual understanding and sympathy. In particular, he demonstrates a keen understanding of 'ordinary life' by mentioning some of the mundane things that worry people, as well as the things people think and do, like make a cup of tea in moments of crisis. Finally, in this particular talk, he acknowledges the fact that he is talking to his audience at one of their most private moments, having not quite started the day, and he emphasises his awareness of their feelings of vulnerability at this time: dreading the arrival of more bills, dreading a possible confrontation with a superior at work, feeling unsightly, a mess, feeling unwilling or even unable to face the day. Catching his audience at their most vulnerable, Rabbi Lionel Blue is able to profit from radio's intimate relationship with its audience to convey often highly personal information on matters such as death, loss, love, sex, faith, loneliness or illness, providing solace, hope and understanding to listeners he does not know. It is significant that Lionel Blue feels able to discuss his own intimate concerns and experiences on the radio without any sense of discomfort or impropriety and, in so doing, requires his listeners to ponder for a moment their own attitudes, beliefs and actions. Radio, because of its intimate acquaintance with its audience, can tackle such issues without seeming to invade its listeners' privacy, without offence, without seeming over-bearing. It is not simply because it reaches vast numbers of people that radio serves as a perfect medium for Rabbi Lionel Blue to spread the message of common sense and contemporary religious or moral values and, at the same time, bring comfort to many of his listeners. It is because listeners regard the radio as an integral part of their lives, because they regard radio as being in touch with their lives, that the medium is able to address intensely personal issues and bring comfort and reassurance to so many. And whilst for Lionel Blue this represents perhaps the most effective means at his disposal of offering spiritual guidance, his talks enable BBC Radio 4 to establish closer relations with its audience, reaffirming the view that radio understands them, talks directly to them as individuals and wants them to 'feed back'. Such talks help to maintain the sense of radio as a two-way, interactive and, above all, intimate medium.

The democratic medium?

The intimate relationship between radio and its audience is not simply due to the fact that radio is a significant (if taken for granted) part of daily life, a companion (and something to talk to) in periods of solitude. It is also because radio offers numerous ways for listeners to respond and even interact with its output (e.g., phone-ins, letters, faxes, e-mail, helplines, etc.) and because it speaks to its audience as individuals rather than as a collective group, addressing its listeners as though they were involved in an act of two-way communication rather than simply a one-sided conversation. With the increasing fragmentation of the radio industry and the steady growth in competition, it has become essential (an economic necessity) for radio stations to target specific audiences, to 'find a niche', and to achieve greater levels of listener loyalty. Attracting and retaining audiences is likely to become increasingly difficult the larger and more fragmentary the industry becomes. The drive towards intimacy and reciprocity would therefore seem to be part and parcel of radio's future development and its longevity. As such, we can expect to see new ways of establishing closer and more intimate links between broadcasters and listeners in the future. And if the future of radio truly lies in the bond it is able to build up between itself and its audience, it would appear that listeners are to perform an ever greater role in broadcasting.

We can see already the extent to which increasing levels of competition in radio broadcasting in Britain resulted in the rise of the radio phone-in once radio stations recognised not only that these were one of the cheapest forms of programming but also, and more importantly, that they enabled stations to build up a large and loyal listenership. Whilst the station gains and retains an audience, listeners get to have their say; they literally become the voice of the station and everything on that station (jingles, music, presenter personalities, advertisements, etc.) becomes geared towards establishing a suitable context within which the voice of the listeners (callers) can best be accommodated. In this process, the listeners themselves are the driving force behind both the content and style of the radio station: they are, ultimately, the power behind the broadcaster's throne – hence such comments as 'Radio is much more democratic than the rest of the mass media' (Hayes 1994: 40) and 'radio's capacity for the "empowerment" of listeners as active and participating members of society is considerable' (Wilby and Conroy 1994: 33). Both of these comments establish radio as the most democratic mass medium: one which offers its audience an unrivalled opportunity not only to participate in the production of broadcast output but also to determine the content and style of radio services. However, to what extent is this more illusory than real?

Is it not the case that even in radio at its most democratic – that is, during the phone-in – behind the apparent freedom of the caller to have her or his say it is actually the broadcaster that has all the power? It is unarguably the presenter or host who sets the terms of the debate and steers its course throughout the radio talk-back show. There are many ways in which these programmes can be seen as being much less empowering or emancipating for listeners than they might at first appear (or sound). First, the station has control over the selection of its callers. Those who ultimately end up on the air voicing their opinions and interacting with the radio presenter have already been vetted. Second, once on air, the presenter is usually able to control what is said by the caller. Callers can be faded out if they prove to be too controversial (or too boring) or, more often, the presenter is in a position to dominate the discussion, being able to speak over the caller when he or she wishes. This is also, of course, due to the presenter having more experience and greater confidence in speaking on air than the caller: the caller far more likely being nervous and disorientated by the unfamiliar experience of speaking on the radio. The host is trained and experienced in the specifics of broadcasting and presentation, cool and confident before their studio microphone (giving them better sound quality). The caller, meanwhile, nervous, disorientated and self-conscious on the other end of a telephone, is less likely to be able to wrest the terms of the debate away from those prescribed by the host. Under such conditions, the caller is in anything but an equal or democratic relationship with the host. It is perhaps not surprising then that whilst some commentators (particularly those who are, or have been, professional broadcasters themselves) have made a case for the democratic and emancipating qualities of radio, others have argued strongly against the notion of radio (particularly commercial radio) as being liberating or empowering for its audience.

One of the most in-depth and authoritative examinations of radio phone-in programmes was undertaken in the late 1970s by Christine Higgins and Peter Moss. Their research into the precise nature of the interactive communication structures between radio phone-in hosts and callers on Australian commercial radio (and the power structures involved in such relationships) culminated in their book *Sounds Real* (1982). Here they write that 'not only has radio not helped democratize culture, despite its potential, but that even in talk-back radio programmes the ability of people to make their own culture is inhibited rather than enhanced' (Higgins and Moss 1982: 32). The main reason for this, they argue, is because the comments and values of the callers are invariably overpowered by 'accepted, authoritative messages', resulting in the transmission of 'a certain mediated vision of the world' (Higgins and Moss 1982: 32–3). In their opinion, the callers' views are filtered through the (covert) dominant ideology of the programmes: an ideology which is itself determined ultimately by consumerism. Perhaps the most enlightening aspect of their research lies in their demonstration of the fact that

> despite their apparent haphazardness and what often seems an extraordinary counter-point between snippets of news, commercials, personal narratives, songs and comments, there is evidence of planned *flow*, of a deliberate sequence of signs and images whose purpose is to transmit certain cultural messages.
>
> (Higgins and Moss 1982: 33)

What appears on the surface to be a random and discontinuous assortment of programme segments in fact conspires to establish a coherent (albeit covert) effect. The disparate and apparently unrelated elements of the talk-back or phone-in programme coalesce and, as an entirety, such programmes confirm capitalist ideology. As such, rather than represent the unmediated dissemination of audience opinions, views and ideologies – which would truly constitute the democratic or empowering dimension of radio broadcasting – 'talk-back programmes can be seen as a way of forming and supplying the opinions of the people and their consumer habits' (Higgins and Moss 1982: 34). Hence, rather than enabling listeners towards self-empowerment, self-determination and autonomy, etc., these shows dictate patterns of consumerism, fostering a culture in which problems are solved by purchasing mass-produced goods rather than individual action, intervention or the free circulation of information and opinion.

The point about *flow* and its disempowering role (effects) within mainstream commercial radio broadcasting has also been noted within the Canadian context by Jody Berland, who describes herself as 'a musician with a professional interest in media and politics' (Berland 1993: 210). Without actually referring to the concept of 'flow' articulated by Raymond Williams in relation to North American commercial television (see Williams 1974), Berland argues that radio 'teaches us addiction and forgetfulness' through its 'continuous rhythm of sound' which 'is more powerful than any single item' (Berland 1993: 211). The effects she describes – addiction and forgetfulness (in other words, effects associated with passivity and impotence) – are certainly similar to those associated with Williams's conception of 'flow', and her subsequent comments alert us to the ideological effects of flow when she speaks of the 'carefully managed rapidity and predictability of pattern' characteristic of mainstream radio broadcasting, Canadian and otherwise (Berland 1993: 211). Radio form emerges here as an orchestrated flow of rapid and predictable items in a continuous sequence (rather than a sequence of discrete and discontinuous items) inducing – and intended to induce – passive listening: a form of listening which, precisely because it is passive, is accepting (rather than questioning, sceptical or discerning) and, hence, vulnerable to any form of persuasion. Berland's comments on Canadian radio broadcasting when set beside those of Higgins and Moss on Australian commercial radio give us a clear indication that, despite what might be appearances to the contrary, modern radio broadcasting is not empowering its listeners throughout the world but actively disempowering them.

These ideas are perhaps most fully developed in the extensive research and conclusions drawn by Higgins and Moss in their book *Sounds Real*. Here, references are made directly to Raymond Williams's concept of 'flow', employing the term in the dual sense of (i) integrated sequences of items rather than discrete programmes and (ii) a flow of cultural meanings across programmes. The latter, Higgins and Moss claim, was not developed fully by Williams in his book *Television: Technology and Cultural Form* (1974) and is something which they are keen to pursue further. Through analysis of the morning programmes of a Queensland commercial radio station on 15 May 1979, they reveal a pattern which, although apparently random, is in fact structured in such a way as to 'facilitate the transmission of certain dominant messages' (Higgins and Moss 1982: 36). Here they claim that a thematic unity has been created from what would otherwise appear to be unconnected items. This, they argue, is 'the *real* internal organization', one that is 'undeclared' and is not apparent to the listeners of these programmes unless they analyse carefully the true nature of the relationships between the programme items – something, of course, they are unlikely ever to do.

Where Higgins and Moss detect evidence of a *planned* flow is in the juxtaposition of commercials and calls: a juxtaposition which produces two distinct sets of messages flowing through the discourse as a whole. The first message is that of the callers. Their stated opinions, experiences and values may contradict those of other callers rather than forming a homogenous discourse, but these unrelated personal narratives establish what is essentially a single theme: basically that life is tough. The second message which emerges in these programmes is, in contrast, 'the bright, brash positivism of the commercials', offering listeners the possibility of a better future, a more controllable set of problems with immediate and tangible resolutions (that is, if they buy the product or avail themselves of the services advertised) (Higgins and Moss 1982: 37). In short, Higgins and Moss argue that the full range of programme items (the songs, the news bulletins, presenter chat, interviews, etc.) 'may coalesce to produce a flow of compatible consumer messages' (Higgins and Moss 1982: 37). They see all of these as welded together to form a unified cultural statement and, moreover, they suggest that the second flow of messages (made up of the advertisements, songs and presenter inanities) constantly overwhelms the first (i.e., the 'life is tough' message of the callers and news bulletins).

What needs to be emphasised here is Higgins and Moss's belief that this is not simply an incidental effect of such programmes but, on the contrary, part of their prescribed function. This is evinced in their remark that the 'advertisements always stand in juxtaposition to the cries for help and expressions of frustration with the *present* and offer their illusory but powerful promise of the future ... ' (Higgins and Moss 1982: 47). In other words, talk-back radio creates a context in which the persistent voicing of dissatisfaction and anxiety are set alongside the advertisers' promise to improve the quality of listeners' lives with their products and services. Therefore, as Higgins and Moss argue, even though the advertisements appear to compete with and contradict the calls they are actually complementary in that they add up to a single statement: buy and everything will be all right.

Higgins and Moss argue that talk-back radio helps to create a 'pseudo-reality' which does not attempt to foster a community of discourse capable of sustaining argument and tension, nor awareness, commitment or potency. Talk-back radio programmes are, if anything, opposed to such goals. What they produce is not a community of active and interactive individuals involved in transforming their own lives for the better (and the good of the community as a whole) but a community of alienated consumers, powerless to transform or improve their own lives (sublimating their own lack of control over their lives through consumerism). According to Higgins and Moss such programmes 'stifle the private voice and make it impossible for people to grow' (Higgins and Moss 1982: 59).

It is interesting to compare the findings of Higgins and Moss once again with the views expressed by Jody Berland in her article 'Contradicting media: towards a political phenomenology of listening'. This gives us an impression of the empowering/disempowering effects of mainstream commercial radio on a more global scale and in a more contemporary context, since Berland has spoken specifically of the role of radio broadcasting in Canadian life in the early 1990s. Emphasising the mobility and transience of modern life (its fractured urban spaces, its centralisation and marginalisation), Berland has suggested that for many people who tune in to radio what is most required at the current time is that it be 'boundlessly hospitable'. Radio can transcend the boundaries separating individuals and provide them with a sense of being part of a community: a listening community. She writes that, 'We listen to radio . . . to keep from being depressed or isolated, to feel connected to something, to enfold ourselves in its envelope of pleasure, information, power' (Berland 1993: 211). In other words, we have grown accustomed to using our radios to stave off the depressing and isolating effects of modern living and, in the process, we hope to achieve a sense of belonging to a community. But clearly such a community, in the real sense of the term, does not exist. It is a myth we are willing to subscribe to despite the obvious fact that there are few opportunities for the members of this community to communicate and interact with each other – which is surely an essential prerequisite for any authentic community. Jody Berland goes on to argue, moreover, that

> the absence of any spontaneous or innovative event, or of any specific (vs. abstract) intimacy, contributes ultimately precisely to depression, which afterall is merely a sideways description of powerlessness, of being prevented in various ways from achieving anything spontaneous or innovative, of having or living a new idea.
>
> (Berland 1993: 211)

Listeners are therefore caught in the proverbial 'catch-22' situation. Drawn to their radios to stave off depression and alienation, and yet excluded from any genuine act of communication, listeners run the risk of being confronted by further evidence of their alienation.

The arguments of the media theorists conflict with those of the media professionals on this issue of radio as a democratic and emancipating medium. There are, it seems, arguments both for and against. Whether radio is or is not a democratic medium and whether it is or is not empowering for its listeners is a vexed question. It is certainly not as clear-cut as Brian Hayes makes out in his essay 'The role of the public voice in present-day radio' (1994) or as Pete Wilby and Andy Conroy suggest in *The Radio*

[handwritten marginalia: counter argument for issue 6 & environmental (issues 5 too)]

Handbook (1994). What emerges from the debate between the theorists and the professionals are two opposing views. Whilst broadcasters claim that radio is the most democratic of all the mass media, offering listeners unprecedented opportunities to make a direct impact on the style and con-
 ˙radio programmes, the theorists insist that radio is, like all the mass
 ˙ insidious force in modern society, stifling freedom of thought and
 a force all the more insidious because it masquerades as being
 ﹍d empowering whilst rendering its audience passive, impotent
 y) vulnerable to exploitation by advertisers and big business.
 nd, we have a view of radio as being essentially democratic in
 ﹕ans for individuals to voice their concerns and opinions both
 ﹍e listening community and to those in positions of authority
 ﹐ politicians, heads of industry, etc.). The impression given
 ﹍ork in this mass medium is that there is a consistent move-
 reasing access for listeners and an increasing recognition of
the need for broadcasters to understand and respond to the needs, attitudes and lifestyles of their audience. On the other hand, we have a view of radio as a disempowering medium which contrives to offer its audience a semblance of power and democracy. From this perspective, radio emerges as a medium offering solutions to lived experiences which simply uphold the social forces that have created the problems in the first place. Furthermore, it appears to offer a sense of a listening community which is not an authentic community in any true sense as, in reality, it thrives on isolated listening and makes no attempts to foster communication and interaction between listeners. In this light, radio appears to dispel listeners' loneliness, alienation and helplessness while actually maintaining the isolation (hence powerlessness) of each individual listener. In short, contemporary radio – for all its apparent commitment to democracy, audience empowerment and community – would seem to rely for its success on these very conditions, as these are the conditions under which radio broadcasting is most likely to gain and maintain an audience.

So which of these viewpoints do we accept? It may seem hard to accept the views of media professionals themselves in this instance, given that they obviously have a vested interest in promoting their industry and defending it from the charges of manipulation typically advanced by the theorists and academics. But then the case could also be made that just as media professionals have a vested interest in promoting the radio industry on the grounds of democracy and empowerment, the media theorists also have a vested interest in demonstrating that unless we educate ourselves to understand the process at work in the consumption of the mass media we run the risk of being manipulated (hence supplying the academics with students on their media courses and readers of their books). This is undoubtedly a cynical view to take in respect to either party, and maybe the reason for the contradictory views of radio as a democratic medium can in fact be located elsewhere. Perhaps, for instance, these conflicting opinions arise out of a (somewhat paradoxical) condition at the very heart of modern radio broadcasting: that it exists by attracting a multitude of isolated listeners (whose very isolation is a source of powerless due to the basic principle of power being vested in mass rather than individual action) and yet can only attract this audience by offering them a sense of potential empowerment.

Perhaps what emerges most strongly from this apparently conflicting and contradictory debate is a notion of the radio industry offering a semblance not just of companionship but also of empowerment to isolated listeners. Another way of putting this would be to say that radio stations seek a multitude of isolated listeners but will lose them if they draw attention to their isolation – and the impotency of their isolated state – and therefore strive to give them a sense of power by presenting them with not just vocal but often vociferous callers as representatives of the listening community at large (and thus of themselves). It is no wonder that broadcasters are at such pains to promote radio as a democratic medium capable of empowering its listeners, since this is the very illusion which talk-radio seeks to foster amongst its audience. This, moreover, is precisely the image which the listeners wish to have of themselves. Few avid radio listeners are likely to identify with the audience described by the media theorists: most would undoubtedly see themselves as active, free-thinking individuals who have found their way on to the airwaves in order to voice their concerns and opinions, their disagreements with the previous caller or studio guest. Most of us who listen day after day and week after week to such radio shows (always listening, never calling) can take comfort in being part of such an active, vocal and vociferous community, as we mutter our own opinions to ourselves. Thus whilst radio stations want to be seen to be empowering their listeners, their listeners want to see themselves as being empowered by using radio. The irony is, of course, that the moment listeners become truly empowered (as active participants within their own communities) they are most likely to leave off listening to their radios.

Finally, what also emerges from this debate is that radio stations have recognised only the need to *appear* more accessible and reciprocal: to *appear* more democratic and empowering than other media (if they are to compete with other media). But the question remains as to just how democratic and empowering they need to *be* in order to out-do the competition. As we have seen, only a small portion of radio's audience need be given actual access to the airwaves and only a fraction of these, if any, need be allowed to dictate the terms of the discussion for this appearance to be achieved. In effect, radio can lay claim to being the most democratic medium without actually having to confer more than a semblance of power on its audience. Despite whatever appearances to the contrary, the power within radio broadcasting surely remains one-sided.

Mediation and consensus

The callers aired on radio phone-ins are there not only to have their say but also to represent the rest of the listening community. At the same time, they help to create a notion of an active, participatory and empowered listenership, enabling individual members of the audience to forget their own solitude (and disempowered state) and identify themselves with something altogether more potent and interactive. Listeners are unlikely to identify with each and every caller or with everything that the callers say. Nevertheless, listeners *are* likely to identify with the callers collectively, simply because they appear to be active and participatory members of the radio community. Phone-ins are therefore rather unusual in that they provide listeners with other listeners (i.e., callers) to identify with. Elsewhere across radio's programme output, the listeners' on-air representative is ordinarily the presenter or disc jockey.

Across a broad spectrum of radio broadcasting, presenters form the link between, on the one hand, the station and its audience and, on the other, each individual listener and the rest of the listening community. As such, they perform a vital role. They are the voice (and, in a sense, the face) of the radio station. Whilst forging links between the separate programme items (i.e., between record and interview, interview and advertisement, advertisement and news bulletin, etc.), presenters speak to the audience on behalf of the radio station itself, not so much expressing as embodying the character of the station (i.e., national, regional or local; commercial or public service; serious or frivolous; trendy or middle-of-the-road; highbrow or populist, etc.). Yet whilst representing the character and interests of the station, the presenter's role is equally to represent the listeners: their concerns, attitudes, interests and ideals. To achieve this, presenters must understand (and be seen to understand) their audience. Their every utterance must convey an awareness of their listeners' needs, desires, experiences, opinions, manners (particularly in terms of speech modes) and lifestyles. This does not necessarily mean, however, that the presenter (or the radio station) is concerned with presenting an authentic version of their listeners' lives.

Much of contemporary mainstream radio broadcasting would seem to be driven by an ambition to provide listeners with a means of escape from real life: from the tedium, drudgery and loneliness of daily life. In so doing, presenters are often more concerned to provide listeners with an antidote to reality rather than an accurate reflection of it. This is particularly true of music radio, which removes the more negative and disturbing aspects of life from its programmes and concentrates on something altogether more idealistic and romantic. As Stephen Barnard puts it, 'Music radio obliterates the nasty and discomforting by means of simple exclusion . . . and by celebrating fantasy and romance in its stead' (Barnard 1989: 154). As he also points out, 'music radio glories in an insulatory kind of good-time camaraderie, marshalled by the disc jockey and reinforced by the paraphernalia of listener response – competitions, phone-in requests, outside broadcasts' (Barnard

1989: 154). Nowhere is this more strongly felt than in daytime music radio aimed at predominantly female audiences. The use of male disc jockeys on these shows is anything but coincidental, as Dorothy Hobson suggests in her essay 'Housewives and the mass media' (1980).

> Within the overall picture of isolation which has emerged in the lives of the women in this study, the disc jockey can be seen as having the function of providing the missing 'company' of another person in the lives of the women. As well as helping to combat isolation it is not too far fetched to see the DJ as also playing the role of a sexual fantasy-figure in the lives of the women.
>
> (Hobson 1980: 107)

Implicit within Dorothy Hobson's statement is the notion that music radio's function as escapist romantic fantasy rests largely with the presenter or DJ, who is required to operate (in part, at least) as a romantic male figure in the lives of listening housewives. The specific role of the daytime music disc jockey would appear to be to accompany women through each day's round of humdrum domestic tasks, adding a touch of spice to an otherwise dull day and thereby making the tedium of housework more bearable.

A similar picture of daytime music radio has been presented by Rosalind Coward in her book *Female Desire* (1984). Here, Coward argues that

> Nowhere is sexual desire more obviously scripted and stage-managed than in the mishmash of music and chat directed at women during the day on popular radio. Sexual desire and love dominate not just as themes in the music but also make up a large part of the DJ's chatter. Forthcoming marriages, broken hearts, happy memories – these are the meat of radio discourse; relationships are at the heart of phone-ins; and radio dedications are from lover to lover. Popular music is broadcast into homes and workplaces during the day, presupposing a certain kind of predominantly female audience. The packaging of the music engages the emotions of this female audience, focusing attention on sexual relationships and in particular requiring the listener to think about her own sexual and emotional involvements.
>
> (Coward 1984: 145)

What is clear from Coward's remarks is that the presenters of these programmes take their cue from the music itself, from the pop songs they play: songs which tend to concentrate almost exclusively on the pleasures and pains of romantic relationships. The familiar themes of yearning, desire, heartache, pleasure, despair and hope are almost invariably conveyed as a direct address between the performer and the listener (e.g., 'You were always on my mind') establishing an intimate (and apparently heartfelt) dialogue between the two. Both the themes of the pop songs and the intimacy in which those themes are expressed by the pop performers are echoed in the patter of the DJs. As Coward writes, the DJs talk in a way which reinforces the sense that all this – the records, the lyrics, and his chatter – are addressed just to you as an individual. It is as if somehow, the DJ knows all about you and is talking just to you. . . . The address is never to a collective but always to an individual. It reinforces the sense created by the records. It is *your* life being talked about, the emotions generated by the records are for *you*, the problems to be addressed will be *yours*.

(Coward 1984: 146)

This intimacy, so typical of radio as a whole, is at its most intense in these daytime music programmes aimed largely at women (and, more specifically, at housewives). But why the almost relentless focus in these programmes on love and sexual desire? The most obvious reason is that these are themes which appeal equally to all classes and types of women and therefore enable radio stations to address a mass audience whilst appearing to talk to each listener on an intensely personal level. As Coward says, 'The listener is lured by a promise; you are special (the individual listener addressed) but your life and experiences are exactly the same as everyone else's' (Coward 1984: 149).

Coward also describes in *Female Desire* the way in which music radio seeks to remind housewives of their past, recalling a time of independence, youthful sexual and romantic experimentation, and freedom from family commitments, from marital and parental responsibilities, thus offering them an escape from their present lives through romantic nostalgia. However, such nostalgia could easily lead to disaffection with the present and, therefore, whilst evoking the 'golden years' these programmes seek to simultaneously reassure their listeners that, no matter what sacrifices they have made, they have ultimately made the right decision. In contrast to their past, listeners' lives may seem more burdened by responsibility, loneliness, frustration and sheer drudgery but still this was the right course to take, because it is the course all women take. As Coward writes,

Daytime radio tells women who are isolated and at home, and possibly very fed up, that the choices which they made were OK. Everyone makes these choices all the time. And sexual relations, women are told, are after all the most important, most universal aspect of our selves. Sexual relations are presented in such a way as to suggest a national interest, a collectivity with identical interests and identical experiences.

(Coward 1984: 150)

The reassurance which music radio offers its female listeners is the reassurance of consensus and of belonging to a community of women who have all made similar sacrifices and found themselves in similar situations. Comfort is to be found not merely in accepting their isolated state as natural but in belonging to a community: a community of isolated housewives all tuned in to a particular radio station; a community sharing similar romantic memories and fantasies; a community sharing the same romantic fantasy-figure in the form of a particular radio DJ. As Dorothy Hobson puts it:

> The disc jockey, as well as providing relief from isolation, links the isolated individual woman with the knowledge that there are others in the same position. Similarly, this can be seen as a functional effect of 'phone-in' programmes ... These programmes not only provide contact with the 'outside' world, they also reinforce the privatized isolation by reaffirming the consensual position – there are thousands of other women in the same situation, in a sort of 'collective isolation'.
>
> (Hobson 1980: 108)

Thus radio would appear to offer solitary listeners a sense of belonging to a collective: a collective of isolated listeners whose relationship to each other exists exclusively via the mediating presence of the disc jockey. There is, of course, an obvious contradiction here: if listeners are only ever addressed as individuals (rather than as a group) how can they derive from this experience a sense of belonging to a collective or a community? The answer lies in the fact that the collective or community constructed here is an extraordinary (and, indeed, contradictory) kind, for it is one in which isolation – a very special type of 'privatized isolation' born of personal sacrifice – is a prerequisite for membership. The sense of the universality of this condition, reflected in the lyrics of the music, the chatter of the DJs and the similarity of the concerns expressed by callers on phone-ins, ensures that solitary listening grants radio listeners membership to a unique type of club: a club where the members never meet or communicate directly. The club, of course, like any club, has its rules, its rituals, its codes of conduct and its abiding principles, beliefs and values. Club membership entails conformity to a consensual view.

Both 'collective isolation' and consensus form important parts of the radio experience, extending well beyond the scope of daytime music shows for housewives. Across the board, radio is instrumental in constructing consensus: that is, in constructing an acceptable collective view. Moreover, a large part of the task of constructing consensus falls to the presenters, who are required (in most cases) to 'assume the identity of the moderate, politically neutral member of a value consensus, projecting the unassailable logic of "common sense"' (Wilby and Conroy 1994: 131). Here the presenter not only presents a view that is acceptable to both the station itself and its audience but also one that individual members of the audience can accept as being that of the community in general. Part of the presenter's task, therefore, is to enhance (wherever and whenever possible) radio's capacity to 'construct, through ideological work a "common ground" from which listeners may engage in the radio experience' (Wilby and Conroy 1994: 132).

As Pete Wilby and Andy Conroy point out in *The Radio Handbook*, through the operations of the presenter (and particularly the disc jockey) 'the radio experience effectively masks the necessary action on the part of the listener to adopt a specific, consensual mode of reception in order that he may understand and fully relate to the values and terms of reference of the programme that he is tuned into' (Wilby and Conroy 1984: 132). The listener's adoption of a consensual view is masked by the nature of the disc jockey's job: that is, the DJ's primary function of maintaining a constant flow of output, smoothing over transitions from one item to another and preventing any breaks or gaps in the sequence of sounds which emanate from the station. In this way, listeners simply have no time to stop and think about what they are actually hearing. As Wilby and Conroy write, 'spontaneity is the key to the reproduction of the consensual experience of listening' (Wilby and Conroy 1994: 132), constituting what Jody Berland has referred to as 'addiction and forgetfulness' (Berland 1993: 211).

The more the construction of a collective view is masked by the spontaneity (the incessant interventions) of the presenter, the more the listener is likely to accept what is heard as the consensual view. Even if the views expressed on the radio (either by callers or the presenter) do not conform entirely to those of the individual listener, the individual listener can still be made to believe that these are the views which are acceptable to the listening community more generally, and that, ultimately, is what is most important. What is important to acknowledge here is the fact that the presenter alone does not construct the consensual or collective view. Indeed, as Wilby and Conroy have written, 'the radio experience is only partially constructed by the presenter; the listener contributes through making the transition from the idiosyncratic world of the individual to the structured, "common sense" world of the consensus' (Wilby and Conroy 1994: 139).

What is implied here is that each individual listener must recognise that their own personal views must be modified in some way if they are to conform to the more general views held by the community, and that this practice is both a necessary and acceptable part of communality. In this way, each listener is complicit in the establishment of consensus. Moreover, listeners agree to comply with the consensual views (and values) expressed by the radio station/programme/presenter because consensus brings with it its own rewards. First among these is the fact that consensus represents a state of belonging to a community – a community of shared values – which is, in itself, reassuring. The reassurance of belonging to this community may well be such that individual listeners are prepared to forfeit some of their own personal ideals, values and beliefs in order to be part of the community. The radio station, its programmes and its presenters are instrumental in articulating the values which the listening community can most readily agree upon. At the same time, radio and, in particular, radio presenters make it easier for their listeners to accept a consensual view by a constant flow of output which allows listeners little time to pause for thought, creating a listening situation which is therefore most conducive to agreement and acceptance. This process (i.e., 'flow') makes it easier for listeners to suspend their own thoughts and feelings and accept those broadcast over the airwaves and into their own personal spaces.

Radio presenters therefore do not construct a consensual view and impose it on their listeners. What they do is present what they perceive to be the views shared by the station and the listening community in general, and then make it as easy as possible for individual listeners to comply with these views (despite whatever specific reservations they may have). This is clearly a considerable task confronting radio stations, and more so today as the competition (for audiences) increases and the industry fragments, serving more and more specific (or 'target') audiences. The need to understand the values of the listening community has become of crucial importance to radio broadcasters in their bid to survive in a more competitive environment. Whilst it is crucial that broadcasters achieve this understanding, this is not something that comes naturally or easily to a medium that has traditionally not had to listen to its audience. As Robert McLeish has written, 'Radio is not a good medium by itself for establishing a genuine two-way contact' (McLeish 1994: 153). Radio is clearly successful in conveying the impression of being intimate and democratic. However, the question of whether or not broadcasters are genuinely able to understand and reflect the specific values and character of their audience is another (and altogether more problematic) issue. After all, the obvious problem with conducting a one-sided conversation is that the person doing all the talking is never really sure of what the other person is actually thinking.

Things to do

1 Listen to a phone-in (talk-back) programme and consider the following questions. Who has the power? Who determines the agenda? Compare and contrast the voice of the presenter with that of the caller. How would you define this relationship? Who is the listener more likely to identify with, the presenter or the callers?
2 Conduct a survey into the popularity of daytime music radio presenters. The purpose of the survey should be to discover which DJs on daytime music radio shows are the most popular and why. Devise a set of questions which will establish the kinds of relationships listeners have with their favourite DJs. Is there a difference in the reasons why male and female listeners like certain DJs?

Note

1   Rabbi Lionel Blue, 'Another Monday morning', first broadcast on BBC Radio 4, 9 January 1989, and now available on a BBC audio-cassette, *Rabbi Lionel Blue: 50 thoughts for the Day*, BBC Radio Collection. London: BBC Enterprises Ltd, 1990. Side 2.

|7|

Case studies

Throughout *On Air*, readers have been introduced to various themes, theories, codes and conventions of radio and have, hopefully, gleaned a broad insight into the history, advantages and disadvantages, and highs and lows of mainstream radio broadcasting. But all too often this insight can be somewhat abstract, particularly for those readers who have never set foot inside a radio studio. In many cases, what is represented in theory to the reader and what actually occurs in practice can seem poles apart. It is hoped that this chapter will demystify the practice of radio broadcasting by giving readers a 'fly-on-the-wall' insight into some of the more common radio practices and in turn exemplify much of the critical theory associated with the study of the radio mass medium.

The radio time-line: history at a glance

On Air opens with an examination of the various concerns and developments that have shaped today's radio industry. Students can follow the metamorphosis of the medium through technological, social and aesthetic changes and ascertain the most significant influences that have impacted the growth of radio broadcasting. The following case studies are 'living' examples of some of these stages, such as the development of pirate, regional and community radio and niche broadcasting. Also, an examination of the history of radio reveals how the activity of radio listening changed dramatically in the 1960s from an interactive, group/family activity to a passive, solitary activity with the popularisation of television. *On Air* does not dispute this occurrence, but the following case studies will challenge the perception that that status has remained unchanged by citing examples of the existence of an interactive radio community.

The power of local radio[1]

The following case study discusses the development of a pirate/community radio station in the Republic of Ireland. Gerry Gannon was the station's founding member.

> *In 1981 in Ireland, County Tipperary, we set up a community radio station. It was in our first week of existence and not many people knew about us and we didn't get much publicity. Anyway, it was a very bad winter and a whole portion of South Tipperary, in fact a significant part of Ireland, was hit by a bad winter. People were snowbound and we recognised this as an opportunity to improve our 'metal' or value in the community, by keeping people informed about what was going on. Suddenly, for some unknown reason, people started tuning in. The word had got out that the local radio would tell you what was happening in your neck of the woods. We started getting phone calls from people who were badly marooned. We organised an army helicopter through the auspices of a local MP (quite an achievement considering we weren't exactly 'legal'!), to do a food drop to one particular community and where there was one newspaper, a smaller one than the other main newspapers in the community, that actually had owned shares in our station, so when we organised the helicopter we organised a photographer and journalist to cover the story and report what was happening. The worst of the storms lasted a week and during that time we were able to inform people that some sort of relief effort had been mounted. We also could keep people up to date about what was going on, when the shops and schools would be open and more importantly when the roads would be open. It was immediate, it was all the time. We broadcast for twenty-four hours and my staff slept in the station on sleeping bags and mattresses. Everybody knew that this moment would establish us as a legitimate broadcaster playing a legitimate role in the community.*

The radio community[2]

The following example challenges the view that radio is a solitary activity. It is true that the listener will often be alone when listening to the radio but, nevertheless s/he is at the same time part of a listening community – one that shares a common interest in the programme to which they are tuned and a concern for other citizens sharing their city. 'Grapevine' is a talk-back programme which began in Perth, Western Australia, in 1995 broadcast on the Australian Broadcasting Corporation's (ABC) 6WF. It began as a way of helping listeners find various items or services through on-air appeals and it highlights the way in which radio listeners can actively become involved with radio through telephone, facsimile, letters and e-mail.

'Grapevine's then (1998) producer, Rosemary Greenham, explains how 'Grapevine' developed from a type of 'swap' or flea-market programme into a community service that, at the same time, offered an interesting, informative and entertaining programme for radio audiences. She remembers how a caller to 'Grapevine' had been part of the listening community for several weeks. This particular caller had a distinctive accent and an unusual first name (i.e., his anonymity was therefore not ensured), and he told the presenter quite early on that he was suffering with a serious illness. By about the third call he let it be known that his illness was AIDS. Several weeks after this revelation, he told the presenter, and in turn the 'Grapevine' listening community, that he had fallen in love and that his partner was also an AIDS sufferer. In some cases, one would expect to receive some complaints from listeners who did not wish to hear such personal, and to many, controversial details made public, but obviously, this particular caller felt comfortable enough to reveal himself to such an extent. He was part of the community, an extreme part of the community, but a member of it none the less, and he and his life were accepted. Using radio in such a way gives it an almost healing quality where a caller can speak openly and be accepted even in circumstances that may not be accepted by one's own family.

Another 'healing' property of radio is using it as an avenue for action. Greenham explains how another caller, who had once been a street kid with a AUS$1000-a-day amphetamine habit was using the programme to help other street kids. As a young man, he had been taken under the wing of a biker and weaned off drugs, a story in itself which questions the clichéd image of the 'couldn't care less', drug-offending, 'rabble-rousing' biker gang member. With some strong guidance and a lot of time and patience he eventually kicked the drugs and went on to become a successful advertising executive. This former 'junkie' wanted to give his hell's angel turned guardian angel something back, but the only reward the biker requested was that he do the same for someone else one day. 'Dave' eventually decided to give up his advertising job and work full time with street kids, repairing bikes and computers with spare parts donated in response to appeals on 'Grapevine'. This work gave the street kids a sense of purpose and value by making other lives better and, in turn, improving their own.

Greenham points out that 'Grapevine' was not simply a 'do-gooder' programme. She agrees that such programmes can degenerate into exclusively dealing with 'worthy causes' and 'parish pump' notices which may service the community but will do little to entertain a radio audience.

To avoid such an occurrence it must be produced carefully. The use of two presenters (as is the case with 'Grapevine'), can build a rapport and 'lighten' the atmosphere. For example, on 'Grapevine', first-time callers, or 'virgin breakers', were required to sing a song the first time they were on air; it's taking the temperature (of the programme), all the time. People listen to 'Grapevine' and feel better in a world when so much news makes them feel that they are living in a serious, dangerous world. We're not denying that these issues do exist, but it's not just hard and tough and frightening but that most of the people are mostly good, most of the time.

Greenham claims that 'Grapevine' would not work on television.

It's too immediate, it doesn't require pictures. If someone rings up and is looking for an old *Goon Show* programme or a Frank Zappa track I can run to the sound library and get it out, but only because I run very fast! Or someone may ring in to say that they've just bought a house and would like to know the history of their plot of land or building. Television could get an old still but it would really be hopeless. It just wouldn't work on TV, it couldn't sustain a thirty-minute programme without good vision.

Niche broadcasting: an example of interactive radio

In 1994 in Hong Kong, the author produced a pilot children's radio programme on Radio 3, RTHK (Radio Television Hong Kong), called 'Kids' Time'. Listeners were encouraged to take part in a segment that encouraged them to listen to the radio, familiarise themselves with the print media and combine their own imagination with that of other children on air. The competition involved writing contributions to a fictional story that 'grew' over several weeks. Initially, a paragraph was written by the producer about a young girl called Zena who lived in outer space. The paragraph was printed in a national, English-language newspaper as well as being read out on air. Children were asked to write the next paragraph and post or fax their contribution to Radio 3. Several paragraphs were read out and the best were put into a hat: one 'lucky' entry would be printed in the newspaper the following week. Over several weeks a story outlining the trials and tribulations of Zena's life grew through an interactive, communal effort that called on children to use their imagination to create 'pictures' for the radio.

'Kids' Time' grew from being a half-hour segment inside a two-hour 'Drive Time' programme, to a one-hour, self-contained daily programme called 'Live & Loud' which became an integral part of Hong Kong's English-speaking children's community. The programme introduced many children to radio for the first time and encouraged them to participate on air and behind the scenes. Children became involved in competitions, projects (such as developing a cook book made up of children's recipes) and OBs where the listening community could meet. 'Live & Loud' also went to local schools where children could help present 'their' programme.

RTHK's children's radio programme is an example of radio listening as both an active and an interactive activity, and contradicts the common opinion that listening to the radio is a solitary, passive experience.

Words, speech and voices

Without words, radio would have little significance, and Chapter 2 of this book examines the various aspects of speech and the 'radio voice' and its relationship with audiences. The following case studies exemplify much of this research by outlining some of the various techniques employed by presenters and producers to appeal to the listener.

Sign-posting

When a presenter is on air, it is vital that s/he remind the listener who s/he is listening to and to what station they are tuned. Once you have the listener's 'ear', the aim is to keep it. To do this, the presenter must make the programme sound as interesting as possible but, at the same time, take care not to give too much away, i.e., use teasers to whet the appetite of the listener and entice them to stay tuned. An example of this technique follows.

> *Good morning, it's five to ten and you're listening to Mary Ordinary on Rational Radio. Coming up after the news at ten o'clock we'll be speaking with[3] a young mother who has taken on her local council and won a £5000 compensation case over her son's education, or rather, lack of it; the Zeds will be in the studio talking about their recent European tour; your chance to win £500 in our 'joke-du-jour' competition and of course, as always, more of your favourite music like this one from ...*

This simple and friendly approach has achieved a great many things. The listener knows:

- what station they are listening to
- who is presenting the programme
- what the time is
- that they will be able to catch the news in only five minutes (so, no point changing the dial!)
- what items will be on after the news. If the listener is interested in a particular item, then it is very likely that s/he will stay tuned in order to catch it. The 'trick' that the presenter uses is not to be too specific about the time when each item will be broadcast, so that the listener does not switch stations and only re-tune at the time of the item of interest. Instead, the presenter will keep reminding listeners what is coming up soon (ish!)

- what style of music the station plays so that s/he can decide if it suits their taste.

It is of vital importance that the sign-posting is done at an opportune time, i.e., when audience numbers are at their peak, such as just before or just coming out of the news.

Sign-posting is done at various times during a presenter's shift. The above is an example of 'live' sign-posting, done by the presenter of the programme. However, this technique can also be pre-recorded, using promos and trailers for other programmes or particular items. Jingles and stings can also be used to sign-post an item and a regular listener learns to identify a particular tune with a particular programme or segment such as traffic, the weather report, the BBC news pips or the theme tune to *The Archers*. Another sign-posting technique is when the presenter has a 'two-way' (i.e., two-way conversation as opposed to a one-to-one interview) with the presenter of another programme as they change shifts, and they discuss some features of the next programme's line-up:

> *Thanks for spending the morning with me. That's it for now but don't go away, Jo Walsh will be joining you after two o'clock to take you through to 'Drive' . . . Oh! and here she is right now. Jo, any surprises in store today?*

On a more informal news station, two-ways can also take place between the news reader and the presenter about what is coming up in the next hour. And a final example of sign-posting is the sponsorship jingle, e.g., 'Tom's Tyres presents today's episode of "XYZ".'

Chapter 2 of this book also discusses the question of scripted speech, in particular the contradictory philosophy of sounding natural and unrehearsed while reading out a prepared presentation: 'when they give their talk at the microphone they should avoid just reading out what they've written and converse, really converse, with someone who isn't there' (Evans 1977: 16). How do presenters achieve this? What is it like to speak to a microphone and imagine that you are speaking to a friend? Students of radio will understand how difficult it is. So many find their first time behind the microphone to be excruciating or embarrassing, particularly the first time they hear their recorded voice played back (especially in front of their peers!). Do I really sound like that? Is my voice that high? Did I really say that?

All experienced presenters have been 'first-timers' at some stage in their careers. A good presenter should be able to ad lib in almost any situation, but a scripted speech offers a kind of security blanket for the nervous radio rookie. The trick is to not write out scripts word for word, nor to read them verbatim. There are exceptions, of course. Drama, news, features and documentaries all require word-perfect narration, but general chit-chat does not; in fact, the opposite applies: perfection sounds imperfect! A sure-fire technique is to jot down points or simple ideas to jog the memory about subjects up for discussion, and then 'talk around' them. Also, be personal; everyday occurrences in the presenter's life such as traffic jams or late trains on the way into work, bank queues and Saturday-morning shopping are more than likely shared by the listener, which adds a sense of intimacy and friendship or familiarity to the presenter/listener relationship.

Visualisation is another very common technique. A former colleague of mine says that he imagines a person standing in a room in a house, listening to the radio. He usually imagines the kitchen because that is his memory of growing up with radio. His 'listener' can be a man or a woman and he simply talks to them but *never*, he says, 'give that person a familiar face because you are then being too specific. The way that you may talk to that particular friend may not be suitable for all your listeners.'[4]

Another technique, which sounds quite strange but works, is motion. Gestures are normal in everyday speech, so why not use them at the microphone? Some presenters even stand up while they are on air for more freedom of movement. One last, albeit perhaps strange technique, is posting a picture of a friend or loved one on the desk and talking to the image. Perhaps some personalities have pictures of themselves!

The mind's eye

Students of radio will be very familiar with the term 'blindness' which is used to theorise radio broadcasting in most popular media textbooks. However, *On Air*'s Chapter 4, 'The mind's eye', opens with an extract from the colourful and poetic text Dylan Thomas's *Under Milk Wood*, a classic example of the way in which radio can evoke pictures. The following case studies continue to challenge the perception that the radio listener is somehow 'blindfolded' or disadvantaged by radio's so-called 'blindness'.

Creating 'vision' for radio

A classic example of the power of radio in reference to imagination is Orson Welles's production of *The War of the Worlds*. His radio play about a Martian attack on earth so convinced listeners that national panic occurred. To replicate such an event, however, may be a little ambitious for the beginner radio student! Perhaps a more attainable exercise would be to create a feature for radio that one would assume would work *only* for a visual medium. An example of such was produced by the author in 1993: a radio feature about a photographic exhibition. In that year, in Perth, Western Australia, the doors on a piece of the state's history (albeit a tragic part of history), were closing; one of Australia's first penal prisons was to be closed and re-opened to tourism. To document the event, a leading local photographer was asked to develop an exhibition looking at the prison's chequered past and recent history. Armed with my Uher (see Glossary), I attempted to produce a feature for the ears about an exhibition created for the eyes – a daunting task. How does one reproduce photography with the spoken word? After much thought, I approached the project by imaging that I was taking a 'blind' person through the exhibition. What would s/he like to know? What details would be of most interest? How could I make the images come to life?

The exhibition was in a large room in one of the oldest buildings in the historic town of Fremantle. The walls were high and heavy and the floors made of solid wood; the acoustics of such a room created a vacuous, hollow, empty sound, perhaps reminiscent of the emotions of an inmate. The photographer was a woman who was required to spend time with the prisoners, a detail in itself worth investigation. How did she feel being the only woman inside the jail? What struck her the most? How was she treated by men who were jailed for theft, murder, even rape? She was the best person to take myself, and my listener, on a journey through history, and that is exactly what we did. The two of us walked from photograph to photograph, describing selected pieces for someone who could not see. We were told about the thoughts and philosophies of the men in the image as well as those of the photographer. We were taken into the prisoners' private space, their bedrooms; their public space, the dining rooms; and their most terrifying space, solitary confinement. The ambience of our voices in that large room, the sound of our feet on wooden floors, and the ache with which any Australian listener carries our colonialist history created a sensuous, entertaining and informative feature. The images of the photographs were putty for the listener to shape into any form she desired. A television feature on the same topic would of course be spectacular, but I would challenge anyone who might claim that the viewer would be required to call on their imagination in the same way as the radio listener.

Truth Claims

The process of editing has always been, and continues to be, a problematic and controversial area of broadcasting. Chapter 5 of this book examines in depth the many questions that surround truth, reality and their relationship with radio broadcasting. The following case studies attempt to exemplify and demystify some of the meanings and methods associated with 'liveness', ethical broadcasting and the representation or manufacture of 'truth'.

Unethical editing

Q: Do you believe in abortion?

A: It's very hard to give a definitive answer as there are so many factors that relate to this question. ... *Yes*, but I believe that it is the woman's choice,

and in most cases it must be a hard decision. *There are so many single moth-
ers in society and many reasons why a young woman would want to abort.*
Perhaps if they had had the option of an abortion without the stigma then
they may have taken it, mainly because of their tender age, their inability to
care for their baby because of the expense, or to avoid being forced to give
the baby up for adoption if they found that they couldn't cope; for many,
this is worse than abortion. *In the case of rape I definitely believe in it.* But
what we mustn't forget is the father's feelings. It is his baby too, and what
goes without saying is that we are talking about a human life. It's difficult,
I can genuinely see both sides. There are those who believe that *the world
would be better off without unwanted children* being born to children, and
then there are those who say 'a life is a life'.

Q: Are you in favour of the death penalty?[5]

A: That's very difficult to say. *Yes . . .* I suppose so, under certain circumstances, but it's an awful thing to take a life, whatever that person has done.
When you're dealing with *murderers and rapists who will probably kill and
rape all over again as soon as they're released . . .* I don't know, maybe *they
should be executed.* But there are always those who are genuinely sorry for
what they've done and are serving their time – while there's life there's hope,
they might change. But it's the others, *the maniacs and fanatics who can't
stop killing – they're a menace to us all,* but on the other hand, that's what
prisons are for, isn't it?

To read only what is in italics indicates an uncompromising viewpoint, and
to report only that would be to quote the interviewee out of context and
possibly cause an outcry with such contentious issues. An interviewee who
is not familiar with how the media works can be excused for making comments that could so easily be misquoted. Others, however, who work with
the media regularly (for example, politicians) prepare their answers with
great care to prevent them being taken out of context. Ideally, politicians
request questions before an interview in order to prepare; this of course is
not always possible, particularly at press conferences and 'door stopping'.[6]
Also, many journalists, particularly those at the top (because they can afford
to), will refuse to prep interviewees with a preview of their questions, claiming that it detracts from the spontaneity and 'liveness' of an interview if the
talent is too rehearsed. However, in such cases the politician is usually very
familiar with the interview subject and will anticipate any potentially contentious questions.

Ethical editing

All current affairs producers attempt to develop a programme that is
dynamic, contemporary, challenging, investigative and relevant. One technique is 'on-the-spot reports', i.e., 'We were there', 'We work hard to bring

you up-to-the-minute news'. Ideally, most programme makers would like to have journalists based in the trouble spots to seek out and report the latest news from that particular region. Unfortunately budgets and logistics do not always allow for this. The next best thing is to find an informed member of the public living in that particular area to work as a stringer. If the stringer is from the town to which the programme is being broadcast then the producer has struck gold because this adds a dimension of familiarity.

In 1992, at the height of the Gulf War, the producer of the 'Morning Programme' (a topical news and current affairs programme broadcast 8.30 a.m. to 12 noon, Monday to Friday, by the Australian Broadcasting Corporation, Perth, Western Australia) found such a person living and working in Iraqi-occupied Kuwait. He was an accountant originally from Perth who spontaneously phoned the producer to give her a piece of vital information and detail about the occupation that had not been reported. She asked him if he would be willing to go on air, and he agreed, but with one proviso, that the interview be pre-recorded. He had a severe stutter and insisted that his speech be edited to disguise it or at least play it down. Such a request uses up valuable time but the informer's knowledge and intelligent understanding of the war compensated for any editorial inconvenience, so we agreed to the conditions. I did many of the interviews and, with the help of a technician, the editing. It was a long process, but the end product was an informative, polished feature, aesthetically unrecognisable compared to the raw interview, but edited without changing the context.

Here, we see an example of ethical editing in that the words were not twisted, nor was syntax tampered with to change context, tense or themes. But the material was altered none the less, so were we presenting the 'truth'? The fact is that stuttering is a disability that thousands of people deal with every day. Is their battle to be understood and accepted made harder by the editing blade rendering the speech pattern more 'acceptable' to the listener? Should we not present the world as it is? People with disabilities are constantly fighting to be accepted as they are, as 'normal', functioning, sociable human beings. If the media constantly 'beautifies' with technology what they consider to be 'unappealing', are they not making the battle for 'normality' and the acceptance of difference more difficult?

A producer will justify such editing by claiming that limits to airtime make it necessary to remove such impediments. This of course is true, particularly in this age of 'soundbite' culture – a culture that encourages people to say 'everything' in a few choice words that can be neatly packaged and edited into thirty- or forty-second grabs. It is common practice for a reporter during a pre-recorded interview to ask the interviewee to summarise their answer if the original answer is too long or too difficult to edit because of 'mistakes' or digression. In their desire to receive good publicity and to sound coherent, most interviewees are only too happy to oblige.

The grey areas

The following example is taken from an interview conducted in Hong Kong in 1994 with an English prostitute working in the former British Colony. The interview took place in the wake of stories investigating the increasing incidence of foreign domestic workers, mainly from the Philippines, Thailand and India, being forced into prostitution. The women were being lured to Hong Kong under false pretences and imprisoned into underground brothels and the police could do little to control the crime. However, despite this tragic, darker side of the sex industry, many women from the first world are attracted to the big money available in the 'high-class' side of prostitution in the wealthy, glamorous city of Hong Kong. The author interviewed one such woman, an unassuming, attractive, articulate, drug-free, middle-class, 27-year-old English woman with a degree from Bristol University. Hardly the clichéd image of a 'hooker'. Why does a young, educated expatriate make the conscious decision to sell her body? (Apart from the £200 to £400 per hour!) What does it feel like to be bought? What kind of men pay for sex? Does she set any ground rules? What are they? Does she ever enjoy herself? What does she hate the most? What about her own personal relationships? Do boyfriends understand? What do her parents think she is doing? How would they react if they knew? What about AIDS and other sexually transmitted diseases? Has she ever been frightened for her safety? Would she want the same for her own daughter if she were to have one?

The interview was fascinating, all two hours of it. However, it had to be packaged into two fifteen-minute features. There was also another catch: the interviewee demanded complete anonymity, which not only included a false name (she was called 'Jacquie' for the sake of the interview) but also that her voice be disguised or that an actress re-voice her answers. So, what decision was made and what impact did that decision have on the question of truth? A voice is disguised by means of a device that turns it into something that would not be out of place in a science fiction film. In many cases this is quite acceptable for short interviews broken up with the narrator's voice, music, SFX, etc., because the listener gets some relief from the unnatural-sounding voice. Also, if the feature is only five to seven minutes long then the listener does not have to endure the strange, harsh-sounding voice for too long. However, with a fifteen-minute one-to-one, where the interviewee is doing nearly all the talking, such a situation would be too distracting for the listener, so the decision was made to re-voice 'Jacquie' using an actress. This decision raises many questions. Is this not falsely representing the interview? Is not using a disguised voice, albeit sounding somewhat 'abnormal', closer to the truth? After all, it *is* the talent who is *actually* speaking. What is more important, reality or audio quality? In this particular case, the latter was prioritised so that the interview would hold the listener's attention and nothing would detract from the content.

With that decision made, the ethical question now raised concerned selection. How does the editor represent reality by discarding one-and-a-half hours of tape? During the editing process all questions and answers had to be transcribed, rearranged into a coherent, linear sequence (it is normal to digress in nearly two hours of conversation), and then re-voiced. This not only included an actress reading 'Jacquie's' answers but the interviewer had to re-ask the questions so that the sound quality was compatible. (The original interview was done in a café; the re-voicing was recorded in a studio.) Is it possible to *re-create* an interview absolutely? What about intonation? Natural voice characteristics? Hidden meanings behind particular emphasis or inflection? Or perhaps, as long as the *essence* of the interview and detail of questions and answers is re-created, then all of the above is irrelevant? Does it really matter that the listener is oblivious to the editing process? Does the listener really want to be burdened with the details of editing technicalities? 'Jacquie's' story was fascinating; would exposing the editing process give the listener a clearer view of the truth or only spoil the pleasure of listening?

Readers should also understand that so-called 'grey areas' occur in the manipulation of 'live' interviews. Many would assume that a live interview would perhaps offer the closest representation of truth because the talent's words do not go 'under the blade', but this is not the case. In fact, the presenter's finger often takes the place of the editing blade. I cite an example[7] of a BBC Radio 4 interview where the guest who was speaking about theatre was instructed to refrain from discussing the politics of Northern Ireland (where he had worked for seven years). Also, it was made clear that when the presenter held up her finger it meant that she wished to speak and that when she gave the wind-up signal (see Glossary), the guest must finish speaking. Also, in preparation for the interview with the presenter, the guest was interviewed twice by the producer. This case reflects common practice in the industry and exemplifies the 'control' that a producer/presenter has over the content and direction of an interview both inside and outside the studio.

Listening and talking back

The following excerpts exemplify theories of the (dis)empowerment experienced by many callers to talk-back radio which are examined in Chapter 6. Both examples have the added dimension of language, where English is the *second* language of the caller.

Dis/empowerment

'The Lunch-Time Programme' was a magazine-style programme, broadcast Monday to Friday from 1.10 p.m. to 2 p.m. on RTHK (Radio Television Hong

Kong), Radio 3 and presented by the author. The first excerpt is taken from a programme broadcast on the Monday of a long weekend which included a pre-recorded interview with an authority on Chinese traditions/celebrations followed by open talk-back. **P** stands for presenter and **C** for caller.

P Hello, we have another caller on the line.

C Yes, I want to say that you should not speak of Chinese people.

P Um, I don't understand.

C You say you want Chinese culture to die.

P I did not!

C You say in the interview that Chinese culture should die.

P No I did not; I asked about the impact of western culture in Hong Kong on young Chinese.

C You say you want Chinese culture to die.

P I asked if more and more young Chinese would prefer to go out with their friends or listen to pop music or something, rather than take part in the Grave Sweeping[8] with their families! And therefore are we seeing many traditions dying out!

C You do not know about Chinese culture.

P Are you calling me racist?

C You are not Chinese, you should not talk of Chinese things.

P No, I'm not Chinese but I live in Hong Kong and many non-Chinese are enjoying a public holiday today for the Grave Sweeping and I think that it is important that we know more about the culture in which we live.

C But you are not Chinese, you should not speak of things that you don't understand.

P But I am trying to understand by doing the interview which I will point out was with a Chinese anthropologist at the Chinese University!

C . . . (*trying to speak*)[9]

P If you are accusing me of stating that Chinese culture should die, tell me when I said that! When did I say that?

C I don't think you should speak of Chinese things.

P The Chinese stations speak of non-Chinese subjects. I had an American on the programme yesterday, was that wrong? This is ridiculous! I think that too many westerners live here and don't know enough about Chinese culture. . . . We should learn more and if you don't like what I do then you can always switch to another station!

ANALYSIS

After making the last comment quoted above, the presenter closed the fader, which meant that the caller could hear the presenter but he (the caller) had no further opportunity to speak. At the same time, the presenter indicated to the technician to cut the telephone line so that the fader could again be opened to allow the next caller to speak. The first caller had no opportunity to redress.

We see here how technology, and the use of that technology, guarantees the presenter complete control over the development of the programme. The caller is given a false sense of empowerment. S/he believes that the opportunity to call and speak on the air gives them the chance to voice opinions freely with the anonymity that radio offers (because they can give a false name and they know that their face will not be seen). In reality, it is up to the producer/presenter how the programme will pan out. This is obvious from the start, when calls are initially screened by the producer before they go to air. It is up to the producer whether the caller will be put through to the presenter. Criteria for successful calls can depend on subject matter, listener appeal and personality of the caller; but one thing is certain: if the producer thinks that a call is unsuitable then it will not be put to air. Once a caller is patched through, the presenter is in a position to determine how long s/he can speak. Also, the presenter has more experience on air and a first-time caller may be intimidated and may therefore come across as unconfident, shy, quiet and tentative, which will automatically give the presenter the upper hand.

In this particular case, the caller was not only dealing with an unfamiliar medium but also speaking in his second language. In retrospect, the presenter was wrong to finish the call so abruptly; however, it is often a case of 'good radio'. The 'shock jock' style of presenting developed by Howard Stern in America, where the presenter attempts to be controversial, is often appealing to the listener because it allows the listener to be involved by being outraged or amused without being responsible for the controversy. But it is important that the presenter finds a balance between *good* radio and *fair* radio. Radio should not only be entertaining, but also informative and humane. The danger in talk-back radio is exploitation of the caller. Confrontation on radio between caller and presenter is often regarded as good radio because it provokes a reaction (of whatever kind) in the listener. In this particular case, the altercation was responded to by a series of calls from listeners wanting to make their own point. Such a response can indicate to the producer that the segment has been successful, albeit unplanned, but s/he must ensure that while trying to produce good radio s/he does not take advantage of the inexperienced or intimidated caller or alienate those listeners who may be offended by confrontation. A confrontational presenter may discourage potential callers who fear that they may be dealt the same treatment if they voice an opposing view on air. It is the presenter's job to be a *facilitator* of information and entertainment, not to impose an authoritative view. To play devil's advocate is an acceptable method of encouraging and facilitating debate, but to bully the listener is the perfect way to lose her.

The power of the listener

While the previous example clearly outlines how the talk-back caller can be disempowered by radio, the following example is one where the guest has been able to manipulate the medium to suit their own agenda. The example is taken from 'The Morning Programme', broadcast on the Australian Broadcasting Corporation, 1992.

The interview in this case study was based on research carried out on various charity organisations. Researchers were looking to determine how much of the donor's dollar actually finds its way to the charity and how much is swallowed up in administration. In turn, the researchers hoped to establish what kind of influence these findings had on the public's decision whether to reach into their hearts and pockets or to keep their cheque books tightly shut! After collecting background material, the interviewer found that the general public was quite sceptical about giving because they were cynical about how their donations were used. The interviewer pre-recorded this part of the interview and then tried to find a high-profile charity to support these claims. A local charity for the homeless was approached and the head of the organisation, a rather well-known, colourful, if somewhat maverick priest, agreed to speak out. He agreed 'off air' that this was the case; that often, many people were sceptical about the handling of their donations and, as a result, sometimes found it difficult to give. It was planned that the priest's role in the feature would be a live interview after the introductory pre-recorded interview with the researchers had been aired. However, when it actually came to the time of the interview the priest changed his mind on air, in a bid to get some free publicity for his organisation, and spoke about the generosity of people and how their much-needed dollars were used and appreciated. His change of heart also changed the entire nature of the feature and caused great embarrassment for the researchers, who were listening to the programme and felt that because their part of the interview was pre-recorded, they were unable to defend their research. The priest had, in effect, misrepresented his intentions so that he could encourage people to keep giving to his appeal. He was a popular personality in the area to which the interview was being broadcast, so to challenge or criticise him on air could have angered many listeners: the interviewer's hands were tied. The outcome of this feature was that a formal complaint against the interviewer was lodged with the station by the two researchers and the local parish priest got some free publicity!

Talking to millions but speaking to one

It may seem a little contradictory that radio is regarded in terms of one-to-one (as outlined in Chapter 6),[10] when literally tens of thousands of people could be listening simultaneously. Radio is a medium of mass communication,[11] but presenters and producers learn to deliver to one person, *the listener*.[12] An example of how this technique 'speaks to one but is heard by millions' follows.

'Helper's Helpline' was a national programme that was broadcast on

RTHK (Radio Television Hong Kong), Radio 3, every Wednesday for fifty minutes in 1993 and 1994. The programme was part of 'The Lunch-Time Programme' (Monday to Friday, 1.10–2p.m.), and was presented by the author throughout 1994. Once a week the entire programme was dedicated to the half-a-million-strong (mainly) Filipino community of domestic helpers living and working in Hong Kong. These workers (mainly women) are forced, due to economics, to leave their families in the Philippines in search of work, and Hong Kong offers salaries five times those attainable in the Philippines (although by Hong Kong standards these salaries are extremely minimal). Many of them may have left their towns and villages for the first time and are particularly vulnerable to those who choose to exploit their ignorance with regard to employment regulations and politics. Thousands of women find themselves with exploitative and abusive employers and, for many, the radio is their only source of information. 'Helper's Helpline' was designed to give domestic helpers an avenue of therapy through talking, and advice through expert guests, in areas of law, health, human rights and trade unionism. Listeners called in with their questions, problems, advice and experiences (but thankfully not all stories were sad ones). The listener might call with a *particular* problem but, in reality, her problem was shared by hundreds or thousands of other workers.

For example, on one particular occasion, we had a caller who was being forced by her employer to sign a receipt for her (minimum) monthly salary of HK$3000 when in fact she was only receiving HK$1200. Her employer told her that if she did not accept this situation he would send her back to the Philippines. Afraid of losing her job, and not having the confidence or experience to report her employer to the Labour Service, she called our programme for help. The advice is given one to one, i.e., we speak to one woman about *her* life, *her* job and point out the options *she* has. What is happening in reality however, is that many more domestic helpers are listening and sharing in a common and wide-ranging problem of exploitation. The situation therefore becomes *their* life, *their* job and now *their* advice. Radio is a confidant, a source of entertainment, information and company. It is imperative that the presenter be conscious of the fact that s/he has thousands of listeners, that the medium is *mass* communication but the *technique* is one of intimacy: one to one. The presenter must ensure that the listener feels that s/he is being spoken to directly, that the programme is inclusive.

The studio interview

One-to-one communication can also take place inside the studio, when the presenter has a studio guest. The guest might be a doctor giving advice on general health issues, a financial adviser or perhaps a pop star. For example, a BBC Radio 1 interview with Madonna is a one-to-one interview between the star and the presenter, but the presenter is conscious that s/he is asking questions to which thousands of fans may want to know the answers. What was the inspiration behind a particular lyric? What does she listen to at home? Where is her favourite holiday destination? This information is being relished by the fan, who may be sitting at home, alone, listening to the one-to-one live interview, but her listening experience is being simultaneously experienced by thousands of radio listeners.

The practical interview

With this case study, we again challenge the concept of radio being a 'blind' medium by examining a programme that actually 'showed' the listener how to do something. During a weekly environmental segment on 'The Morning Programme' (ABC Radio) a regular guest came into the studio to talk about recycling in the home. This guest was a home-maker who through creative reuse and avoidance of waste reduced her family's weekly 'garbage' to about 10 per cent of the average. Her skill did not come from university courses or council funding or even community projects, but from straightforward economic necessity: with a family of seven to care for she simply had to be thrifty. This 'ordinary' woman became one of the programme's most popular guests as more and more listeners phoned in to speak with her and get practical advice on alternative uses for 'rubbish' and ways to actually avoid accumulating it in the first place (by thinking about what they actually bought at the supermarket, i.e., how it was packaged and whether they really needed it). The callers asked questions that were on the lips of thousands because the general audience were all living in the same city and contending with many similar problems/existences. I would challenge anyone who might claim that this programme would be equally effective on television. With the latter being so reliant on pictures there would be limits to the topics that could be dealt with each week because of the detailed preparation required to produce images. With radio, however, *anybody* could call at *any time* and ask about *anything* to do with recycling and receive advice – advice that was shared by thousands following a question asked by one. *Act locally, think globally!*

Notes

1 Extract taken from a face-to-face interview by the author, Cindy Wieringa, with Gerry Gannon, 6 p.m., Tuesday 27 January 1998, Perth, Western Australia.

2 All case studies and quotes in this section are taken from a face-to-face interview by the author, Cindy Wieringa, with the producer of 'Grapevine', Rosemary Greenham, 3 p.m., Tuesday 27 January 1998, at the Perth headquarters of the Australian Broadcasting Corporation.

3 Note that the presenter uses the phrase 'speaking with', rather than 'talking to'. This discourse has a greater sense of inclusiveness and intimacy.

4 Face-to-face interview by the author, Cindy Wieringa, with Gerry Gannon, Perth, Western Australia, 6.00 p.m., 27 January 1998.

5 Example taken from Boyd 1994: 245.

6 To 'door-stop' is to approach an interviewee with microphone in hand when the interviewee has not invited and is not expecting questions. The term is taken from a confrontational approach where the journalist may knock at a door and put their foot in the door when it is answered to prevent it from closing in their face.

7 Face-to-face interview by the author, Cindy Wieringa, with Dan Baron Cohen, 5 p.m., Thursday 5 February 1998, London.

8 Chinese celebration in respect to the dead.

9 The caller had something to say but the technology is such that as soon as the presenter speaks into her microphone the listener's voice is over-ridden and therefore cannot be heard. This is known as a 'Gate'. Also, it is common for the presenter's voice level to be set higher than that of the caller; and, of course, the technology through which the presenter's voice is broadcast gives it a much clearer and richer quality.

10 See also 'Sign-posting', this chapter.

11 Mass communication is the transmitting of programmes to be heard simultaneously by an indefinitely large number of people (this definition is specific to the electronic media).

12 During production meetings the audience is referred to as *the* listener or *our* listener, discourse that reinforces the intimacy of radio.

Glossary

This glossary has been compiled from the author's own experience and with reference to the following books: Baker 1995; Boyd 1994; Hughes et al. (eds) 1992; McLeish 1994; Wilby and Conroy 1994.

AAP Australian Associated Press. Syndicated news service.

Acoustic The properties or furnishings of a room (e.g., carpet, high ceilings, sound-proofing) which influence the quality of sound it is possible to produce within that room.

Actuality The unscripted sound recorded on location, i.e., the 'actual' sound present at an interview or broadcast. This sound is often cut and used to 'colour' a recording.

Ad Advertisement or commercial.

Ad lib Improvised speech.

Aerial Device for transmitting or receiving radio waves.

Afternoon A shift that runs from approximately 2 p.m. to 4 p.m. This format is generally music-based; i.e, 'easy listening'.

Agence Française French syndicated news service.

AM See **Frequency**.

Analogue recording Where audio is stored by a continuously changeable magnetic flux on moving tape, e.g., reel-to-reel tape.

Anchor Person presenting the programme.

AOR Adult-orientated rock, i.e., music targeted at an adult audience. Usually refers to mainstream music from the 1970s, 1980s and 1990s.

AP Associated Press. Syndicated news service.

Assemble editing Recording audio on to completely blank tape. This is also known as dump editing, i.e., sound is 'dumped' from one source on to another.

Atmos Abbreviation for atmosphere. The natural sound at the place of an interview or broadcast, e.g., beach, pub, school, field. A few minutes' recording of the atmosphere should be taken at the time of an interview for editing purposes. Also known as 'wild track'.

Audio Sound, or the reproduction of sound.

Audio frequency Audible sound wave. Accepted range 20Hz–20kHz.

Auditory Received by the ear.

Automatic level control Device to keep audio signal at a particular level. Available on studio and portable equipment.

Back announcement (Back anno.) Referencing the item just broadcast, i.e., naming song(s) just played.

Base Location of the on-air studio where input from all audio sources is channelled.

Bass cut Device in microphone which electrically removes the lower frequencies.

Bed Instrumental background music to which narration or vocals are added.

Bi-directional microphone A microphone that is sensitive in front and back but will not pick up side audio, e.g., ribbon microphone.

Bi-media Any broadcast or campaign that includes more than one medium, e.g., radio and television. Also applies to reporters who service more than one medium.

Boom Wheeled microphone support using a long arm to hold microphone over performance.

Booth A very small (often with room only for one person), sound-proof studio for recording (mainly) voice work.

Breakfast A shift that runs from approximately 6 a.m. (after the 'graveyard shift') to 8 a.m. or 8.30 a.m. This time is traditionally 'light' entertainment and contains news bulletins.

Breakthrough Undesirable audio 'breaking' or 'interrupting' a soundtrack.

Brief Background information for a presenter on a particular topic. Generally used in current affairs programmes so interviewer can ask appropriate and intelligent questions.

Broadcasting The transmitting of programmes to be heard simultaneously by an indefinitely large number of people.

Bulk eraser A machine which uses a magnetic coil to wipe sound or vision from a tape.

Bulletin A broadcast which provides the latest information on a topic, usually news, weather and traffic.

Cans Slang for headphones.

Capacitor mike Versatile microphone that requires a battery.

Capstan The drive spindle of a tape recorder.

Cardoid mike Microphone most responsive to sound directly in front and to either side.

Cart Short for cartridge. A tape of 20, 40, 70, 90 or 100 seconds used to record jingles, advertisements, etc. Longer carts are available for recording music. The tape is on a loop and will keep turning until it is finished and ready to start again automatically. This system is slowly being replaced with computer and digital technology. Carts are played on a cart machine.

Cassette 3 mm recording tape generally used for domestic purposes.

CD Compact disc (often referred to simply as 'disc'). Digital recording and playback medium.

Channel The complete circuit from a sound source to the point in the control panel where it is mixed with others.

Chinagraph Wax pencil used to mark tape during editing.

Clip A short piece of audio taken from a longer recording, also known as a 'soundbite'.

Colour Generic term for various techniques used to 'brighten up' a programme, e.g., SFX, music.

Commentary Live broadcast in which reporter describes an event, e.g., sport, parade, etc.

Community radio A style of broadcasting that adheres strictly to the requirements peculiar to a definitive community (e.g., small village, council, island). Station operates through sponsorship, advertising and voluntary work.

Compressor Technology that 'reduces' range of audio signal, which generally gives better-quality audio, e.g., used if the master recording is too low.

Condenser mike See **Capacitor mike**.

Contra A 'you scratch my back and I'll scratch yours' deal. A presenter may plug an item, event, restaurant, product, etc. and receive 'gift' rewards, e.g., free meal. The system is not illegal but does raise ethical issues in connection with impartiality.

Copy Written speech for news story, or narration for advertisement or promo.

Copyright The legal ownership of creative work by the author, composer, publisher or designer.

Cough key/button Switch that allows the presenter to cut the microphone circuit for a fraction of a second if s/he needs to cough, sneeze, etc.

Cross-fade The fading in of a new source while fading out the old. Generally refers to discs and is also known as 'spilling'.

Cue A signal to begin. May be a verbal, written, musical or light (cue light found on desk) signal, or a gesture.

Cue sheet Document giving introductory script or technical information about an audio item, e.g., introduction to pre-recorded interview with duration, and first and last three words.

Current affairs Broadcasting that relates to news events but, unlike news production, does not rely on topical, recently 'broken' stories; rather it discusses issues that are current but not necessarily new.

Cut Signal given by producer to presenter to immediately end broadcast item. Signal is index finger drawn across throat.

DAT Digital Audio Tape. Small tapes which record superior-quality digital sound.

Dead air Unintentional silence during broadcasting. Could be due to a number of reasons, e.g., CD does not play when fired, presenter's microphone is not working and therefore no sound is being broadcast, etc. Sometimes, however, dead air is used for effect.

Deadline The time by which a journalist/presenter/producer must deliver a broadcast.

Dedication An item dedicated to a particular person or event, e.g., 'This song goes out to X with love from XX on your anniversary.'

Delay Used during live phone-in and interviews as a safeguard against potentially libellous or offensive remarks. It refers to the delay time between when a caller speaks and when her or his speech is broadcast, i.e., heard by the listener. The delay time is usually seven seconds – long enough for the presenter to push the 'Dump' button which will delete the comment and have it replaced by the presenter's voice or a 'bleeping' tone.

Demographic The profile of a station or show's average listener, i.e., age, profession, income, musical taste, etc. This profile is particularly important when attracting advertising and sponsorship. An advertiser will not necessarily invest in a station with the largest audience but will look for the best target audience or demographic for their product, e.g., youth stations will not be best placed for advertising expensive cars.

Desk Control panel 'driven' by a presenter or technician when broadcasting a programme or shift. The desk brings together all the different components in the broadcast, e.g., voice, music, features and selects or mixes them to transmit.

Digital radio A strong signal of CD sound quality and interference-free reception. Digital radio not only offers superior sound quality but also more programme choice, greater ease of tuning and data services such as PC-compatible 'teletext'.

Digital recording Sound encoded and stored using a computerised numerical system as opposed to analogue recording. Copies can be made of a recording without losing a 'generation' i.e., quality.

Directional microphone A mike which is sensitive in only one direction, the front.

DJ Disc jockey or presenter, i.e., person who presents a programme. DJs, however, present predominantly music programmes; 'presenter' is the term used for genres such as talk, news, etc.

Documentary A factual or news-based feature-length programme, e.g., 'political', 'wildlife', 'music' documentary, etc.

Dolby System which reduces 'hiss' on audio recordings.

Double header A style of presentation using two presenters.

Drive-time (Drive) A shift that runs from approximately 4 p.m. to 6 p.m. and is aimed at listeners driving home from work. The format is generally informative and 'newsy' with little emphasis on music. 'Drive' in Britain can often run to 7 p.m. because of motorway and city gridlock.

Drop-out Loss of sound due to tape damage. Generally occurs on over-used tape.

Dry run Programme rehearsal.

Dub To make a copy of an audio recording.

Dump button See **Delay**.

Duration Length of time of a programme or a programme item.

Easy listening A style of broadcasting where the language and music are unobtrusive, inoffensive, recognisable. Music is middle of the road, i.e., not of extremes.

Editing The rearrangement of recorded material to produce a polished piece of work. An edit is a 'join' made in that process.

Editing block Specially shaped metal guide which holds the tape in position during cutting and splicing.

Embargo An impediment or ban. Often used in news production when certain information has an 'embargo' on its broadcast, e.g., a news room may receive a press release with information that cannot be broadcast for a certain period of time. To break an embargo can sometimes mean fines, and usually the service will be deemed unethical and unworthy of future information.

ENG Electronic news gathering.

Evenings 7 p.m. to midnight. It is during this time that many stations differ by offering a selection of genres from specialist music or speech programmes to radio drama, comedy, competitions, etc., but with little emphasis on news.

Executive producer Overall controller of programming.

Fade When the presenter slowly reduces the output of a song or feature as it finishes, thereby, 'fading' it out. The control switch for this activity is known as a fader. Using the same source, presenters can 'fade in' by slowly increasing output.

Feature A broadcast devoted to a particular topic. Longer than a story in a news bulletin but shorter than a documentary.

Feed Process of sending audio from one source to another.

Feedback A loud piercing sound caused by the microphone picking up the output from speakers or headphones, creating a loop of sound.

File Generally a term used in the production of news and current affairs when a journalist records a story either back at base or by 'filing' the story down a telephone line.

Fill The presenter of a live programme may need to 'fill' a few moments for various reasons, e.g., a pre-recorded programme needs to be cued, the producer needs a few moments to settle a late guest or get an interviewee on the telephone, a CD or cart has not 'fired' correctly or airtime between the end of one item and the beginning of another, e.g., a news bulletin, needs to be occupied. The presenter can 'fill' by ad libbing or by playing a jingle or promo, etc. This is not the same as **Filler**, below.

Filler A 'light-weight', short programme, used to fill gaps in a schedule. Often used when normal programming fails, or to give 'light' and 'shade' to current affairs programmes.

Fire To start a piece of recorded audio, e.g., CD, cart, reel.

Format Guidelines or rules drawn up by the management of a radio station referring to its style, mission, genre. Also, the means of storing audio, i.e., cart, tape, etc.

FM See **Frequency**.

Freelance Self-employed broadcaster, also known as a 'stringer'.

Frequency Measurement of radio waves denoting the number of cycles per second expressed in units called Hertz (Hz). A station's frequency denotes its position on the dial although this may be calibrated by wavelength. Frequencies on the AM band (including medium and long wave transmissions) are expressed as kHz (kilohertz), and on the FM band as MHz (megahertz). FM is considered superior due to less interference.

Gain A dial on the desk which increases the audio signal.

Generation The number of copies of a recording are known as generations, i.e., when you first copy a recording that copy is known as the second generation.

Generic Term used to name a particular product/technology that is general and not label-specific, e.g., 'Revox' refers to a 'reel-to-reel' regardless of the manufacturer's name on the machine; also, 'Walkman' is a generic term used to describe a portable cassette recorder/player and does not specifically mean Sony Walkman.

Grab A short piece of audio, usually speech, taken from a longer interview. This term is generally used in the context of news and current affairs.

Graveyard shift Radio shift between midnight and breakfast.

Gun mike Microphone that resembles a long-barrelled shotgun. It is multidirectional and is generally used when audio source is distant.

Heads Components of an audio recorder which erase, record or play back.

IBA Independent Broadcasting Authority. Body that regulated all non-BBC broadcasting prior to the 1990 Broadcasting Act. Now regulated by the Radio Authority.

ID Short for identification and used for Station ID, Presenter ID. Also known as 'ident'.

ILR Independent Local Radio, non-BBC local radio. Began in 1973 and is regulated by the Radio Authority.

Input Sound going into a desk to be broadcast or recorded.

INR Independent National Radio, non-BBC national radio. First in Britain was Classic FM.

Insert See **Grab**.

Insert edit To 'insert' sound on to a tape in between audio grabs already recorded on the tape.

Interviewee Person being interviewed about a particular topic. Also known as 'the talent'.

Intonation Relating to the quality of the voice, specifically modulation or accuracy of pitch.

IPS Inches per second. Refers to the speed at which tape travels past the recording head.

Jingle Short musical item that has a variety of uses, e.g., station ID, 'colour' for an advertisement.

Kissing-the-red Slang phrase which indicates the best output level, i.e., when the 'VU' needles just touch or 'kiss' the red, or middle-range, meter reading.

Lacing Threading audio tape on to a machine such as a reel-to-reel.

Landline Circuit between two points for communication purposes. Used to 'feed' audio from one source to another.

Lead The main story in a news broadcast.

Leader Coloured plastic tape that can be added to a recording in much the same way that splice editing is done and is used as a marker/guide to particular recordings. It is also used to give extra length to a tape so that it can be laced on to the machine.

Level The volume or output of an audio source. Presenters will test their 'level' before speaking to check that it is of broadcast quality.

Limiter A device which prevents the level exceeding a certain point.

Link A segment which 'takes' the listener from one item to the next, e.g., music to interview. Usually done by the presenter but may take the form of a pre-recorded jingle or sting.

Lip mike 'Hands off' microphone worn on the head and held very near the presenter's lips, favoured by sports commentators.

Listener Generally 'the listener'. Refers to the audience. Presenters think in terms of one listener to give presentation style a sense of intimacy.

Live When the broadcasting of a programme and the receiving of it by a listener are simultaneous, i.e., the programme is not pre-recorded.

Log Written record of station output, very important with regard to needle-time.

Lunch-time A shift that runs from approximately midday until 2 p.m. This programme is traditionally in a 'magazine' style and often aimed at women.

Magazine A style of programming that generally deals with 'lifestyle', human interest stories.

Mainstream A style of broadcasting that caters to popular, middle-of-the-road tastes, particularly music, i.e. not alternative or specialist, e.g., Top 40.

Marantz Generic term for a portable recording machine which uses cassettes. Derived from the manufacturer's name of the most commonly used machine.

Mass communications A means of communicating to the 'masses', e.g., radio, television, cinema, internet, literature (i.e., newspapers, magazines, books journals, etc.).

Master Original copy of final edited recording.

MD (Mini disc) Digital recording device using a miniature compact disc.

Media release Document sent to stations, usually to the news room, offering a potential news story, also known as a press release.

MHz See **Frequency.**

Mike noise Microphone noise. Refers to various sounds which can interfere with the final quality of a recording. Noises generally refer to noises created by presenter, e.g., 'popping' (see below) or wind noise during OBs.

Middle of the road Term used for popular, mainstream, easy-listening music. Does not necessarily mean current chart music but generally refers to music that has been in the charts.

Mixer A machine which can fade up and down and mix together the output of sound or video channels; technique is called mixing.

Morning A shift that runs from approximately 8 a.m. to midday and has two main formats. One concentrates on news and current affairs and has half-hourly news bulletins and generally consists of informative speech, both live and pre-recorded and with little emphasis on music. The second has a lighter approach and a less 'newsy' style with more music.

Muzak Musical 'bed' used to accompany/underlay narration.

MW (Medium wave) See **Frequency.**

Nagra Brand name for high-quality, portable reel-to-reel recording equipment.

Nat-Snd (Natural sound) The 'natural' or background sound recorded on location, e.g., crowd noises, nature, cars, etc. Also known as **Atmos.**

Needle-time A station's permitted usage of commercial records. Expressed in hours or minutes per week.

Network Station that broadcasts nationally or a large broadcasting operation on a regional or national level characterised by links between individual radio stations capable of sharing source material and output.

News Items of information that deal with factual new/topical information.

News release See **Media release.**

OB (Outside broadcast) A broadcast that takes place outside, e.g., radio roadshow.

Off air A device that enables a presenter to monitor the audio which is actually being transmitted, i.e., what is being received by radio sets, rather than simply listening to the audio that is broadcast in the studio. It is advisable for presenters to listen 'off air' to ensure that what they are hearing in their headphones is the same thing that the listener is hearing, i.e., to ensure that there has not been a breakdown in transmission. Presenters tend to dip in and out of 'off-air' listening because the quality is not as clear as the studio sound and often has a slight delay (and therefore can be somewhat disconcerting when trying to present a programme). 'Off air' is also the opposite of '**on air**', i.e., when a presenter has her microphone off and is not broadcasting *she* is 'off air' and when the shift has finished the *programme* is 'off air'.

Off mike When the sound source is working outside a microphone's most sensitive range, i.e., a presenter could be speaking when the microphone is too low, too high, etc., resulting in poor levels.

Omni-directional mike Microphone sensitive in all directions. Also applies to transmitters and aerials.

On air Time when programme is being broadcast. An 'on air' sign will light up outside the studio door when a programme is being broadcast.

Open-ended A programme without a pre-determined finishing time.

Out-cue The last few seconds (words or SFX) of a programme. The presenter or producer must know how a programme will finish so they can come in with the next item.

Output Sound which is being broadcast.

Package A recorded, self-contained feature item.

Panel Studio mixing desk, control board or console.

Peak The highest desired output level of sound.

Phone-in 'Interactive radio' where the listener can phone the programme and speak to the presenter or guest and take part in the discussion. Also called talk-back.

Pilot Inaugural programme of a new series, used as an indicator of the series' potential popularity.

Pirate radio Unregulated or unlicensed broadcast (see Chapter 1).

Pitch Quality of sound according to rate of vibrations controlling it. In broadcasting, pitch relates to quality of voice, i.e., high or low.

Playlist List of tracks to be played during a shift. Playlist is put together according to audience (i.e, musical preference) and record company demands, (i.e., royalty payment/needle-time).

Plug Free advertisment. See **Contra**.

Popping An explosive sound produced by someone speaking too close to a microphone or occuring if the levels of the microphone are too high. Popping generally occurs on plosives, i.e., p, b, t, etc.

Prefade A device on a radio desk which enables a presenter to audition audio while s/he is on air without interfering with current output, for example, the presenter may be playing a disc and may wish to sample the beginning of the next disc to be played.

Pre-recorded Programme is recorded in a studio or on location prior to its broadcast.

Presenter Person who hosts a programme 'on air'.

Press release See **Media release**.

Producer The person responsible for/in charge of 'producing' or putting a programme together before and during broadcast. The producer will decide on the content of the programme, find and set up related interviews, brief the presenter, co-ordinate feature items and 'stringers', and oversee the programme while it is being broadcast.

Producer's choice A BBC policy where the producer is required to produce the programme within a certain budget. This means 'buying in' particular services, e.g., technical, music, etc., which are often cheaper from outside the BBC than from within. Producer choice treats each operation inside the BBC as an autonomous business unit.

Promo Abbreviation of promotion, which advertises or 'promotes' a future programme/item/event/service.

Public Service Broadcasting (PSB) 'The operation of a broadcasting service as a means of information, education and entertainment' (as defined by parliament in the BBC's Licence and Charter). It also 'carries certain defined rules on how much of each there should be' (McCabe and Stewart 1986: 70).

Quarter-inch Tape used for analogue reel-to-reel recording tape.

Radio Authority Statutory body that licenses and regulates the independent radio industry.

Radio microphone A mike which requires no cable connection. Useful for OBs and television work.

Ratings A survey measuring the number of listeners to a specific programme or station. The results of these surveys are particularly interesting to potential advertisers.

Reader A type of news story that, on radio, is simply read out without the use of 'grabs' or SFX. On television, it is a story read straight to camera without pictures.

Received Pronunciation (RP) A mode of speech that was once considered desirable for radio presenters. It refers to a standard of elocution considered 'good English' and often associated with middle-class, 'Home-Counties' speak.

Reel A storage and playing unit for audio tape. Reels vary in size from approximately that of a CD to that of a vinyl LP, the size of the reel relating to the length of the audio tape, e.g., fifteen, thirty or sixty minutes. Reels can be made from either plastic or metal and play tape on reel-to-reel machines.

Relay Simultaneous transmission of a programme originating from another station.

Repro Reproduction of audio.

Resonance The echoing, resounding quality of sound. A resonant voice is one that is 'full' and rich.

Reuters First international syndicated news service, named after its founder.

Reverberation (Reverb) The continuation of sound after its source has stopped transmitting; echo.

Revox Brand (and now generic) name for a reel-to-reel recording machine.

Ribbon mike High-quality microphone, fixed on a stand or hanging from a ceiling, that will pick up more than one speaker.

Rundown Chronological list of items (discs, interviews, etc.) included in a programme or shift. Also denotes source (CD, 'live' phone-in, etc.) as a guide to radio team (producer, presenter, technician, etc.). Also known as a **running order,** but this generally relates specifically to a news bulletin, i.e., order of stories.

Running order See **Rundown**.

Running time Duration of a programme.

Run-through See **Dry run**.

Sampling The 'grabs' of music used to colour a programme. Producers must adhere to copyright laws when using commercial music.

Scripted Radio speech that has been prepared and written out for the presenter to read, as opposed to **ad lib**.

SFX Sound effects, i.e., pre-recorded music, sound, noise used during editing to 'colour' a feature or drama.

Shift Time that a presenter will spend on air, e.g., Drive-time shift, 4 p.m. to 6 p.m.

Sibilance A whistling quality heard during the pronouncement of the sound 's'. Generally more common in women than men. Most microphones have a built-in mechanism that will play down this sound as it is considered undesirable.

Sign-posting Telling the listener what is coming up later in the programme.

Sig-tune (Signature tune) A jingle which identifies, or 'sign-posts', a particular programme.

Slug Short identifying title given to an item. Particularly used to name news stories.

Soundbite See **Grab**.

Spill or Spilling See **Cross-fade**.

Spin doctor A 'minder' or press officer attached to a politician.

Splicing Editing which will cut and remove or cut and add audio, using a blade, chinagraph pencil and splicing tape.

Sting Single music chord. Used for dramatic effect, colour or ID.

Stretch To lengthen a live item. The producer may need the presenter to 'fill' a few moments and indicates this by making a horizontal figure of eight with her two index fingers and thumbs and then slowly pulling the two halves apart, as if 'stretching' an elastic band.

Stringer See **Freelance**.

Stylus Small diamond- or sapphire-tipped arm protruding from a gramophone pick-up. In contact with the record surface it conveys the mechanical vibrations to the cartridge for conversion into electrical energy, i.e., sound.

Syndicated news service A news-gathering service that employs journalists all over the world to collect news stories and electronically send them to a central collection agency which relays those stories to news stations/networks world-wide (radio, TV and print) who subscribe to the service.

Tail-out A method of protecting quarter-inch tape by storing it back-to-front so that the recording side of the tape is on the inside, i.e., winding audio tape backwards so that its 'tail' is 'out', or at the beginning of the reel.

Talent The interviewee or guest.

Talk-back See **Phone-in**. Also, a two-way system between studios through which a presenter or voice-over artist can communicate with the producer. This can be done verbally through an internal microphone system or visually through computer screens.

Talk radio A style of broadcasting that is predominantly speech.

Technician A person who is responsible for the technical production in audio broadcasting.

Tighten The opposite of 'stretch'. The producer may need a live item to be shorter than planned and indicates this to the presenter by moving her palms towards one another without them actually touching. This command is different to 'wind-up' because it does not mean that the item should finish, only that it needs to be 'tighter'.

Time call When the presenter tells the listener the time.

Tone Electronically generated sound to test recording levels. Also quality of voice, i.e., 'warm', harsh, etc.

Trail Abbreviation for trailer, an item which promotes a forthcoming programme or item.

Transcript The text of a broadcast, e.g., verbatim script of an interview (verb: to transcribe).

Transcription A high-quality tape or disc recording of a programme, often intended for reproduction by another broadcaster.

Turn-around The time it takes to record, edit and present a programme. Generally a term used in the production of news.

Two-way Conversation or interview between two studios some distance from each other. A presenter may be speaking to an interviewee or to a specialist correspondent about a particular issue (generally done through talk-back system).

Uher Trade name for a portable recording machine which uses quarter-inch tape.

UHF (Ultra-High Frequency) Radio or television transmission in the range of frequencies from 30 MHz to 3000 MHz.

Underground radio Not to be confused with pirate radio. An underground service is one that is considered 'subversive' or illegal. Often, underground services are found inside oppressive political regimes as a means for citizens to 'speak out' or to receive information.

UPI (United Press International) Syndicated news service.

VHF (Very High Frequency) Radio or television transmission in the range of frequencies from 30 MHz to 300 MHz.

Visual talk-back Communication between a producer and presenter using a keyboard and screen, i.e., the producer can type comments, suggested questions, etc., while a presenter is speaking.

Voice-over Voice commentary generally behind documentaries or commercials. Also used in TV news.

Voice report News item recorded by the journalist using his/her own voice.

Vox pop From the Latin: 'voice of the people'. Usually a collage of comments from people on the street and edited together.

VU meter Indicators found on a radio desk that show level of output (see **Kissing-the-red**).

Warm-up Initial chat between presenter/interviewer and talent before commencement of interview designed to make talent feel comfortable and, if done on air, to ease the listener into the programme.

Wavelength The distance between two similar points in adjacent cycles in a sound or radio wave. Expressed in metres. Also known as **Frequency**.

Wild track See **Atmos**.

Windshield Protective foam cover for microphones during OBs or field work. Helps reduce wind interfering with quality of recording. Also called a 'wind sock'.

Wind-up Signal given to presenter by producer to finish a broadcast item, e.g., interview, disc. Producer uses a cue light on the desk or more commonly an index finger moving in a tight circle.

Wipe To erase tape, cart, reel, etc.

Wire service See **Syndicated news service**.

Wow Slow speed variations discernible in tape or disc reproduction. (The sound is similar to that heard when a vinyl record is started at a low speed and the correct speed is engaged while the record is playing.)

Wrap A short piece of actuality audio 'wrapped' with a vocal introduction and a back announcment, or a short news-in-brief item outlining several stories which 'wraps up' some of the day's news. Also a finished prerecorded item: 'That's a wrap'.

References and bibliography

Adams, D. 1985: *The Hitch-hiker's Guide to the Galaxy: the original radio scripts.* London and Sydney: Pan Books.

Arnheim, R. 1936: *Radio.* Salem, NH: Ayer Co. Publications Ltd.

Augaitis, D. and Lander, D. (eds). 1994: *Radio Rethink: art, sound and transmission.* Canada: Walter Phillips Gallery.

Baker, P. 1995: *Making it as a Radio or TV Presenter.* London: Judy Piatkus.

Barnard, S. 1989: *On the Radio: music radio in Britain.* Milton Keynes and Philadelphia: Open University Press.

Beckett, S. 1990: *The Complete Dramatic Works.* London and Boston: Faber & Faber.

Berland, J. 1993: Contradicting media: toward a political phenomenology of listening. In Strauss, N. *Radiotext(e).* US: *Semiotext(e)* 6, 1, 209–17.

Boyd, A. 1994: *Broadcast Journalism: techniques of radio and TV news.* Oxford, Boston, Johannesburg, Melbourne, New Delhi and Singapore: Focal Press.

Brecht, B. 1932: Der Rundfunk als Kommunikationsapprat. In *Blattaer der Hessischen Landestheaters*, Darmstadt 16. Repr. and trans. in Strauss, N. 1993: *Radiotext(e).* US: *Semiotext(e)* 6, 1, 15–17.

Briggs, A. 1979: *History of Broadcasting in the United Kingdom.* Oxford: Oxford University Press.

Burns, T. 1977: *The BBC: Public Institution, Private World.* Macmillan.

Coward, R. 1984: *Female Desire.* London, Glasgow, Toronto, Sydney, Auckland: Paladin, Grafton Books.

Crisell, A. 1992: *Understanding Radio.* London and New York: Routledge.

Crisell, A. 1994: *Understanding Radio.* London and New York: Routledge.

Crisell, A. 1997: *An Introductory History of British Broadcasting.* London and New York: Routledge.

Curran, J. and Seaton, J. 1991: *Power Without Responsibility*, 4th edn, London and New York: Routledge.

Davies, J. 1994: *History of Broadcasting and the BBC in Wales.* Cardiff: University of Wales.

Ditingo, V. 1995: *The Remaking of Radio.* Boston, Oxford, Melbourne, Singapore, Toronto, Munich, New Delhi and Tokyo: Focal Press.

Donovan, P. 1992: *The Radio Companion*. London: Grafton.

Drakakis, J. (ed.) 1981: *British Radio Drama*. Cambridge: Cambridge University Press.

Dyson, F. 1994: The genealogy of the radio voice. In Augaitis, D. and Lander, D. (eds) *Radio Rethink: art, sound and transmission*. Canada: Walter Phillips Gallery 167–86.

Esslin, M. 1971: The mind as stage. *Theatre Quarterly* 1, 3, 5–11.

Evans, E. 1977: *Radio: A Guide to Broadcasting Technique*. London: Barrie & Jenkins.

Felton, F. 1949: *The Radio Play: its technique and possibilities*. London: Sylvan Press.

Graddol, D. and Swann, J. 1989: *Gender Voices*. Oxford: Basil Blackwell.

Gray, F. 1981a: Giles Cooper: the medium as moralist. In Drakakis, J. (ed.) *British Radio Drama*. Cambridge: Cambridge University Press, 139–57.

Gray, F. 1981b: The nature of radio drama. In Lewis, P. (ed.) *Radio Drama*. New York and London: Longman, 48–77.

Hargrave, A.M. (ed.) 1994: *Radio and Audience Attitudes: Annual Review, 1994*, Broadcasting Standards Council: Public Opinion and Broadcasting Standards Series 5. London: John Libbey & Company Ltd.

Hayes, B. 1994: The role of the public voice in present-day radio. In Hargrave, A. M. (ed.) 1994: *Radio and Audience Attitudes: Annual Review, 1994*, Broadcasting Standards Council: Public Opinion and Broadcasting Standards Series 5. London: John Libbey & Company Ltd, 40–4.

Higgins, C.S. and Moss, P.D. 1982: *Sounds Real: radio in everyday life*. St Lucia, London and New York: University of Queensland Press.

Hind, J. and Mosco, S. 1985: *Rebel Radio: the full story of British pirate radio*. London and Sydney: Pluto Press.

Hobson, D. 1980: Housewives and the mass media. In Hall, S., Hobson, D., Lowe, A. and Willis, P. (eds) *Culture, Media, Language*. London: Routledge, 105–14.

Horrie, C. and Clarke, S. 1994: *Fuzzy Monsters: Fear and Loathing at the BBC*. Mandarin.

Hughes, J.M., Michell, P.A., Ramson, W.S. (eds) 1992: *The Australian Concise Oxford Dictionary*. Melbourne: Oxford University Press.

Hutchby, I. 1991: The organization of talk on talk radio. In Scannell, P. (ed.) *Broadcast Talk*. London: Sage, 119–37.

Lewis, P. (ed.) 1981a: *Radio Drama*. New York and London: Longman.

Lewis, P. 1981b: The road to Llareggub. In Drakakis, J. (ed.) *British Radio Drama*, Cambridge: Cambridge University Press, 72–110.

Logan, T. 1994: Radio daze: a clear view from below. In Hargrave, A.M. (ed.) 1994: *Radio and Audience Attitudes: Annual Review, 1994*, Broadcasting Standards Council: Public Opinion and Broadcasting Standards Series 5. London: John Libbey & Company Ltd, 52–6.

MacCabe, C. and Stewart, O. 1986: *The BBC and Public Service Broadcasting*. Manchester: Manchester University Press.

Matheson, H. 1933: *Broadcasting*. London: Thornton Butterworth Ltd.

McLeish, R. 1994: *Radio Production*, 3rd edn, Oxford: Focal Press.

McWhinnie, D. 1959: *The Art of Radio*. London: Faber & Faber.

Moss, P.D. and Higgins, C.S. 1984: Radio voices. *Media, Culture and Society* 6, 4, 353–75.

Pease, E.C. and Dennis, E.E. (eds) 1995: *Radio, the Forgotten Medium*. New Brunswick: Transaction Publishers.

Pinter, H. 1991: *A Slight Ache and Other Plays*. London and Boston: Faber & Faber.

Raban, J. 1981: Icon or symbol: the writer and the 'medium'. In Lewis, P. (ed.) *Radio Drama*. New York and London: Longman, 78–90.

Reith, J. 1924: *Broadcast over Britain*. London: Hodder & Stoughton.

Scannell, P. (ed.) 1991: *Broadcast Talk*. London: Sage.

Scannell, P. 1996: *Radio, Television and Modern Life*. Oxford: Blackwell.

Scannell, P. and Cardiff, D. 1991: *A Social History of British Broadcasting: Volume 1, 1922–1939, Serving the Nation*. Oxford: Basil Blackwell.

Schlesinger, P. 1978: *Putting 'Reality' Together*. London and New York: Methuen.

Seymour-Ure, C. 1991: *The British Press and Broadcasting Since 1945*. Oxford: Blackwell.

Strauss, N. 1993: *Radiotext(e)*. US: *Semiotext(e)* **6**, 1.

Thomas, D. 1995: *Under Milk Wood*. London: J.M. Dent & Sons Ltd.

Valentine, C.A. and Saint Damian, B. 1988: Gender and culture as determinants of the 'ideal voice'. *Semiotica* **71**, 3/4, 285–303.

Wilby, P. and Conroy, A. 1994: *The Radio Handbook*. London and New York: Routledge.

Williams, K. 1998: *Get Me a Murder a Day: a history of mass communication in Britain*. London and New York: Arnold.

Williams, R. 1974: *Television: technology and cultural form*. Glasgow: Fontana.

Williams, R. 1990: *Television: technology and cultural form*, 2nd edn, London: Routledge.

Index

THE
SCRUFFS

Bromley Libraries

30128 80286 841 7